God's Plot

God's Plot

PURITAN SPIRITUALITY IN THOMAS SHEPARD'S CAMBRIDGE

Edited by Michael McGiffert

Revised and Expanded Edition

University of Massachusetts Press
Amherst

Printed in the United States of America
ISBN 0-87023-926-0 (cloth); 915-5 (pbk.)
LC 94-2899

Library of Congress Cataloging-in-Publication Data

Shepard, Thomas, 1605-1649.
God's plot : Puritan spirituality in Thomas Shepard's Cambridge / edited by Michael McGiffert. — Rev. and expanded ed.
p. cm.
Includes bibliographical references and index.
Contents: Thomas Shepard, the practice of piety — The autobiography — The journal — The people speak, confessions of lay men and women — The confessions.
ISBN 0-87023-926-0 (alk. paper) — ISBN 0-87023-915-5 (pbk. : alk. paper)
1. Shepard, Thomas, 1605-1649. 2. Puritans—Massachusetts—Cambridge—Clergy—Biography. 3. Puritans—Massachusetts—Cambridge—History—17th century. 4. Cambridge (Mass.)—Church history—17th century. 5. Massachusetts—Church history—17th century. I. Title.
BX7260.S53A32 1994
285.8'092—dc20
[B] 94-2899
CIP

British Library Cataloguing in Publication data are available.

This book is a revised and expanded edition of
God's Plot: The Paradoxes of Puritan Piety, Being the Autobiography & Journal of Thomas Shepard, edited by Michael McGiffert
and published in 1972 in
The Commonwealth Series,
Winfred E. A. Bernhard, General Editor

In Memory of
Arthur Cushman McGiffert, Jr.,
1892–1993
Father and Teacher

CONTENTS

PREFACE: GOD'S PLOT REVISITED

For the Reverend Thomas Shepard and his congregation in Cambridge, in the colony of Massachusetts Bay, God's plot was the great plan of human salvation. Framed in scripture and developed in Christian theology, the plot centered in the sacrifice of Christ. Extended to humanity, it embraced all who accepted it as true and committed themselves to its terms. Shepard and his people envisioned a divine scenario governing the living of their lives and the saving of their souls. They became actors with parts to play in a cosmic drama of redemption. God wrote the script, cast the parts, directed the staging; Christ took the starring role; religion explained each act and scene. The emotions and ideas invested in this plot, the meanings made of it, the ways it was lived—these were constituent and dynamic elements of Puritan spirituality.

The documents in this volume illustrate the Puritans' sense of the plot's design. The first text—Shepard's autobiography—was left in manuscript by the Cambridge minister at his death in 1649; it is reprinted here in full from the first edition of this book (1972). The second comprises selections from Shepard's journal. The third section presents thirty-three confessions of the men and women of Shepard's congregation from the earliest years of its existence. In these records of the pastor and his people you will find the heart of Puritan passion and the secret of Puritan power.

A note on the historiography will help put the documents in perspective. Contemporary interest in American Puritan spirituality dates from Perry Miller's master study of the New England "mind," more than a half-century old and still rewardingly read today.[1] Miller's vision long ruled, but by 1972, when the first edition of *God's Plot* was published, his authority was being contested. Younger scholars were raising revisionist questions. Some charged that Miller neglected the social life of early New Englanders. Others objected that he slighted the New England Puritans' inward experience. New inquiries were being projected amidst declarations

1. Miller, *The New England Mind: The Seventeenth Century* (New York: Macmillan, 1939).

that tearing down the Miller "monolith" was essential to the liberty of scholars and the progress of scholarship.[2]

From this creative ferment, and from other sources, came both a new social history of New England, led by studies of village communities, and a new concern with the Puritans' religious psychology and devotional practice. Miller had identified a deep "strain of Augustinian piety" but left it to others to explore the psychological stresses that made Puritanism both problematic and potent.[3] A call then went out for the recovery of "the emotional, the experiential, and ultimately the mystical element . . . of Puritan evangelical religion."[4]

God's Plot helped answer this call, although I was not so much consciously responding to it as simply looking for work. I had read Shepard's sermons as an undergraduate. I knew where to find his journal—in the rare book collection of the New York Public Library; I knew, too, that few if any scholars had looked at it; neither had I. I got the idea, in the mid-1960s, of transcribing the journal, coupling it with Shepard's autobiography, which was already in print, and trying to get a publisher interested. These two texts, each virtually unique for its time and place, presented an opportunity for a young historian to try to make a contribution and, maybe, a mark.

The venture turned out to be worthwhile. Shepard's journal, revealing the inner workings of God's plot, has become a key source for Puritan consciousness and conscience. Shepard's autobiography, which finds in providence the ordering principle for the tumultuous events of his life, shows the plot's outer workings. When the two documents were juxtaposed in print, so that each could be read directly in terms of the other—with harmonies and contrasts fully exposed—their dialogue spoke to scholars in ways that helped cue a new generation of American Puritan studies. *God's Plot* took the question of assurance—how can I know I am saved?—to be

2. For a contemporary report see Michael McGiffert, "American Puritan Studies in the 1960's," *William and Mary Quarterly,* 3d Ser., XXVII (1970), pp. 36–67.

3. Miller, *New England Mind,* chap. 1.

4. James F. Maclear, " 'The Heart of New England Rent': The Mystical Element in Early Puritan History," *Mississippi Valley Historical Review,* XLII (1956), p. 622. Maclear's call was prompted in part by new work on English Puritan piety.

central to the inquiry into Puritan spirituality. The question was not new; subsequent studies of the patterning of piety have expanded and deepened the inquiry.

The Shepard materials, for all their interest, had a drawback. We had learned from Miller and other scholars a great deal about the thought of ministers—more than enough, some believed. In the 1970s, historians were challenging the clerical monopoly in Puritan studies. They were asking whether the clergy, as a professional elite with an agenda of its own, really spoke *for* their people as well as *to* them. Was there a genuine meeting of minds between pulpit and pews? Shepard's writings compounded the question. Were his spiritual torments at all representative? Did layfolk share his quest for evidences of God's grace? Can we legitimately speak of Puritanism as a single sensibility embracing both clergy and laity? Was there a real consensus?

Answers came in 1981 when George Selement and Bruce C. Woolley edited fifty-one testimonies of religious experience and life events that were given by applicants for membership in Shepard's church during the 1630s and 1640s. A further group of sixteen confessions was printed ten years later.[5] These texts have profoundly influenced our understanding of the Puritan spirit.

The confessors were a fair cross-section of the Cambridge congregation and community: young and middle-aged, women and men, farmers and farm wives, artisans, sailors, servants, Harvard students. These were people whom Shepard advised and admonished; his language was their language, his spirit, their spirit. Although each story is of course unique, together they meld into a mood of piety like his. Tracing the hard road of regeneration, they exhibit the same dynamic interface of anxiety and assurance. They confirm Shepard's problematizing of relations with the deity and show that ordinary men and women, too, felt agonizingly at risk. The lay confessions reinforced the thesis of Puritan consensus. They

5. George Selement and Bruce C. Woolley, eds., *Thomas Shepard's Confessions,* Colonial Society of Massachusetts *Collections,* LVIII (Boston, 1981). Mary Rhinelander McCarl, "Thomas Shepard's Records of Relations of Religious Experience, 1648–1649," *William and Mary Quarterly,* 3d Ser., XLVIII (1991), pp. 432–66. Selement had addressed the subject in "The Means to Grace: A Study of Conversion in Early New England," Ph.D. diss., University of New Hampshire, 1974.

also helped prompt the writing of a new religious history, one crucially concerned with popular experience and expression.[6]

The result has been a great surge of interest in American Puritan spirituality using clues often drawn from the Shepard materials. Major works to date—annotated in the bibliography at the back of this book—include Charles Hambrick-Stowe, *The Practice of Piety: Puritan Devotional Disciplines in Seventeenth-Century New England* (1982), Patricia Caldwell, *The Puritan Conversion Narrative: The Beginnings of American Expression* (1983), Charles Lloyd Cohen, *God's Caress: The Psychology of Puritan Religious Experience* (1986), David D. Hall, *Worlds of Wonder, Days of Judgment: Popular Religious Belief in Early New England* (1989), Andrew Delbanco, *The Puritan Ordeal* (1989), Amanda Porterfield, *Female Piety in Puritan New England: The Emergence of Religious Humanism* (1992), and Janice Knight, *Orthodoxies in Massachusetts: Rereading American Puritanism* (1994). These studies, along with Thomas Werge's *Thomas Shepard* (1987) and others noted in the bibliography, highlight a field of scholarship that is distinguished for both continuity and creativity.

Overall, in this recent work we see the dialectic of anxiety and assurance still foregrounded, but with a change of emphasis—more, now, on assurance than on anxiety, more on the resolution than on the problem. Supporting this shift are studies that set the institutional supports of piety in place and deepen our sense of piety as a developmental process involving continuous conversion, a life of growth in grace. Finally, we are achieving a better comprehension of the relations of clergy and laity, and of the laity's faith and practice, in early New England.

These advances should be taken not as terminal points but as benchmarks for the further study of Puritan spirituality. We have no reason to suppose that all the surviving documents have now turned up: Mary McCarl's utterly accidental discovery of lay con-

6. See George Selement, "The Meeting of Elite and Popular Minds at Cambridge, New England, 1638–1645," *William and Mary Quarterly,* 3d Ser., XLI (1984), pp. 32–47, with comments by David D. Hall, "Toward a History of Popular Religion in Early New England," and Darrett B. Rutman, "New England as Idea and Society Revisited," ibid., 49–55, 56–61. See also Darrett B. Rutman, *American Puritanism: Faith and Practice* (Philadelphia: J. P. Lippincott, 1970).

fessions in a file of Richard Mather's papers at the American Antiquarian Society tells us differently. We certainly have no call to imagine that scholarship has spoken the last word—answered all questions, knotted all loose ends. Thomas Shepard urged his people at Cambridge: "Be always converting . . . , always pulling up foundations."[7] Their assignment was constantly to learn and relearn their roles in God's plot, always practicing, always perfecting. Scholars are like that, too, in their own way, within the unfolding scenario of their profession: there will be many new occasions for their own plot to ripen and thicken.

This edition of *God's Plot* reprints the introduction to the 1972 edition, Shepard's autobiography in its entirety, and nearly fifty percent of the journal. To these documents are added thirty-three confessions of Shepard's parishioners.

I am indebted to the First Church in Cambridge, Congregational, for permission to reprint the autobiography and to the Rare Books and Manuscripts Division of the New York Public Library for permission to reprint selections from the journal. Twenty-four confessions come from among the fifty-one held by the New England Historic Genealogical Society, Boston (Mss Cb 1017); originally published by the Colonial Society of Massachusetts, they have been freshly transcribed and annotated for this volume. The remaining nine were among sixteen discovered in the Mather Family Papers (Box 13, Folder 7) at the American Antiquarian Society and edited by Mary Rhinelander McCarl in 1991 for the *William and Mary Quarterly,* a publication of the Institute of Early American History and Culture. I am grateful to the NEHGS and the AAS for permission to print the documents. For the editorial apparatus I have drawn on the scholarship of Selement, Woolley, and McCarl. Charles L. Cohen, David D. Hall, Janice Knight, and Donald Weber have given valued counsel and support. Donald Weber's suggestion to the University of Massachusetts Press prompted the reissue of this book. David Hall proposed including the lay con-

7. Shepard, *The Parable of the Ten Virgins* (1660) in *Works,* ed. John A. Albro (Boston, 1853), II, 632.

fessions. Charles Cohen invented the new subtitle and gave aid in transcribing the confessions. All shared thoughts on the new format and prefaces.

Michael McGiffert
Williamsburg, Virginia

October 1993

God's Plot

THOMAS SHEPARD: THE PRACTICE OF PIETY

FEW WRITINGS admit the modern reader so directly to the heart of a Puritan as do the *Autobiography* and *Journal* of Thomas Shepard (1605–1649), a minister of the first generation of settlers in Massachusetts. Shepard encountered great disorders in both his inner and outer worlds. His life defined itself in images of chaos, and he responded by straining to order his experience through exercises of public service and private devotion. These efforts included the recording of his life, retrospectively in the *Autobiography,* immediately in the *Journal,* each the only document of its kind that is known to have survived from the early pioneer period in New England.

The *Autobiography* dramatizes what Shepard called "God's great plot" of reformation and redemption, making vivid the faith in divine design by which Puritans affirmed their sense of the moral order of existence in an age of revolutionary turmoil, defined their parts in the play of God's purpose, and affirmed the cosmic dimensions of their experience. The *Journal* lays bare the passion of a Puritan who labored to bring himself wholly into a right relation with the God Who not only imposed direction and pattern on outward events but also by His grace composed the discords of the troubled, sinning soul.

I

The striking feature of his life, as Shepard recalls it in the *Autobiography,* was its unsettledness.[1] When he was three years old, plague broke the family in which he had been "the youngest and best beloved."[2] A year or so later his mother died, and the little boy,

1. My interpretation of Shepard's character, and of the character of English Puritanism in Shepard's generation, is indebted to Michael Walzer's brilliant book, *The Revolution of the Saints: A Study in the Origins of Radical Politics* (Cambridge: Harvard University Press, 1965).
2. Except as otherwise noted, quotations are from Shepard's *Autobiography.*

who had been shuffled from relative to relative, suffered the distempered administrations of stepmother and schoolmaster. At age ten he was orphaned by the death of his father, for whose life the child had prayed "very strongly and heartily . . . as knowing I should be left alone when he was gone." Thereafter his case improved, but his ruling anxieties were already fixed. It would be hard to invent a more persuasive provenance for the guilt he betrays in the *Autobiography* in attributing his misfortunes to his own "childishness" or for the fragility and terror of self, the longing for security, and the thirst for acceptance that are revealed in his *Journal.*

Puritanism spoke to these needs. It offered release from the agitation of the self through commitment to a commanding cause; a fellowship of judgment and compassion; and an authority above all human powers, permitting Thomas Shepard to appeal from the father who had betrayed him—first by bringing home "another woman who did let me see the difference between my own mother and a stepmother," and later by dying, despite his son's prayers—to the Father Who, though He might often turn away His face in sorrow or wrath, at least behaved consistently and, when sufficiently entreated, would return in the fullness of His love. Yet if Puritanism helped meet Shepard's emotional needs, it also confirmed them, for the Puritan ethos embodied the ailments of its adherents as well as the remedies they painfully worked out, and often a perpetuation of the ill was included, as Shepard's experience suggests, in the prescription of the cure.

Graduating from Emmanuel College, Cambridge University, where he underwent conversion, Shepard began his ministry at a time when hopes for the purification of the English Church were flickering low and dissenting clergymen had to live hole-and-corner. His early career was typical in its direction, though probably atypical in the frequency of its disruptions, of a growing company of reformers who longed to build Jerusalem in England or, failing that, on the American coast. Taking the latter course, John Winthrop's ships set sail in 1630; later that same year Shepard was barred from preaching by William Laud, Bishop of London and rising at that time to direct the campaign for Anglican uniformity. (Shepard's account of his terminal interview with Laud, though not part of the *Autobiography* proper, is printed below with the text of the *Autobiography.*) For the remainder of his time in England, until 1635, the young minister shifted from place to place—"tossed," he wrote, "from the south to the north of England" and back again—often just a jump ahead of Laud's pursuivants, preaching publicly when he could, otherwise privately in the homes of Nonconformist patrons. These trials confirmed him in Puritanism—specifically the warmly evangelical Puritanism of Perkins, Sibbes, Preston, and Goodwin, whose preaching Shepard called "most spiritual and excellent"—and finally drove him to risk the trans-Atlantic venture. "Although it was true I should stay and suffer for Christ," he reflected, "yet I saw no rule for it now the Lord had opened a door of escape." He never dressed his decision in the colors of courage but frankly confessed his yearning for peace and security beyond the reach of Laud's long ecclesiastical arm.

In view of the traumas of his childhood and the disturbed experience of his young manhood, it is hardly surprising that Shepard did not become one of those bluff pugnacious parsons who, as someone has said, next to the Kingdom of Heaven love a good fight. He had little talent or desire for combative Nonconformity, and none at all for revolutionary enterprise. The conventional Puritan image of the *miles Christianus,* girt in God's armor and warring against the hosts of Anti-Christ, utterly fails to fit him. Wanting Miltonic grandeur and Cromwellian militancy, Shepard was not cut out to be a prophet, a rebel, or a martyr, but was rather a priest who, leaning on rules and rituals, drew strength from settled patterns of authority, role, and status. His proper place, defined by his fears as by his gifts, lay within the sheltering walls of the institutional church in a society where the church, suitably reformed, enjoyed the generous support of civil law and popular sentiment.

Explicitly teleological and didactic, Shepard's autobiographical narrative declares that the vicissitudes of experience—the fragmentary, incoherent, superficial doings of men—have significance only in relation to Providence: their meaning lies entirely out of themselves. That is why the *Autobiography* stresses episodes of crisis, God's hand being most plainly seen in gratuitous deliverances from great dangers. The horse falls from the flooded bridge, but God saves the rider. The pregnant wife tumbles down the stairs, but God keeps both mother and unborn child from harm. The gale-lashed ship drives ashore, and the despairing sailors point to the place where all aboard will drown, but God averts the wreck. The man contemplates suicide, but God comes "between the bridge and the water."[3] Laud's agents close in, but God gives a means of escape.[4] Antinomians and Indians assail the infant colony, but God shields His people. From each incident a lesson of contrition and obligation was to be taken. Apparent accident was seen to be a piece of divine stagecraft, and even the malice of Laud worked out to Shepard's good.

New England, "a land of peace, though a place of trial," gave Shepard the physical security, stable identity, and public acceptance that he needed. There until his early death at age 43 he served as pastor of the church at Cambridge, raised successors in the ministry as unofficial chaplain of Harvard College[5] (and as a father, three of

3. Shepard, *Certain Select Cases Resolved* (1648), in *Works*, ed. John A. Albro (Boston, 1853), I, 327. The reference is autobiographical: see below, p. 46 n.16.

4. Shepard's closest call may have occurred while he was waiting ship at Ipswich. Edward Johnson tells the story: ". . . some persons eagerly hunting for Mr. Thomas Shepard began to plot (for apprehending of him) with a boy of sixteen or seventeen years of age, who lived in the house where he lodged, to open the door for them at a certain hour in the night. But the Lord Christ, who is the Shepherd of Israel, kept a most sure watch over his endeared servants, for thus it befell, the sweet words of grace falling from the lips of this reverend and godly Mr. Thomas Shepard in the hearing of the boy (the Lord's working withal), he was persuaded this was an holy man of God and therefore with many troubled thoughts began to relate his former practice, although he had a great sum of money promised him only to let them in at the hour and time appointed. But the boy, the more near the time came, grew more pensive and sad, insomuch that his master, taking notice thereof, began to question him about the cause of his heaviness, who being unwilling to reveal the matter held off from confessing a long time, till by urgent and insinuating search of his godly master with tears he tells that on such a night he had agreed to let in men to apprehend the godly preacher. The good man of the house forthwith gave notice thereof unto them, who with the help of some well affected persons was conveyed away by boat through a back lane." Johnson, *The Wonder-Working Providence of Sions Saviour in New-England* (1654), ed. J. Franklin Jameson (New York: Charles Scribner's Sons, 1910), pp. 94–95. Shepard's omission of reference to any such episode in his *Autobiography* suggests that the tale may be apocryphal.

5. Harvard was located at Cambridge (then Newtown) in part because of Shepard's presence there. See Johnson, *Wonder-Working Providence*, p. 201, and Cotton Mather, *Magnalia Christi Americana* (Hartford, 1855), I, 386. In addition to directing students in the paths of righteousness, Shepard served as overseer of the College, begged books from England, countered objections to the reading of "heathen authors," and helped save the infant institution from insolvency by proposing to the Confederation of New England in 1644 a "motion of beneficence" whereby each family in the associated colonies was asked

whose four surviving sons became clergymen), published many sermons and tracts, and proved himself a strong protagonist of the new order of righteousness which he helped create in Massachusetts. The last of these commitments seems to have yielded him especially large satisfactions. Whether defending the New England Way against Presbyterian criticism from the mother country and denouncing the toleration of sectarians there in the 1640s, or suppressing Antinomians and other dissidents nearer home, or preaching an election sermon to the General Court, or instructing magistrates, or admonishing his congregation for breaches of the communal covenant, Shepard could account himself—and be accounted by others—a profitable servant of a godly cause. New England made him, in effect, a new man. Released from the frustrations of underground existence in England, he could bring all his energies and abilities into action, focus them, and see his work bear fruit. What he was, people valued; what he had to say, they wanted to hear; what he did they rewarded with respect. He became a highly esteemed practitioner of a highly esteemed profession; his "painful" Christianity set a model for laymen and clergymen alike. In later years, sitting in his "city on a hill" and thinking back over his life, Shepard likened his migration to resurrection: the Lord had let him "live among God's people as one come out from the dead, to his praise."

In his Cambridge ministry Shepard acquired a reputation—the more remarkable because forged in the face of chronic ill-health—for exceptional evangelical efficacy. "Pastor Evangelicus," Cotton Mather called him, and Edward Johnson, the chronicler of early Massachusetts, glowingly memorialized him as "that gracious,

---

to give to the College annually a quarter-bushel of wheat or its monetary equivalent, a scheme that yielded nearly £270 over the next nine years. Only in respect of the misdeeds of the first master, Nathaniel Eaton, did Shepard's vigilance fail—an oversight that gave him acute pain. Students: Edmund S. Morgan, *The Diary of Michael Wigglesworth, 1653–1657* (New York: Harper and Row, Torchbook Edition, 1965), pp. 108–19. Books: Shepard to Hugh Peter, Dec. 27, 1645, in *American Historical Review,* IV (Oct., 1898), p. 106. "Heathen authors": Shepard to John Winthrop, c. 1642, in *Winthrop Papers,* IV (Boston: The Massachusetts Historical Society, 1944), p. 346. "Motion of beneficence": Samuel E. Morison, *The Founding of Harvard College* (Cambridge: Harvard University Press, 1935), pp. 314–18. Eaton affair: ibid., ch. 17, and James Kendall Hosmer, ed., *Winthrop's Journal* (New York: Charles Scribner's Sons, 1908), I, 310–14.

sweet, heavenly-minded and soul-ravishing minister . . . in whose soul the Lord shed his love so abundantly that thousands of souls have cause to bless God for him . . . who are the seal of his ministry . . ."[6] Harvard students, among others, testified to the power of his precept and example: "After his death," wrote one, "I thought God might just speak to me now no more. . . ."[7] John Winthrop reports that "one Turner of Charlestown," where Shepard often gave the weekday lecture, committed suicide after "being wounded in conscience at a sermon of Mr. Shepard's."[8] There was a tradition, preserved by the eighteenth-century New England preacher Thomas Prince, who published a portion of Shepard's *Journal,* that Shepard "scarce ever preached a sermon but someone or other of his congregation was struck in great distress and cried out in agony, 'What shall I do to be saved?' "[9] We may allow for exaggeration[10] and still admit the extraordinary power of this "poor, weak, pale-complexioned man"[11] who occupied the pulpit at Cambridge. The secret of his accomplishment will be found in his *Journal* on whose pages, as in the "little book" that he kept during his conversion, he "writ down what God taught me." Knowing himself so well, he knew how to minister to others whose spiritual problems resembled his.

By the early 1640s, when Shepard wrote the only volume of the *Journal* that is known to exist—did he write others, since lost or destroyed?—tranquillity had settled on the Wilderness Zion. The early physical hardships were long past; also survived were the threats of Indians and heretics—those agents of Satan whose ruin Shepard relates, and gloats over, in the *Autobiography.* Church and state had been stabilized; a few years more, and the New England Way, both civil and ecclesiastical, would be codified in the Laws and

6. Mather, *Magnalia Christi Americana,* I, 380; Johnson, *Wonder-Working Providence,* p. 107.
7. Morgan, ed., *The Diary of Michael Wigglesworth,* p. 119.
8. Hosmer, ed., *Winthrop's Journal,* II, 55.
9. Quoted by John A. Albro, "Life of Thomas Shepard," in Shepard's *Works* (Boston, 1852–1853), I, clxxx.
10. Prince, a promoter of the Great Awakening, treated Shepard as a prototype of Jonathan Edwards, who, it is worth noting, found much to value in Shepard's evangelical writings. See John E. Smith's observations in his edition of Edwards' *Religious Affections* (New Haven: Yale University Press, 1959), pp. 53–57.
11. Johnson, *Wonder-Working Providence,* p. 136.

Liberties of Massachusetts and the Cambridge Platform of Church Discipline. Though New Englanders were facing economic difficulties resulting from the falling off of immigration, and though the towns and churches were not always models of concord, Shepard had ample cause to rejoice in New England's serenity. Whether he looked back to the trials of the preceding decade or abroad to England where civil war raged, he found reason to praise God that "the churches are here in peace; the commonwealth in peace; the ministry in most sweet peace; the magistrates (I should have named first) in peace."[12]

II

Though peace had fallen on Shepard's outer world, his inner weather continued stormy. His *Journal* conveys this unsettledness of spirit by oceanic similes that evoke the biblical chaos of waters before God moved upon their face: "I . . . saw how apt my heart was to be like the sea, troubled and unquieted with cares, with griefs, with thoughts of future events, with men, with God. . . . Fickleness of spirit is like a sea wave or froth: it's blown with any wind. . . . If God's spirit breathes, it follows that; if Satan [it] follows that." This was not by any reckoning the condition of a man in whose "quiet still heart" the Paraclete delighted to dwell.[13] More than once Shepard writes of his longing to "depart out of this world and to be with God, perfectly near him where no more shaking is or shall be."[14] He cannot believe his faith is right or his actions—his "duties"—acceptable. He confesses pangs of envy, vanity, and anger; frivolous impulses of mirth; cravings for mundane indulgences of pleasure, profit, and honor. He finds fault with his preaching and counseling. Above all—embracing and shaping all his perturbations—he wants desperately to learn, and employs the *Journal* to discover, if he is, to quote one of his English sermons, "one of that small number whom God hath picked out to escape this wrath to come"—a number calculated by him at one to every thousand

12. *New Englands Lamentations for Old Englands present errours* (London, 1645), p. 4.
13. *Journal,* pp. 129–30: this and subsequent citations are to the present volume.
14. Ibid., p. 83.

damned.[15] "How may I know I am saved?" is the distinguishing question of a spiritual log that is at once wholly personal and characteristically Puritan.

Though apparently utterly eligible for Heaven, Shepard suffered privately the anticipatory torments of the damned. Cotton Mather's report of Shepard's "daily conversation" as "a trembling walk with God" describes the tenor of his piety but misses the anguish of a man whom God often left to walk alone, unsustained by plain evidence of grace,[16] and who found it "a hard thing to walk in a midway between deep disconsolations for the Lord's desertions of me and extreme slighting of them."[17] Shepard puts the key question, "Is this God in Christ mine or no?" and makes it a case of conscience: "For I knew it was my duty so to examine myself as to bring my thoughts unto an issue one way or other."[18] It was a rule, he explained to his congregation, "that the saving knowledge of Christ is dependent upon the sensible knowledge of a man's self."[19]

Shepard's self-examination nakedly exposes both the terrors of a Puritan in mortal doubt of God's love and the psychological strategies, more or less consciously exploited, by which assurance of salvation was sought and at least temporarily attained. Shepard's *Journal* allows us to describe the Puritan ethos as one of anxiety and assurance. On the one hand, Puritans like Shepard responded with intense anxiety to worlds, both outer and inner, that were experienced as radically disordered and dangerous. On the other hand, they devised ways not only to live more or less equably with their agitations but even to turn them to productive account.

Puritans looked for security from and within a system of ideas that was fairly clear, consistent, and stable—intended, like all such systems, to explain and organize experience—and they reinforced it by strenuous efforts to resolve differences of opinion among

15. *The Sincere Convert: Discovering The small number of true Beleevers, And the great difficulty of Saving Conversion,* 4th ed., in Albro, *Works,* I, 45.
16. Mather, *Magnalia,* I, 380.
17. *Journal,* p. 115.
18. Ibid., p. 121. Cf. William Perkins, *A Case of Conscience, the greatest that ever was; How a man may know whether he be the Childe of God, or no* (London, 1595).
19. *The Parable of the Ten Virgins opened and applied* (1660), in Albro, *Works,* II, 127.

themselves and to eliminate residual obscurities. They held hard to the common principle of ideological uniformity—"there is but one truth (you know)," Shepard reprimanded the tolerating Independents of England[20]—and this need for union on a solid ground of orthodoxy was enhanced by the Puritans' sensitivity to chaos defined as diversity. Yet this theological system on which they relied contained such anxiety-arousing or anxiety-expressing doctrines as Original Sin, Total Depravity, and Limited Atonement—three of the five basic points of seventeenth-century Calvinism as prescribed by the Synod of Dort (1618–19). It also included the tenet of double predestination, and though in New England the odds on grace were no doubt rather better than Shepard's English figure of one thousand to one, even in that New World Canaan and even discounting for homiletical hyperbole, the reckoning of chances for any individual was not likely to improve that individual's complacency. Nor was confidence enhanced by the discovery that God cloaked his decrees of election and reprobation in mystery, making uncertainty the elementally disturbing condition of a Puritan life. "The secrecy of God," said Shepard's father-in-law Thomas Hooker, "does drive men to much trouble. It is like an unbeaten way to the seamen; they must sound every part of it."[21] Not least important, Protestant theologians taught that men were saved by faith, not by works—faith being defined as belief, trust, loyalty, and dependence on God. By shifting the requirement of salvation from doing penance to being penitent, these spiritual mentors drove back the problem of assurance from outer appearance to inner reality, from public act to private attitude, and so made the search for assurance a radically inward undertaking, challenging each devotee to sound the bottomless deeps of his own heart.

Shepard sees in himself grave symptoms of infidelity to the fundamentals of Christian conviction—the existence of God, the Sonship of Christ, the veracity of Scripture, the authenticity of miracles.[22] He voices some startlingly modern, relativistic mis-

20. Shepard to Hugh Peter, Dec. 27, 1645, in *American Historical Review,* IV (October, 1898), p. 106.
21. Quoted in Perry Miller, *The New England Mind: The Seventeenth Century* (New York: Macmillan, 1939), p. 374.
22. See, e.g., *Journal,* pp. 102, 109, 112.

givings—"whether if I had been educated up among the Papists I should not have been as verily persuaded that Popery is the truth . . ." Again and again he records his fear that "I had no faith [or] that I had mistaken faith," and he confesses that "this wound . . . of secret atheism," though sometimes "skinned over," is never fully healed but festers as an "old sore of carnal objecting and of unbelief."[23] He worries lest his faith, infirm as he knows it to be, turn out to be his own fabrication—rather than Christ's gift—and thus damnable like all human works. He finds it hard to live by faith when his faith is jarred by the opacity of God's decrees, leading him earnestly to "desire that the Lord would speak immediately to me as to the prophets, that so I might certainly feel and know this living God."[24]

Shepard's quest for credible information of grace had its rationale in the concept of the Covenant of Grace, which the late master of American Puritan studies, Perry Miller, has called "the foundation for the whole history and structure of Christian theology" in early New England.[25] Waiving an elaborate discussion of this basic idea, it is enough to note that the Covenant was intended to clarify and underwrite the terms of assurance for true believers. It declared that salvation did not depend on the good behavior or character of the saved sinner, and it guaranteed that God would sustain those whom He had chosen. Thus it reflected the fourth and fifth points of Dort Calvinism—Irresistible Grace and the Perseverance of the Saints. Self-critical Puritans found it immensely reassuring to consider that, after all, they did not control their own destinies—if they did, they were doomed—but that they were upheld "by the strength of the Covenant of Grace,"[26] and that this Covenant could never be annulled by any failing of theirs, short of the unpardonable and almost unthinkable sin of ultimate apostacy. "The Psalm 25 came to mind," Shepard wrote in his *Journal,*

23. *Autobiography,* p. 44; *Journal,* pp. 126, 103, 120.
24. *Journal,* pp. 128.
25. See Miller's *The New England Mind: The Seventeenth Century,* chap. 13, and his earlier essay, "The Marrow of Puritan Divinity" (1935), in *Errand into the Wilderness* (New York: Harper and Row, Torchbook Edition, 1964), chap. 3.
26. Shepard, *Ten Virgins,* II, 353.

"wherein God promiseth the meek and humble to show them his covenant, and so I saw the Lord at that time revealing his covenant unto me, on which I was to build [my] assurance, not on my performance . . . by my own strength or graces."[27] Through the Covenant God saved those whom He willed to save, and though "saints may fall," Shepard told his people, "yet never to another lover, for they cannot fall into any sin that breaks Covenant between them and the Lord. . . ."[28] God's grace could be neither earned nor forfeited, for to allow human agency any influence in the forensic counsels of the Trinity would impeach God's majesty and diminish Christ's death.

The Covenant comprised the pledges made by God to His elect in the Scriptures, to which Shepard constantly repaired:

> I was earnest in prayer for God's favor and love, and doubting of it for myself and for others (because I looked to God's secret decree). At last I saw it was God's decree in the gospel and his will that whoever come to Christ should have life and favor and so answer to all prayer for himself and others—which gave me some sweet assurance.[29]

The *Journal* shows that Shepard found solace most abundantly in the Psalms and the Fourth Gospel, as, for example, in Psalm 34:18, "The Lord is near unto them that are of a contrite heart, and will save such as be afflicted in spirit"; John 4:10 (the text most often cited), "Jesus answered and said unto her, If thou knewest the gift of God, and who it is that saith to thee, Give me drink, thou wouldest have asked of him, and he would have given thee water of life"; and John 6:37, "All that the Father giveth me, shall come to me; and him that cometh to me I cast not away." Similar passages of evangelical promise are cited from Leviticus, Proverbs, Isaiah, Jeremiah, Hosea, Amos, Matthew, Romans, I John, and Revelation.

God's *promise* of salvation contained a binding guarantee that He would *perform* salvation. ". . . The covenant of grace is absolute," Shepard explained, "wherein the Lord doth not only promise the

27. *Journal,* p. 93.
28. *Ten Virgins,* II, 362.
29. *Journal,* p. 88. It is needful to stress this biblical base of Puritan piety if only because too many scholars, not excluding Miller, have managed to minimize it.

good, but to begin and perfect and fulfill the condition absolutely without respect of sin *ex parte creaturae.*"[30] The condition is faith, and God's promise to fulfill the condition means that He will implant saving faith in the souls of the elect. Therefore, said Shepard, "the covenant runs not only thus, viz., 'If thou believest, thou shalt be saved, but also, I will enable [thee] to believe.' "[31] It followed that the saints had the "unspeakable comfort" of knowing that

> if the Lord had put it over unto thee to believe, it is certain thou shouldst never have believed. But now the work is put into the hand of Christ; that which is impossible to thee is possible, nay, easy with him. He can comprehend thee when thou canst not apprehend him . . .[32]

The comprehended believer could expect an encouraging glimpse of God's predestinating purpose, for "the Lord's heart is so full of love (especially to his own) that it cannot be contained so long within the bounds of secrecy . . . but it must aforehand overflow and break out into the many streams of a blessed Covenant. . . ."[33] God reaches across the chasm of sin to mitigate man's estrangement. "Oh, the depth of God's grace here," Shepard exclaimed,

> that when he [man] deserves nothing else but separation from God, and to be driven up and down the world as a vagabond or as dried leaves, fallen from our God, that yet the almighty God cannot be content with it, but must make himself to us, and us to him, more sure and near than ever before.[34]

Piety could conceive no greater dispensation of divine love.

In actuality, however, and notwithstanding the preachers' celebration of its benefits, the Covenant of Grace left the problem of assurance far from solved. If a man were really in the Covenant, he

30. *Certain Select Cases Resolved,* I, 309.
31. *The Church Membership of Children, and their right to Baptisme* (1663), in Albro, *Works,* III, 521.
32. Shepard, *The Sound Believer. Or, A Treatise of Evangelicall Conversion* (1645), ibid., I, 195.
33. Shepard, Preface to Peter Bulkeley, *The Gospel-Covenant; or, the Covenant of Grace Opened,* 2nd ed. (London, 1651), p. B1 recto.
34. Ibid.

would, as Miller observes, "be through with all doubts and misgivings"; he would have an ungainsayable guarantee of grace.[35] But how was he to be sure that the blessings of the Covenant were really his? The ministers told him that *if* his faith were sound, *if* he earnestly tried to be loving and useful, *if* he were moved by desire for Heaven, *if* he responded gratefully to the good news of the Gospel, then he had substantial assurance of fair estate. Thus Shepard instructed his people that "If you are wrapped up in God's covenant, if any promise be actually yours, it is no presumption to take possession by faith of what is your own."[36] But how, confronting that perilous *if* and fearing to presume on God's loving kindness, could Shepard's listeners feel sure enough? And if unsure, would they make bold to assert with Thomas Hooker that "we have the Lord in bonds for the fulfilling his part of the Covenant" or with John Preston that "you may sue him of his bond written and sealed, and he cannot deny it."[37] Moreover, the Covenant may actually have inhibited the search for assurance on the part of weaker spirits who, too diffident to believe that God had saved them, thought the Covenant's blessings too good to be true: ". . . the saints have many fears," Shepard remarked, "whereby they dare not come. They fear they may presume. They see themselves most vile and unworthy of the least smile. The benefits are so exceeding great to which they are called that they think it is too good for them . . ."[38] One of Shepard's fellow ministers observed that when the Cambridge pastor dealt "with a tender, humble soul, he gives comfort so largely that we are afraid to take it."[39]

Hence there is reason to reject Miller's early view that under the Covenant of Grace Puritans "enjoyed clear sailing to the haven of assurance."[40] Likewise, Shepard's distresses go far toward making nonsense of another writer's assertion (echoing seventeenth-century

35. "Marrow of Puritan Divinity," p. 71.
36. *Sound Believer,* I, 196.
37. Quoted in Miller, *The New England Mind: The Seventeenth Century,* pp. 380, 389.
38. *Sound Believer,* I, 229–30.
39. Quoted in Albro, "Life of Shepard," *Works,* I, clxxxix.
40. "Marrow of Puritan Divinity," p. 71. Miller did not repeat this exaggeration in *The New England Mind: The Seventeenth Century.*

critics of New England's alleged claims to superior sanctity) that the "immigrant Fathers of New England . . . felt no serious doubt of their being . . . 'saints' and the 'elect.' "[41] Hardly less absurd, in the light of Shepard's *Journal,* appear the notions that "Puritans like Thomas Shepard" were "self-assured," and that Shepard himself was "perfectly satisfied with leaving the explanation of the final mysteries of life and death, of salvation and damnation, to a benign, if awesome Creator . . ."[42] God dealt with His saints through the Covenant: that much was clear. But though the Covenant helped make a measure of assurance possible, it did not guarantee it, and in extreme cases it may even have had the unintended effect of enhancing rather than allaying anxiety.

To help their people find out if they were "wrapped up" in the Covenant, Shepard and his colleagues developed schemes of evidence by which inquirers might test their condition. True saints were upright, self-denying, industrious in a warrantable calling; they loved their neighbors, obeyed their magistrates, and honored their ministers. They closely examined their hearts, grieved over sins—their own and others'—begged mercy, thought on holy things. Thus they manifested their "sanctification," that theological term defined by Shepard as the "work of the Spirit in the soul whereby the soul, beholding the glory of Christ and feeling his love, hereupon closeth with the whole will of Christ and seeketh to please him, as his happiness and utmost end."[43] Sanctification was the process by which God made men holy; it was "a most sweet and comfortable evidence . . ."[44] of their redemption or "justification."

But here, too, there was ambiguity. The sanctified were expected to make their sanctification visible in "blessed fruits and works."[45] Thus Shepard reflected that "if I did not walk holily in all things

41. Austin Warren, *The New England Conscience* (Ann Arbor: The University of Michigan Press, 1966), p. 7.
42. Kenneth Lynn, *The American Society* (New York: George Braziller, 1963), p. 1. Babette May Levy, *Preaching in the First Half Century of New England History* (Hartford: The American Society of Church History, 1945), pp. 145–146. Levy's treatment of Shepard is otherwise perceptive.
43. *Ten Virgins,* II, 333.
44. *Sound Believer,* I, 258.
45. Ibid.

before God I should not, I could not, have assurance of any good estate . . ." Yet that was easier said than done, for the works that were performed by people who knew themselves to be incorrigible sinners were never above suspicion. "I saw," Shepard wrote, "if I laid the evidence of my salvation upon my works that it would be various and uncertain as my gracious works were . . ." This was, he confessed, one reason why he was "staggered so much by unbelief."[46] He told his congregation that their "best duties are tainted, poisoned, and mingled with some sin, and therefore are most odious in the eyes of an holy God," and he told himself, "I am accursed for the best duty I do . . ."[47] In point of assurance, the saint's best was never quite good enough.

Opportunities to misinterpret the marks of grace were virtually infinite. In the Puritans' deeply disordered world, things were seldom as they seemed, and when fair hopes proved so often false, canny men prepared to be deceived, knowing, as Shepard informed the saints, that "the veriest reprobate in the world may have as good an assurance of Heaven as thou; there may be better in Hell than thee."[48] Thus in New England, where membership in the Heaven-bound community of saints was highly valued, the contamination of hypocrisy in the churches was taken for granted even while the ministers labored to keep the churches pure. "It is clearer than the day," Shepard wrote, "that many who are inwardly . . . the children of the devil are outwardly . . . the children of God."[49] No pastor grappled more earnestly with this problem than Shepard; his published lectures on the parable of the wise and foolish virgins are the most penetrating treatment of hypocrisy to be found in the writings of the founding generation.

Most instructive from the standpoint of the concern with assurance is Shepard's identification of a class of persons, believed to be numerous, whom he calls "gospel" or "evangelical" hypocrites—not the sly impostors who worm their way into the churches, but the innocent ones who, quite unconscious of their own fraudulence, deceive others unwittingly because they are "close deceivers of their

46. *Journal,* pp. 93, 46.
47. *Sincere Convert,* I, 104; *Journal,* p. 111.
48. *Ten Virgins,* II, 245.
49. *Church Membership of Children,* III, 517.

own souls."[50] The evangelical hypocrite would be a zealous churchman and good citizen, have a choice character, display the insignia of grace, bear the name of Christian and sincerely believe himself to be "wrapped up" in the Covenant; he would, in short, go the whole way to the Celestial Gates, trusting and humble—only to find the Gates shut against him. It is true that Shepard exposed the delusions of hypocrites in order to goad the saints to sharper self-scrutiny, on the principle that "never was yet man deceived but he that was willing to be deceived, that would not use the means, and search," and it is also true that he insisted strongly that "a vast difference" lay "betwixt a sincere Christian and the closest hypocrite."[51] Yet in consideration of the *Journal,* through which Shepard's suspicions of his own evangelical hypocrisy run like threads of fire, the reader will not be surprised at the remark of Shepard's older colleague Nathaniel Ward that "when Mr. Shepard comes to deal with hypocrites, he cuts so desperately that men know not how to bear him; he makes them all afraid that they are all hypocrites."[52] In reality, this notion of evangelical hypocrisy, pressed to its logical conclusion, had desperate consequences: it made hypocritical one's perception of one's own hypocrisy and so destroyed the cognitive basis of assurance.

Probably the keeping of a journal, which seems to have been an important point of Puritan piety, was itself a means of assurance, or was so intended. Ability to sustain this methodical, painful discipline could be regarded as a mark of a gracious soul, and the regularity of the exercise may itself have contributed to the diarist's composure. Day after day Shepard wrote down words that lent objective reality and continuity to his inner life—the goose-quill scribble tracing, so to speak, a life-line of personhood, even sainthood, across unsettling experience. Day after day these pages declared their author's existence both as the self that suffers and as the self that observes, weighs, and tries to understand. Shepard's piety is above all else percipient. Metaphors of light and enlightenment pervade the *Journal.* "I saw" is his characteristic statement: "I saw

50. *Ten Virgins,* II, 246.
51. Ibid., pp. 199, 206.
52. Quoted in Albro, "Life of Shepard," *Works,* I, clxxxix.

how I was without all sense as well as sight of God, estranged from the life of God . . ."; ". . . on Sabbath morning I saw the Lord frowning on me in several providences . . ."; "I saw the Lord had let me see my unbelief and desire the removal of it."[53] Shepard sees, and is seen—a Chillingworth, as it were, and equally a Dimmesdale: there lies Shepard flattened out in wholly genuine anguish, but there, simultaneously, is that other Shepard, perpendicular, cognitively masterful, the seeing I, lifting his pen to make a diagnostic or prescriptive note in his *Journal.* There is something somehow god-like about the second Shepard—something that verges perilously near the abominable sins of presumption and pride. Could the "I" that so clamantly asserts itself lose itself? And if it could not be lost, how could it be saved? The difficulty, unrecognized but perhaps not unfelt, lay at the core of the piety that inscribed journals like Shepard's. The way the journal was kept, responsive to the needs that inspired its keeping, tended to cancel, in point of assurance and emotional aplomb, the value of keeping a journal at all.

III

Given the urgency of the issue and the ambiguities of the evidence, it is hardly surprising that Puritans did not live easy lives. But if anxiety could not be abolished—infused as it was throughout the very structures of thought and feeling by which Puritans sought to master their unsettledness—perhaps it could be so managed as to prevent weak souls from being driven to distraction. Perhaps it could even be made to tell positively on behalf of assurance itself. It became the great problem of Puritan piety to maintain anxiety while simultaneously converting it into assurance. Shepard's *Journal,* read in conjunction with his sermons, shows how the problem could be solved.

For the "spiritual weepers"[54] who knew better, as he did, than to take God's grace for granted, Shepard had words of comfort: their perplexities were normal. True saints could not expect to live in

53. *Journal,* pp. 88, 92, 125.
54. Cf. William Haller, *The Rise of Puritanism* (New York: Harper and Row, Torchbook Edition, 1957), p. 27.

constant beatitude but had to weather many "winter seasons" when it was helpful for them to reflect that "very few living Christians have any settled comfortable evidence of God's eternal love to them in his Son."[55] Though the general design of God's plot was clear, His intentions for individuals were not. Therefore, and properly, there were "disquietings in the hearts of saints after that they be in Christ," so that "a child of God, commonly, after all his prayers, tears, and confessions, doubts much of God's love toward him . . ."[56] As Perry Miller observes, Puritan pastors devoted much effort and time to "telling the people that they should not let themselves be overwhelmed with too great a grief for their sins." None can have studied more conscientiously than Shepard to show the saints how "to turn all crosses to cheerfulness."[57]

If anxiety was normal, it was also mandatory. Those who were not assiduously anxious—the spiritually torpid, for instance, or Antinomians who claimed to have convincing, if private, notice of God's favor—were almost certainly bound for Hell. It followed that the sound believer could measure his assurance by his anxiety: the less assured he felt, the more assurance he actually had. This is the central paradox of Puritan piety; no passage in all the literature of Puritanism more vividly illustrates it than Shepard's almost offhand note in the *Journal* that "the greatest part of a Christian's grace lies in mourning for the want of it."[58] Was Goodman Brown afraid that his graces might be shams? Did he sniff hypocrisy upon the breath of prayer? Did he go around asking himself, "Are not my desires, my faith, my love counterfeit, which I may have and yet go to Hell?"[59] Shepard would assure him that the deeper the doubt, the higher the hope: ". . . the Lord's choicest servants have their complaints, their sighs and groans unutterable; they have their fears, temptations, and tears. Who more abundantly?"[60] Making despair do the office of delight, Shepard thus grounded assurance

55. *Ten Virgins,* II, 211, 78.
56. *Sound Believer,* I, 209; *Sincere Convert,* I, 102.
57. *The New England Mind: The Seventeenth Century,* p. 386; *Journal,* p. 130.
58. *Journal,* p. 123. Cf. Edmund S. Morgan's penetrating observation that "the Puritan's strength lay not in confidence but in the lack of it . . ." *The Puritan Family,* new ed. (New York: Harper and Row, Torchbook Edition, 1966), p. 5.
59. *Ten Virgins,* II, 220.
60. Ibid., II, 243.

on anxiety itself. Like his great contemporary Descartes, though for very different ends, he made doubt the basis of affirmation. For a twentieth-century counterpart one might turn to the theologian Paul Tillich: if "you are desperate about the meaning of life, the seriousness of your despair is the expression of the meaning in which you are still living. This unconditional seriousness is the expression of the presence of the divine in the experience of utter separation from it."[61]

Tempering the wind to the shorn lambs of Cambridge, Shepard stressed the mercy rather than the wrath of God. He had not always done so. As a young lecturer at Earle's Colne he had forged his sermons in the burning pit of Hell. Having discovered in his own conversion the efficacy of fright, he had exploited the ample repertory of brimstone—the day of doom, the last assize, the devouring flames, the horrid concourse of pandemonium—and he had scorched the unregenerate with words that anticipated such masterworks of the fiery genre as Jonathan Edwards' "Sinners in the Hands of an Angry God": "Thou art condemned, and the muffler is before thine eyes. God knows how soon the ladder may be turned. Thou hangest but by one rotten twined thread of thy life over the flames of hell every hour."[62] Significantly, in the American sermons ten years later, one encounters only an occasional brand from this old burning. Shepard continued to remind his hearers that God is angry with the wicked every day, and he did not cease to inculcate the fear of the Lord as a spur to saintly striving, but he used the homiletics of hellfire less and less often, and by the 1640s he appears to have renounced them completely. Though he preached both the law and the gospel—the law to "set out man's sin," the gospel to "set out God's love"[63]—his heart was far more deeply engaged in the latter.

This change may be attributed in part to altered circumstance. Shepard had found Earle's Colne a "poor town" and "blind place," an English counterpart of Gomorrah. There he addressed a larger proportion of unconverted, possibly unconvertible persons than

61. *The Protestant Era,* trans. James Luther Adams (Chicago: University of Chicago Press, 1948), p. xv.

62. *Sincere Convert,* I, 35.

63. *Journal,* p. 126.

would become the case in New England. Probably he felt himself, as a fresh recruit to the embattled Puritan cause, to be preaching God's judgment in a darkening time to a deaf declining nation. Massachusetts, by contrast, would be "God-glutted, Christ-glutted, gospel-glutted," and in his outpost of Zion up the Charles River, speaking to a community overwhelmingly composed of saints and saints' children, whose troubles were attributable less to "want of grace" than to "weakness of it,"[64] Shepard turned his attention from "the constitution of a Christian" to "the conversation of a Christian constituted."[65] He became concerned less to make converts than to improve the sanctity of those already converted.

Explanations of a psychological nature for this change may be adduced from the *Journal*'s report of Shepard's spiritual experience, through which he came to see that "the first thing the Lord reveals to draw the soul to himself is the fullness of grace in himself" and that "we fear and fly from nothing so much in God as his anger, and love nothing more than his love . . ."[66] The motive of terror became suspect: it gave rise to hypocrisy and to "violent affections and pangs," which, said Shepard, "I never liked."[67] Men could not be scared into Heaven; genuine holiness flowed not from fright but from feelings of gratitude and love, these being the right responses of the elect to the offer of redemption. "I should love Christ," Shepard wrote, "and out of love hate my sin, not out of fear of wrath . . ."[68] Therefore, he advised the trembling saints:

> Look to the tender-heartedness of the Lord Jesus, for, beloved, all the doubts of Christians arise chiefly from this head, from a hard opinion of Christ which Satan suggests . . . God's people do not know the tender-heartedness of the Lord Jesus; Satan presents him only in wrath.[69]

64. *Sound Believer,* I, 236; *Journal,* p. 95.
65. The phrases are Giles Firmin's from his *The Real Christian, or a Treatise of Effectual Calling* (London, 1670), p. B3 verso.
66. *Journal,* pp. 86, 120. One sees the change occurring in a letter to a troubled layman that Shepard wrote just before he left England: "Judge ye not rigorously of God, as though he were a bloody, austere God, . . . but look upon God as having a father's heart and affection towards you . . ." *Certain Select Cases Resolved,* I, 325.
67. *Ten Virgins,* II, 234. Cf. II, 435: ". . . it is hypocrisy for a man to be led only by fear, but it is prophaneness . . . not to be terrified at all . . ."
68. *Journal,* p. 133.
69. *Ten Virgins,* II, 84.

It was the sweetness of grace, the tenderness of Christ, that Shepard sought above all to communicate. God is "a sweet portion"; Christ is "mercy and love to all meek, humbled, believing sinners that came to him . . ."; God's "disposition is very sweet; his affection . . . is sweet to us."[70]

So solicitous a Father did not leave His children totally in the dark. Though the evidences of regeneration were far from foolproof and the divine decrees remained ultimately inscrutable, Shepard could assure the saints that "The experience of the work of grace makes men savingly to know what grace is . . ."[71] If they feared themselves damned for their "best duties," he would remind them that men should not presume to judge their own performance, whether good or ill: "Our actions may be most sinful when [God's] working in and about these may be most just and holy."[72] God's plot fixed the meaning and worth of men's acts; thus transcendentally appraised, "those duties you are ashamed to own, the Lord will not be ashamed to crown."[73] Saints must strive to do good while acknowledging that salvation was premised on their utter inability to do good, save by Christ's aid. Hence the paradox of the fortunate fall: "I saw how sin was sanctified and made a blessing, because it made Christ more sweet"; ". . . I saw the reason why the Lord did not take away all sin in the hearts of the faithful presently. It was because he was so fully pleased in the righteousness of his Son."[74] If saints complained that they did not seem to have their share of the graces which were the portion and seal of the elect, Shepard would advise them, as he advised himself, that "I should not be assured from any measure [of grace] received, but rather from sense of Christ's fullness, my own want, and my desire after perfection."[75] But was not this desire for perfection spurious? In some moods Shepard could not believe so: "Why hath the Lord let me see my unbelief and come for strength against it and pray for mercy, if the Lord had no purpose to help me? Why would he let me feel want of the spirit and pray for it if he intended not to succor

70. *Journal,* pp. 87, 92, 123.
71. *Ten Virgins,* II, 473.
72. *Theses Sabbaticae. Or, The Doctrine of the Sabbath* (1649), in Albro, *Works,* III, 90.
73. *Certain Select Cases Resolved,* I, 324.
74. *Journal,* pp. 134, 118.
75. Ibid., p. 128.

and give it me?"[76] So persuaded, the most timorous saint might dare to assert that "if I did desire this gift, the Lord would give it me . . . because 'tis more difficult for the Lord to work in me a desire after the spirit than for him to give the spirit . . ."[77]

At the base of these heartening reflections lay the Pauline paradox. "God doth show his power by the much ado of our weakness to do anything," Shepard explained; hence "the more weak I, the more fit I to be used. . . . When I was most empty, then by faith I was most full."[78] Such was the method of God's plot: through Christ, God "brings contraries out of contraries; he makes darkness light, Hell Heaven, guilt pardon, weakness strength . . ."[79] Though formally oppositional, these polarities were instrumentally connected in God's soteriological strategy: for the saint to be raised up, the Old Adam had to be laid low. Shepard had learned this truth in his own conversion when, at the final crisis, his will demolished and his ego devastated, every defense down and all subterfuges exhausted, there was nothing for it but to lie down at the throne of the living God and, "come what can come, to be quiet there."[80] The insight was subsequently confirmed in his pastoral care of "Christ's weak ones," toward whom, he writes, "my bowels yearned."[81] Thus he perceived the psychological profundity of Irresistible Grace, and so he taught his people to pray, "Say, I am thy clay, Lord, and have been a broken, unclean vessel, unfit for any use, to hold any grace. . . . Now, Lord, undertake for me. Begin thou the work, and take the glory . . ."[82] In this dialectic of contraries resided the secret of assurance.

But if assurance could be drawn from anxiety, it was no less true that anxiety was drawn from assurance or, more accurately, from the saint's feelings of assurance. Shepard nowhere develops a formal psychology of the emotions, and his record of his own fluctuating feelings is anything but intellectually strict. That he deeply distrusts his feelings is plain: they are unreliable because uncontrollably

76. Ibid., p. 125.
77. Ibid., p. 107.
78. Ibid., pp. 98, 106.
79. *Ten Virgins,* II, 228.
80. *Journal,* p. 101.
81. Ibid., p. 95.
82. *Ten Virgins,* II, 563.

subjective, because unstable and ambivalent, because too readily mistaken for faith, because conducive to passivity. But it is also plain that he feels intensely and variably, and it is precisely this condition of intensity and variability that holds the key to the dynamic of Puritan piety. For how could an aspiring saint, hoping beyond hope, come to believe himself saved without feeling great joy and relief? If he did not, his case was very doubtful. And how could these feelings be prevented from dissolving into something very like complacency or even pride? And how could a proud complacent soul be saved? Here the rule of contraries worked in reverse: "I saw also the deceit of man's heart which when it is very bad then it begins to seek to be very good. If it have and feel any good, it grows full and lifted up and loose."[83] Shepard's *Journal* reveals the subtle psychological transaction whereby anxiety is transmuted into assurance which is transmuted into anxiety, in Sisyphean sequence. Thus, typically, he finds that his faith, "formerly closing with Christ by affection, was battered and shaken as if I had sought the righteousness of Christ by my own works and that these shakings came in after the Lord gave me some secret and sweet persuasion that Jesus was the Christ . . ."[84] The two mental states tend to fuse: to be anxious is to be assured; to be assured is to be, or become, anxious.

Sainthood, as Thomas Shepard experienced and observed it, was thus rather a process than a settled condition, and far beneath the superficial daily agitations of consciousness the process was patterned by a dynamic relation of hopeful and fearful emotions, interacting and interpenetrating. The pattern took shape in Shepard's original conversion; his mature piety cyclically reenacted in abbreviated form that initial trauma. The *Autobiography* describes a conversion that runs true to Puritan form; the *Journal* records what Shepard called his "renewed conversions,"[85] these being the best part of sanctification[86] and, it may be added, the psychological

83. *Journal,* p. 106.
84. Ibid., p. 125–26.
85. Ibid., p. 101.
86. Shepard's stress on renewed conversions gives no warrant for historians of Puritanism to equate sanctification with "good works" and "outward behavior," as does E. S. Morgan in *The Puritan Family,* pp. 3–6. Sanctification denoted much more than "good social conduct"; it was primarily and essentially a "work of the Spirit in the soul," and its spiritual meanings should not be subordinated to its ethical or social manifestations.

trigger of Puritan revivalism. In his preaching Shepard insisted on the renewability of conversion—so strongly that he tended to slight the evidential significance of the original experience. He held that God's first caress was not enough; the man who rested on his conversion would almost certainly prove a hypocrite. He also noted that there was always "much self" in "first conversion" and remaining after it, and that the first impulse to holiness was too often the last: ". . . 'tis too common for men at the first work of conversion, oh then to cry for grace and Christ, and afterward grow licentious . . . a hypocrite's light goes out or grows not. Hence many ancient standers take all their comfort from the first work, and droop when in old age."[87] For the saint who strove to grow in grace, however, each fresh conversion yielded great dividends of assurance and reconfirmed the order of experience on which the saint's psychological stability depended.

IV

In the rhythm of renewed conversions there came times—not many but compelling—when assurance was permitted to be perfect. At his first conversion Shepard received Christ "with a naked hand, even naked Christ." In the *Journal* he sets down similar experiences of transfiguration, for which the metaphors of ecstasy alone were apt, when he felt himself "covered with God as with a cloud" or when he would "roll . . . upon Christ" and "lie by him and lie at him" for hours at a time.[88] This mystical impulse is expressed in Shepard's hunger for a "plain intuitive revelation" of grace,[89] in his resort to the Johannine gospel, the most richly mystical of the four, and in his yearning for communion with the Father in a simple unmediated experience, transcending all theological discourse, all squinting at signs and sifting of evidences, all shifts and counterfeits of relations that were less than ultimate, that would lift him wholly out of himself and seat him childlike in the lap of Deity. This was the firmest ground of confidence: at such times, Shepard reports, "my heart was much filled with sweet hopes and comfort-

87. *Ten Virgins,* II, 203, 128.
88. *Autobiography,* p. 48; *Journal,* 96, 132, 134.
89. Ibid., p. 113.

able assurance of peace, of my being at last with Christ whenever death shall seize upon me."[90]

Shepard consistently sets mystical passion above and against the claims of discursive reason. "I have seen a God by reason," he writes, "and never been amazed at God. I have seen God himself and have been ravished to behold him."[91] Noesis could neither sustain the hope of grace nor exorcise anxiety, "for if I doubted the being of God or the coming of Christ or the truth of the scriptures, I saw those reasons might set me at a stand, but yet could not clearly reveal nor persuade, but some doubts would still remain."[92] Noting that men of little faith found their perplexities not merely resistant but vastly magnified and multiplied when they tried to build assurance on rational grounds, Shepard relates the cheats of reason to the teleology of God's plot:

> it was righteous and just for the Lord to entangle and leave all men in the dark that seek for the final determination of any part of his counsel by reason, and . . . hence the Lord in mercy did leave his people to great doubts, both of the scriptures and of their own estates, that rest only or lastly upon this and the power of this to persuade their hearts.[93]

By destroying his trust in his intellectual perspicacity, God drove the saint to his knees; He committed those who relied on reason to "darkness [and] confusion" so that "they may feel a need of him."[94] With regard to high holy things, the Puritan temper was supra-rationalist.

This is not to say that Puritans were foes of rationality. Contending against the truly antirational extremisms of their age, they forcefully asserted the rights of reason. They assumed that the elements of the One Truth were logically coherent, that God addressed men in language men could understand, even if imperfectly, that the means and ends of the design of redemption under the Covenant were rationally related, that the procedures of God's

90. Ibid., p. 115.
91. Ibid., p. 103.
92. Ibid., p. 112.
93. Ibid., p. 113.
94. Ibid.

plot, though paradoxical, were not self-contradictory. Thus against Antinomians and other such "gospel wantons" Shepard emphasized the didactic and disciplinary uses of reason as a means by which "the spirit may let in his light and clear up the truth" and as a curb on wayward excitable emotions. "We know," he remarked, "how men have been kings and lords over their own passions by improving reason . . ."[95] Orthodoxy, piety, and morality thus had a rational basis: God's ways and orders, though mysterious, were not allowed to be absurd. But reason had its upper limits of validity, a point Puritans were prompt to make in combat with the rationalizing theologians of England and the Continent. Nor was the point merely polemical; it was crucial to the spiritual life, for a piety that failed to subordinate reason to faith was by Puritan lights at best irrational and at worst impious.

In expressing the pietistic components of Shepard's religiosity, moreover, the *Journal* reveals susceptibilities that are far more Antinomian than Arminian. As a young man Shepard had been tempted by Grindletonian perfectionism; like Anne Hutchinson—who was believed by the orthodox of Massachusetts to have been infected with Grindletonianism—he craved perfect assurance, and, also like her, he was often strongly tempted "to forsake the scriptures and wait for a spirit to suggest immediately God's inmost thought toward me."[96] These were points of emotional kinship, the all-important difference being that the Establishment minister could not allow his desires to erupt in what he condemned as "Balaamitish ravishments, and hypocritical pangs, and land-flood affections,"[97] like those ascribed to Anne Hutchinson. Perhaps his perfectionist inclinations enabled him to understand, even to sympathize with, her temptations, while his victory over his own temptations led him to condemn her the more sternly for yielding to hers. However that may be, it seems plausible to suggest that in putting down the Antinomian apostate, Shepard was suppressing the Antinomian propensities of his own passionate spirit. He kept his longings private, locked them in his *Journal,* and used the *Journal* to order, interpret, and sublimate them, partly for homiletic ends, in

95. *Ten Virgins,* II, 283.
96. *Journal,* p. 112.
97. *Ten Virgins,* II, 268.

terms of the sovereign schedule of God's plot. It is this revelation and repression of passion—hardly surmisable from the sermons alone—that makes Shepard's *Journal* an exceptionally instructive document.

Finally, for Shepard, language and thought become redundant. The soul that was seized by the Spirit knew God as purely and inexpressibly as the body knew that honey was sweet and fire hot. "There is," Shepard explains, "a light of glory" by which "the elect see things in another manner" than natural men and evangelical hypocrites. "To tell you how, they cannot; it's the beginning of light in Heaven."[98] Such illumination, characteristic of mystical piety in general and related specifically to Shepard's own intense percipience, brought certainty and calm: it was "an experimental knowledge of the work of grace" and convinced even Shepard that "the spirit doth not leave the soul to conjectures it is so and to fears it may not be so, but it is a most clear evidence of truth, as tasting of honey is to the tongue. . . ."[99] That was how Shepard came to believe that he was really "wrapped up" in the Covenant of Grace, for the Covenant was the agency of rapture, and the rapt spirit needed no surer testament of God's reconciling love. Thus God perfected His great plot by resolving its paradoxes, and as the Puritan saint was overwhelmed by ineffable grace, piety became inarticulate.

A NOTE ON THE DOCUMENTS

This is the fourth printing of Shepard's *Autobiography.* Its first editor, Nehemiah Adams (*The Autobiography of Thomas Shepard, the Celebrated Minister of Cambridge, New England* [Boston, 1832]), yielded so far to the scruples of his day as to alter or omit passages which he "conceived to be, both in matter and manner, unsuited to what some call the fastidiousness, but others the refinement and delicacy of the age." Thus Shepard's "whoredom" became Adams' "sin," and all references to biological reproduction—for example, "my wife had conceived and was breeding"—were silently expunged. In 1846 Alexander Young included the *Autobiography* proper, omitting the prefatorial address to Shepard's son and the

98. Ibid., II, 235.
99. Ibid., II, 222; *Journal,* p. 114.

notes that conclude the manuscript, in his *Chronicles of the First Planters of the Colony of Massachusetts Bay,* published in Boston. Unlike Adams, Young updated Shepard's spelling and punctuation; also unlike Adams, he forbore to bowdlerize. A verbatim text, marred by only a few slight errors, was edited with a Shepard bibliography by Allyn Bailey Forbes for The Colonial Society of Massachusetts, *Publications,* XXVII (*Transactions,* 1927–1930), pp. 343–400. In the present edition, a few pages of Shepard's financial accounts, included in the manuscript of the *Autobiography* and reprinted by Forbes, have been omitted. The manuscript is owned by The First Church in Cambridge, Congregational.

The full correct text of the *Journal* here receives its first edition. A portion of it, comprising the entries through December 27, 1641, was published in Boston in 1747 by the Reverend Thomas Prince in his *Three Valuable Pieces* with a preface by David Brainerd. Reprinted in Edinburgh in 1749 and in Glasgow in 1847, this is the version that appears in the third volume of Shepard's *Works* (Boston, 1853). Because Prince was working from a copy, the provenance of which is not known, it is impossible to place responsibility for the numerous unmarked deletions, interpolations, and other amendments that corrupt his transcription. Whether Prince found or made them, the changes were useful to him: his edition was intended to edify those who were "seriously concerned for their salvation and afraid of being deceived in matters of eternal moment." The following comparisons illustrate the character of the alterations:

SHEPARD	PRINCE
January 30, 1641	
I saw I did not cease to be and live that Christ might be and live in me. I saw Christ was to pray, do, counsel, and that I should be wholly careless of myself and careful for this.	I saw I did not cease to be and live of myself that Christ might be and live in me. I saw Christ was to do, counsel, direct, and that I should be wholly diffident of myself, and careful for this, that he might be all to me.

March 11, 1641

March 11. In prayer I was cast down with the sight of our worthiness in this church to be utterly wasted.	March 2. I was cast down with the *Sight of our Unworthiness* in this Church, deserving to be utterly wasted.

May 29, 1641

. . . I considered that as men had their voice, so the spirit his voice by which he spake, whose voice is most sweet.	. . . I considered as Men had their Voice; so that which *he* spake, whose *Voice is most sweet,* is witnessed to the Hearts of his People by the still Voice of his Spirit.

September 8, 1641

This is magnifying of God.	This therefore is magnifying of God, to make him All, the Fountain of all Goodness and Excellency!

The excerpts quoted by Cotton Mather in his *Magnalia Christi Americana* are similarly inaccurate. The manuscript of the *Journal,* a leather-bound volume measuring 3 by 3¾ inches and 1⅛ inches thick, containing 190 tightly written leaves, is in the possession of The New York Public Library.

While maintaining strict fidelity to the substance of the text, I have followed the practice of Samuel Eliot Morison, in his edition of William Bradford's *Of Plymouth Plantation,* in modernizing Shepard's spelling and irregular punctuation in both documents, as well as in the quotations from Shepard and others that appear in this introductory essay. Thus *euill* becomes *evil, vpon vs* becomes *upon us, woorke* becomes *work, honour* becomes *honor.* Abbreviations—e.g., *L.* for *Lord, bec:* for *because, Octob:* for *October*—are spelled out full length. Such words as *ignorance* and *sin,* when capitalized by Shepard, have been reduced to lower case; the pronouns of deity have been left in lower case as Shepard wrote them, and I have also let stand the capitals of terms such as *Law* and *Legal* because of these words' technical theological denotations. Paragraphing follows Shepard's, though editorial discretion has been employed to reflect the sense of the original in a very few instances where Shepard's intention is not perfectly clear. The presence of a few illegible words and phrases is noted within brackets, that is: [one or two words illegible]; editorial interpolations are also bracketed; parentheses and brackets have been inserted to reduce the confusions of Shepard's numberings within numberings. When Shepard quotes the Bible from memory, his quotations usually read closer to the Geneva translation, on which he was raised, than to the King James. In the editorial notes and the introductory essay I have therefore used the former version. Where the dates of Shepard's entries in the *Journal* fall out of chronological order, I have not attempted to correct them. For the identification of years in the *Journal* I have used the Gregorian calendar rather than the Julian calendar of Shepard's time.

ACKNOWLEDGMENTS

My interest in Thomas Shepard dates back more than two decades to the time when, as an undergraduate at Harvard, I had the good fortune to encounter Perry Miller and his studies of Puritan thought. Adopting him as a grand, ungodly, godlike model of a scholar, I attempted a senior thesis on Shepard's role in the Antinomian Controversy. For that immature undertaking I was lucky to have the guidance of Laurence B. Holland; the finished essay was criticized by Edmund S. Morgan and Samuel Eliot Morison. I have now the welcome chance to repay a small part of my debt to these teachers.

I am grateful to The First Church in Cambridge, Congregational, for permission to publish the *Autobiography* and to The New York Public Library—whose Keeper of Manuscripts, Mr. Robert W. Hill, now retired, has been most helpful—for permission to publish the *Journal.* Edmund S. Morgan has kindly deciphered several words and phrases where Shepard's minuscule scribble poses more than usual difficulty. The introductory essay was read in draft by Arthur Cushman McGiffert, Jr., and Stuart B. James, whose criticisms have been immensely valuable. I have been helped on particular points by my colleagues Allen D. Breck,

Charles P. Carlson, Jr., J. Donald Hughes, and Edward A. Lindell, of the University of Denver, and by Everett H. Emerson and Winfred E. A. Bernhard of the University of Massachusetts. Secretarial costs have been partly paid by the Department of History and the Graduate School of Arts and Sciences of the University of Denver.

MICHAEL MCGIFFERT
Denver, Colorado
December, 1971

THE AUTOBIOGRAPHY*

To my dear son Thomas Shepard with whom I leave these records of God's great kindness to him, not knowing that I shall live to tell them myself with my own mouth, that so he may learn to know and love the great and most high God, the God of his father.

In the year of the Lord 1634, October 16, myself, wife, and family with my first son Thomas committed ourselves to the care of our God to keep us one and to carry us over the mighty seas from old England to New England. But we had not been two days on the sea, but that the wind arose and drave our ship almost upon the sands where the Lord did most apparently stretch forth his hands in saving of us from them when we were within a very little ready to be dashed in pieces upon them. And this our danger of sinking and losing all our lives [page torn: words missing] in two several days, [page torn: words missing] not been the infinite wisdom and power of God to help us I do not conceive how possibly we could have escaped in such terrible storms. Now one cause of our going at this time of winter was because my wife was conceived of this second son Thomas, and because we were persecuted in old England for the truth of Christ which we professe[d] there we durst not stay to make ourselves known, which would have been at the baptizing of the child. Hence we hastened for New England, and therefore though thou, my dear son, wast not born then, yet thou wert in the dangers of the sea in thy mother's womb then, and see how God hath miraculously preserved thee, that thou art still alive and thy mother's womb and the terrible seas have not been thy grave. Wonder at and love this God forever.

After that we came from the sea my first son fell sick in passing from the ship to the shore in the boat, of which sickness within a fort[night. Page torn: words missing] after he died at Yarmouth in

* On the first several pages of the manuscript Shepard set down a record of financial transactions, debts, and credits (not here reprinted), in which appears the single date, May 1, 1646.

[page torn: words missing] which was no small gr[ief. Page torn: words missing]. But the Lord preserved us and provided for me and my wife a hiding place from the knowledge of our enemies and from their malice, by the means of Mistress Corbet in Norfolk, in one of whose houses we stayed all that hard winter with our dear friend Mr. Roger Harlakenden[1] and enjoyed a sweet time together in a most retired manner. So the winter being spent and my wife's time of travail in childbed drawing nigh, we were much perplexed whither to go and where to stay that we might not be known, and keep the child so secretly as that it might not be baptized until it came to take of that ordinance in purity in old England. And being thus doubtful what to do, the Lord by letters from London called us to come thither where my wife might have all help in the time of her extremity and my child kept secret. And this we concluded for to do, and therefore took our leave of this our winter house, and in our way to London we went to Mr. Burrows[2] his house, a godly, able minister, where my wife, when she was big and great with child—of thee, my son Thomas—she fell down from the top to the bottom of his stairs with her back so hurt that all of us did think and fear her child could not but be slain or hurt with this sore fall, but herself felt not much hurt and her child had none. Oh, remember, my son, to know and love this God that here did pity and spare thee in thy mother's womb a second time! From this place we went to London, my wife thus big with child very safe and well, and there the Lord provided for my wife and self and friends a very private house where our friends did us all the good they could and our enemies could do us no hurt, where my wife on the Sabbath day, being April 5, 1635, was delivered mercifully of this second son Thomas, which name I gave him because we thought the Lord gave me the first son I lost on sea in this again, and hence gave him his brother's name. And so the mother growing strong, the child began to grow weak, and I did verily think would have died of a sore mouth, which I taking to heart, the Lord awakened me in the night and stirred me up to pray for

1. Roger Harlakenden, a well-to-do Nonconformist, befriended Shepard when the latter was silenced, accompanied him to New England, and took an active part in church affairs and politics until his death in 1638.
2. Jeremy Burroughs, Puritan clergyman, at that time rector of Livetshire, Norfolk.

him, and that with very much fervency, as I thought, and many arguments to press the Lord for his life came in, as:

(1) The glory the Lord should have by betrusting me with this child: he should be the Lord's forever.

(2) Because this kindness would be to me fruit in season, if in the time of my privacy, persecution, sorrow for the loss of my first child He would give me this and that other in this.

(3) Because though it was brought very low, yet then was the Lord's time to remember to help.

(4) Because I thought if the Lord should not hear me now, my soul would be discouraged from seeking to him because I sought for the first and could not prevail for his life, and this was sore if the Lord should not hear me for this.

(5) Because all healing virtue was in Christ Jesus' hands who was very tender to all that brought their sick unto him.

(6) Although my sins might hinder him from doing this, yet I told the Lord his mercy should be the more wonderful if in healing my child of his sickness he would withal heal me of my sins. And thus after a sad heavy night the Lord shined upon me in the morning, for I found him suddenly and strangely amended of his sore mouth which I did expect would have been his death. Oh, the tenderness of our God! Remember, therefore, my son, this mercy of the Lord to thee. Thus the child with the mother having recovered their strength, we set a second time to sea, and when we went the child was so feeble that diverse of our friends did conclude the child could [not] live until it came to New England in a close ship, but the care of God was so great that it was made much better by the sea and more lively and strong. And in this voyage it and all of us were in danger to be drowned by a most terrible leak which the Lord stopped for us. Another danger in the ship that the Lord delivered it from was this: the ship in a storm tumbling suddenly on the one side, my wife having the child in her arms was almost pitched with her head and child in her arms against a post in the ship, and being ready to fall she felt herself plucked back by she knew not what, whereby she and the child were again preserved, and I cannot ascribe this to any other but the angels of God who are ministering spirits for the heirs of life. And thus after a[n] eleven weeks' sail from old England we came to New England

shore where the mother fell sick of a consumption and thou, my child, wert put to [one word illegible] nurse to one goodwife Hopkins who was very tender of thee. And after we had been here diverse weeks, on the seventh of February or thereabout God gave thee the ordinance of baptism whereby God is become thy God and is beforehand with thee that whenever thou shalt return to God, he will undoubtedly receive thee—and this is a most high and happy privilege, and therefore bless God for it. And now after that this had been done thy dear mother died in the Lord, departing out of this world to another, who did lose her life by being careful to preserve thine, for in the ship thou wert so feeble and froward both in the day and night that hereby she lost her strength and at last her life. She hath made also many a prayer and shed many a tear in secret for thee, and this hath been oft her request: that if the Lord did not intend to glorify himself by thee, that he would cut thee off by death rather than to live to dishonor him by sin. And therefore know it: if thou shalt turn rebel against God and forsake God and care not for the knowledge of him nor to believe in his Son, the Lord will make all these mercies *woes* and all thy mother's prayers, tears, and death to be a swift witness against thee at the great day.

Thus the Lord taking away thy dear mother's life, the Lord takes care for thee and preserved thee in health until the spring, May 1, 1636: and now the hand of the Lord was stretched out against my child so that he had for diverse weeks a sore mouth both within and without, cheeks and lips full of blisters so as that he could eat no meat, only suck the breast, by which only he lived a long time, which I did think would have been its death again. But the Lord, being sought unto, recovered him again. And then the humor fell into his eyes which grew so sore that partly by the humor and partly by the ill handling and applying medicines to them his eyes grew stark blind with pearls upon both eyes and a white film, insomuch as it was a most dreadful sight unto all the beholders of him and very pitiful, which was such a misery that methought now I had rather that the Lord would take away my child by death than let it live a blind and a miserable life. But the Lord saw my sorrows, my tears, my poor prayers which were in bitterness for him. And after that I had concluded I must have a blind child to be a constant sorrow to me till my death and was made to be contented to bear the indignation of the Lord because I had sinned, resolving now to fear nor care nor grieve no more, but to be thankful, nay, to love the Lord's will—presently, I say, upon this by a poor weak means, viz., the oil of white pasec, the Lord restored my child to his sight suddenly and strangely—I may almost say miraculously—again, which was no small joy to me and no little encouragement to do the Lord's work that took so much care for me and mine. Now consider, my son, of this great care of God for thee, and remember to lift up thy eyes to heaven to God in everlasting praises of him and dependence upon him, and take heed thou dost not make thy eyes windows of lust, but give thy eyes, nay, thy heart and whole soul and body, to him that hath been so careful of thee when thou couldst not care for thyself.

T. {My Birth and Life} S.

In the year of Christ 1604[3] upon the fifth day of November, called the powder treason day, and that very hour of the day wherein the Parliament should have been blown up by Popish priests, I was then born, which occasioned my father to give me this name Thomas, because he said I would hardly believe that ever any such wickedness should be attempted by men against so religious and good Parliament. My father's name was William Shepard, born in a little poor town in Northamptonshire called Fossecut near Towcester, and being a prentice to one Mr. Bland, a grocer, he married one of his daughters of whom he begat many children—three sons: John, William, and Thomas; and six daughters: An[na], Margaret, Mary, Elizabeth, Hester, Sarah—of all which only John, Thomas,[4] Anna, and Margaret are still living in the town where I was born, viz., Towcester in Northamptonshire, six miles distant from the town of Northampton in old England. I do well remember my father and have some little remembrance of my mother.

3. An error for 1605.

4. Evidently a slip of the pen, since Shepard did not live in Towcester after completing his studies at Emmanuel College.

My father was a wise, prudent man, the peacemaker of the place, and toward his latter end much blessed of God in his estate and in his soul, for there being no good ministry in the town he was resolved to go and live at Banbury in Oxfordshire under a stirring ministry, having bought a house there for that end. My mother was a woman much afflicted in conscience, sometimes even unto to distraction of mind, yet was sweetly recovered again before she died, and I being the youngest she did bear exceeding great love to me and made many prayers for me. But she died when I was about four years old, and my father lived and married a second wife not dwelling in the same town, of whom he begat two children, Samuel and Elizabeth, and died when I was about ten years of age. But while my father and mother lived, when I was about three year old, there was a great plague in the town of Towcester which swept away many in my father's family, both sisters and servants. I being the youngest and best beloved of my mother was sent away the day the plague brake out to live with my aged grandfather and grandmother in Fossecut, a most blind town and corner, and those I lived with also being very well to live yet very ignorant. And there was I put to keep geese and other such country work all that time, much neglected of them, and afterward sent from them unto Adthrop, a little blind town adjoining, to my uncle, where I had more content but did learn to sing and sport as children do in those parts and dance at their Whitsun Ales, until the plague was removed and my dear mother dead who died not of the plague but of some other disease after it. And being come home, my sister An[na] married to one Mr. Farmer, and my sister Margaret loved me much, who afterward married to my father's prentice, viz., Mr. Waples.[5] And my father married again—to another woman who did let me see the difference between my own mother and a stepmother: she did seem not to love me but incensed my father often against me; it may be that it was justly also for my childishness. And having lived thus for a time, my father sent me to school to a Welshman, one Mr. Rice, who kept the Free School in the town of Towcester, but he was exceeding curst and cruel and would deal roughly with me and so discouraged me wholly from desire of

5. Adams and Young read Mapler; Forbes reads Waples.

learning that I remember I wished oftentimes myself in any condition to keep hogs or beasts rather than to go to school and learn. But my father at last was visited with sickness, having taken some cold upon some pills he took, and so had the hickets[6] with his sickness a week together, in which time I do remember I did pray very strongly and heartily for the life of my father and made some covenant, if God would do it, to serve him the better as knowing I should be left alone if he was gone. Yet the Lord took him away by death, and so I was left fatherless and motherless when I was about ten years old, and was committed to my stepmother to be educated who therefore had my portion which was £100 which my father left me. But she neglecting my education very much, my brother John, who was my only brother alive, desired to have me out of her hands and to have me with him, and he would bring me up for the use of my portion. And so at last it was granted, and so I lived with this my eldest brother who showed much love unto me and unto whom I owe much, for him God made to be both father and mother unto me. And it happened that the cruel schoolmaster died and another[7] came into his room to be a preacher also in the town, who was an eminent preacher in those days and accounted holy but afterward turned a great apostate and enemy to all righteousness and I fear did commit the impardonable sin. Yet it so fell out by God's good providence that this man stirred up in my heart a love and desire of the honor of learning, and therefore I told my friends I would be a scholar. And so the Lord blessed me in my studies and gave me some knowledge of the Latin and Greek tongues, but much ungrounded in both. But I was studious because I was ambitious of learning and being a scholar, and hence when I could not take notes of the sermon I remember I was troubled at it and prayed the Lord earnestly that he would help me to note sermons. And I see cause of wondering at the Lord's providence therein, for as soon as ever I had prayed (after my best fashion) then for it, I presently the next Sabbath was able to take notes who the precedent Sabbath could do nothing at all that way. So I continued till I was about fifteen years of age and then was con-

6. I.e., hiccoughs.

7. William Cluer, a graduate of Emmanuel, became master of the school on September 23, 1617.

ceived to be ripe for the University, and it pleased the Lord to put it into my brother's heart to provide and to seek to prepare a place for me there, which was done in this manner: one Mr. Cockerell,[8] Fellow of Emmanuel College in Cambridge, being a Northamptonshire man, came down into the country to Northampton and so sent for me, who upon examination of me gave my brother encouragement to send me up to Cambridge. And so I came up, and though I was very raw and young, yet it pleased God to open the hearts of others to admit me into this College a pensioner,[9] and so Mr. Cockerell became my tutor. But I do here wonder and I hope shall bless the Lord forever in heaven that the Lord did so graciously provide for me, for I have oft thought what a woeful estate I had been left in if the Lord had left me in the profane, ignorant town of Towcester where I was born, that the Lord should pluck me out of that sink and Sodom, who was the least in my father's house, forsaken of father and mother, yet that the Lord should fetch me out from thence by such a sweet hand.

The first two years I spent in Cambridge was in studying and in much neglect of God and private prayer which I had sometime used, and I did not regard the Lord at all unless it were at some fits. The third year, wherein I was Sophister, I began to be foolish and proud and to show myself in the public schools, and there to be a disputer about things which now I see I did not know then at all but only prated about them. And toward the end of this year when I was most vile (after I had been next unto the gates of death by the smallpox the year before), the Lord began to call me home to the fellowship of his grace, which was in this manner:

(1) I do remember that I had many good affections (but blind and unconstant) oft cast into me since my father's sickness by the spirit of God wrastling with me, and hence I would pray in secret. And hence when I was at Cambridge I heard old Doctor Chaderton,[10] the Master of the College, when I came, and the first year I was there to hear him upon a Sacrament day my heart was much affected, but I did break loose from the Lord again. And half a year after I heard Mr. Dickinson common-place in the chapel upon

8. Daniel Cockerell, M.A., 1612, Fellow, 1612–21.
9. Shepard was admitted pensioner on February 10, 1619/20.
10. Laurence Chaderton, Master of Emmanuel, 1584–1622.

those words—I will not destroy it for ten's sake (Genesis 19)[11]—and then again was much affected, but I shook this off also and fell from God to loose and lewd company, to lust and pride and gaming and bowling and drinking. And yet the Lord left me not, but a godly scholar, walking with me, fell to discourse about the misery of every man out of Christ, viz., that whatever they did was sin, and this did much affect me. And at another time when I did light in godly company I heard them discourse about the wrath of God and the terror of it and how intolerable it was, which they did present by fire: how intolerable the torment of that was for a time—what then would eternity be! And this did much awaken me, and I began to pray again. But then by loose company I came to dispute in the schools and there to join to loose scholars of other colleges and was fearfully left of God and fell to drink with them. And I drank so much one day that I was dead drunk, and that upon a Saturday night, and so was carried from the place I had drink at and did feast at unto a scholar's chamber, one Basset of Christ's College, and knew not where I was until I awakened late on that Sabbath and sick with my beastly carriage. And when I awakened I went from him in shame and confusion, and went out into the fields and there spent that Sabbath lying hid in the cornfields where the Lord, who might justly have cut me off in the midst of my sin, did meet me with much sadness of heart and troubled my soul for this and other my sins which then I had cause and leisure to think of. And now when I was worst he began to be best unto me and made me resolve to set upon a course of daily meditation about the evil of sin and my own ways. Yet although I was troubled for this sin, I did not know my sinful nature all this while.

(2) The Lord therefore sent Doctor Preston[12] to be Master of the College, and, Mr. Stone[13] and others commending his preaching to be most spiritual and excellent, I began to listen unto what he said, and the first sermon he preached was Romans 12—be renewed in the spirit of your mind—in opening which point, viz., the change

11. Correctly, Gen. 18:32.

12. John Preston (1587–1628), one of the most influential Puritan preachers and writers of his generation, served as Master of Emmanuel from 1622 to 1628.

13. Samuel Stone (1602–1663) graduated from Emmanuel in the same year as Shepard. Suspended for nonconformity in 1630, he went three years later to New England where with Thomas Hooker he served the churches at Newtown and Hartford.

of heart in a Christian, the Lord so bored my ears as that I understood what he spake and the secrets of my soul were laid upon [i.e., open] before me—the hypocrisy of all my good things I thought I had in me—as if one had told him of all that ever I did, of all the turnings and deceits of my heart, insomuch as that I thought he was the most searching preacher in the world. And I began to love him much and to bless God I did see my frame and my hypocrisy and self and secret sins, although I found a hard heart and could not be affected with them.

(3) I did therefore set more constantly (viz., 1624, May 3) upon the work of daily meditation, sometimes every morning but constantly every evening before supper, and my chief meditation was about the evil of sin, the terror of God's wrath, day of death, beauty of Christ, the deceitfulness of the heart, etc., but principally I found this my misery: sin was not my greatest evil, did lie light upon me as yet, yet I was much afraid of death and the flames of God's wrath. And this I remember: I never went out to meditate in the fields but I did find the Lord teaching me somewhat of myself or himself or the vanity of the world I never saw before. And hence I took out a little book I have every day into the fields and writ down what God taught me lest I should forget them, and so the Lord encouraged me and I grew much. But in my observation of myself I did see my atheism, I questioned whether there were a God, and my unbelief, whether Christ was the Messiah, whether the Scriptures were God's word or no. I felt all manner of temptations to all kind of religions, not knowing which I should choose, whether education might not make me believe what I had believed, and whether if I had been educated up among the Papists I should not have been as verily persuaded that Popery is the truth or Turkism is the truth, and at last I heard of Grindleton,[14] and I did question whether that glorious estate of perfection might not

14. The "Grindletonians," judging from the writings of their leader, Roger Brereley (or Brierley), curate at Grindleton in Yorkshire, were spiritual seekers and perfectionists. They were regarded by their critics as antinomians or "familists" who held "that we must not now go by motives but by motions and that when God comes to dwell in a man He so fills the soul that there is no more lusting." Stephen Denison, *The White Wolfe* (London, 1627), p. 39. John Winthrop attributed the antinomianism of Anne Hutchinson to Grindletonian inspiration. Brereley himself was exonerated of antinomianism by the Archbishop of York in 1628.

be the truth and whether old Mr. Rogers' *Seven Treatises* and the *Practice of Christianity,*[15] the book which did first work upon my heart, whether these men were not all legal men and their books so, but the Lord delivered me at last from them. And in the conclusion after many prayers, meditations, duties, the Lord let me see three main wounds in my soul: (1) I could not feel sin as my greatest evil; (2) I could do nothing but I did seek myself in it and was imprisoned there, and though I desired to be a preacher, yet it was honor I did look to like a vile wretch in the use of God's gifts I desired to have; (3) I felt a depth of atheism and unbelief in the main matters of salvation and whether the Scriptures were God's word. These things did much trouble me and in the conclusion did so far trouble me that I could not read the Scriptures or hear them read without secret and hellish blasphemy, calling all into question and all Christ's miracles, and hereupon I fell to doubt whether I had not committed the impardonable sin. And because I did question whether Christ did not cast out devils from Beelzebub, etc., I did think and fear I had, and now the terrors of God began to break in like floods of fire into my soul. For three quarters of a year this temptation did last, and I had some strong temptations to run my head against walls and brain and kill myself. And so I did see, as I thought, God's eternal reprobation of me, a fruit of which was this dereliction to these doubts and darkness, and I did see God like a consuming fire and an everlasting burning, and myself like a poor prisoner leading to that fire, and the thought of eternal reprobation and torment did amaze my spirits, especially at one time upon a Sabbath day at evening, and when I knew not what to do (for I went to no Christian and was ashamed to speak of these things), it came to my mind that I should do as Christ: when he was in an agony he prayed earnestly. And so I fell down to prayer, and being in prayer I saw myself so unholy and God so holy that my spirits began to sink, yet the Lord recovered me and poured out a spirit of prayer upon me for free mercy and pity, and in the conclusion of

15. Richard Rogers, preacher at Wethersfield, Essex, was a prominent figure in the rise of Puritanism. Haller calls his *Seven Treatises,* published in 1603, "the first important exposition of the code of behavior which expressed . . . the Puritan . . . conception of the spiritual and moral life" (*The Rise of Puritanism* [New York: Harper and Row, Torchbook Edition, 1957], p. 36). The *Practice of Christianity* was an abbreviated edition of the earlier work.

the prayer I found the Lord helping me to see my unworthiness of any mercy and that I was worthy to be cast out of his sight and to leave myself with him to do with me what he would, and there and never until then I found rest. And so my heart was humbled and cast down, and I went with a stayed heart unto supper late that night and so rested here, and the terrors of the Lord began to assuage sweetly.[16] Yet when these were gone I felt my senselessness of sin and bondage to self and unconstancy and losing what the Lord had wrought and my heartlessness to any good and loathing of God's ways. Whereupon walking in the fields the Lord dropped this meditation into me: Be not discouraged therefore because thou art so vile, but make this double use of it: (1) loathe thyself the more; (2) feel a greater need and put a greater price upon Jesus

16. Shortly before his departure from England, Shepard summarized this experience for the benefit of a troubled inquirer:

> . . . you desire me to tell you how myself came to the cure of atheistical thoughts, and whether they did wear out, or whether they were rationally overthrown.
>
> I answer, at first they did wear out, meeting with fruitless and dead-hearted company, which was at the university.
>
> The Lord awakened me again, and bid me beware lest an old sore broke out again. And this I found, that strength of reason would commonly convince my understanding that there was a God, but I felt it utterly insufficient to persuade my will of it unless it was by fits, when, as I thought, God's Spirit moved upon the chaos of those horrible thoughts; and this, I think, will be found a truth.
>
> I did groan under the bondage of those unbelieving thoughts, looking up, and sighing to the Lord, that if he were as his works and word declared him to be, he would be pleased to reveal himself by his own beams, and persuade my heart by his own Spirit of his essence and being, which if he would do, I should account it the greatest mercy that ever he showed me. And after grievous and heavy perplexities, when I was by them almost forced to make an end of myself and sinful life, and to be mine own executioner, the Lord came between the bridge and the water, and set me out of anguish of spirit, . . . to pray unto him for light in the midst of so great darkness. In which time he revealed himself, manifested his love, stilled all those raging thoughts, gave return in great measure of them; so that, though I could not read the Scripture without blasphemous thoughts before, now I saw a glory, a majesty, a mystery, a depth in it, which fully persuaded, and which light (I desire to speak it to the glory of his free grace, seeing you call me to it) is not wholly put out, but remains, while I desire to walk closely with him, unto this day. And thus the Lord opened mine eyes, and cured me of this misery; and if any such base thoughts come (like beggars to my door) to my mind, and put these scruples to me, I used to send them away with this answer: Why shall I question that truth which I have both known and seen?

Certain Select Cases Resolved (1648), in *Works,* ed. John A. Albro (Boston, 1853), I, 327.

Christ who only can redeem thee from all sin—and this I found of wonderful use to me in all my course whereby I was kept from sinkings of heart and did beat Satan as it were with his own weapons. And I saw Christ teaching me this before any man preached any such thing unto me. And so the Lord did help me to loathe myself in some measure and to say oft: Why shall I seek the glory and good of myself who am the greatest enemy, worse than the Devil can be, against myself, which self ruins me and blinds me, etc.? And thus God kept my heart exercised, and here I began to forsake my loose company wholly and to do what I could to work upon the hearts of other scholars and to humble them and to come into a way of holy walking in our speeches and otherwise. But yet I had no assurance Christ was mine.

(4) The Lord therefore brought Dr. Preston to preach upon that text, I Corinthians 1:30: Christ is made unto us wisdom, righteousness, sanctification, and redemption. And when he had opened how all the good I had, all the redemption I had, it was from Jesus Christ, I did then begin to prize him and he became very sweet unto me, although I had heard many a time Christ freely offered by his ministry if I would come in and receive him as Lord and Savior and Husband. But I found my heart ever unwilling to accept of Christ upon these terms; I found them impossible for me to keep that condition, and Christ was not so sweet as my lust. But now the Lord made himself sweet to me and to embrace him and to give up myself unto him. But yet after this I had many fears and doubts.

(5) I found therefore the Lord revealing free mercy and that all my help was in that to give me Christ and to enable me to believe in Christ and accept of him, and here I did rest.

(6) The Lord also letting me see my own constant vileness in everything put me to this question: Why did the Lord Jesus keep the law, had no guile in his heart, had no unbrokenness but holiness there? Was it not for them that did want it? And here I saw Christ Jesus righteousness for a poor sinner's ungodliness, but yet questioning whether ever the Lord would apply this and give this unto me.

(7) The Lord made me see that so many as receive him, he gives power to be the sons of God (John 1:12), and I saw the Lord gave

me a heart to receive Christ with a naked hand, even naked Christ, and so the Lord gave me peace.

And thus I continued till I was six years' standing, and then went half a year before I was Master of Arts to Mr. Weld's[17] house at Terling in Essex where I enjoyed the blessing of his and Mr. Hooker's[18] ministry at Chelmsford. But before I came there I was very solicitous what would become of me when I was Master of Arts, for then my time and portion would be spent, but when I came thither and had been there some little season until I was ready to be Master of Arts, one Dr. Wilson[19] had purposed to set up a lecture and give £30 per annum to the maintenance of it, and when I was among those worthies in Essex where we had monthly fasts they did propound it unto me to take the lecture and to set it up at a great town in Essex called Coggeshall, and so Mr. Weld especially pressed me unto it and wished me to seek God about it, and after fasting and prayer the ministers in those parts of Essex had a day of humiliation, and they did seek the Lord for direction where to place the lecture. And toward the evening of that day they began to consider whether I should go to Coggeshall or no; most of the ministers were for it because it was a great town, and they did not know any place did desire it but they. Mr. Hooker only did object against my going thither for being but young and unexperienced, and there being an old yet sly and malicious minister in the town who did seem to give way to it to have it there, did therefore say it was dangerous and uncomfortable for little birds to build under the nests of old ravens and kites. But while they were thus debating it, the town of Earle's Colne, being three mile off from Essex [*sic:* from Coggeshall], hearing that there was such a lecture to be given freely and considering that the lecture might enrich that poor town, they did therefore just at this time of day come to the place where the ministers met, viz., at Terling in Es-

17. Thomas Weld (1595–1661), then vicar of Terling, was pastor at Roxbury in Massachusetts Bay (1632–41) where he took an active part in suppressing the antinomian dissidents. In 1641 he returned to England with Hugh Peter as agent for the colony. From 1649 to his death he served as rector of St. Mary's Church, Gateshead Parish, in Newcastle.
18. Thomas Hooker (1586–1647) was then preaching at Chelmsford, Essex. Silenced by Laud, he went to Holland in 1631 and to New England in 1633. He was minister at Newtown until his removal to Hartford in 1636.
19. Dr. Edmund Wilson, brother of the Rev. John Wilson of Boston.

sex, and desired that it might be settled there for three years (for no longer was it to continue in any place because it was conceived if any good was done it would be within such a time, and then if it went away from them the people in a populous town would be glad to maintain the man themselves, or if no good was done it was pity they should have it any longer). And when they thus came for it the ministers with one joint consent advised me to accept of the people's call and to stay among them if I found upon my preaching a little season with them that they still continued in their desires for my continuance there. And thus I, who was so young and weak and unexperienced and unfit for so great a work, was called out by twelve or sixteen ministers of Christ to the work, which did much encourage my heart, and for the Lord's goodness herein I shall, I hope, never forget his love, for I might have been cast away upon a blind place without the help of any ministry about me. I might have been sent to some gentleman's house to have been corrupted with the sins in it. But this I have found: the Lord was not content to take me from one town to another, but from the worst town, I think, in the world to the best place for knowledge and learning, *viz.,* to Cambridge, and there the Lord was not content to give me good means but the best means and ministry and help of private Christians, for Dr. Preston and Mr. Goodwin[20] were the most able men for preaching Christ in this latter age. And when I came from thence the Lord sent me to the best country in England, *viz.,* to Essex, and set me in the midst of the best ministry in the country by whose monthly fasts and conferences I found much of God. And thus the Lord Jesus provided for me of all things of the best.

So being resolved to go unto Earle's Colne in Essex after my commencing Master of Arts and my sinful taking of orders about a fortnight after of the Bishop of Peterborough, *viz.,* Bishop Dove,[21] I came to the town and boarded in Mr. Cosins his house, an aged but godly and cheerful Christian and schoolmaster in the town, and by whose society I was much refreshed, there being not one man else in all the town that had any godliness but him that I

20. Thomas Goodwin (1600–80), then Fellow of Catherine's Hall, Cambridge, was second only to Preston at the University as a powerful preacher. Later he became the foremost Independent at the Westminster Assembly.

21. Thomas Dove (1555–1630), Bishop of Peterborough, 1601–30.

could understand. So having preached upon the Sabbath day out of 2 Corinthians 5:19, all the town gave me a call and set to their hands in writing, and so I saw God would have me to be there, but how to be there and continue there I could not tell. Yet I sinfully got a license to officiate the cure of the Bishop of London's register before my name was known, and by virtue of that I had much help. But when I had been there awhile and the Lord had blessed my labors to divers in and out of the town, especially to the chief house in the town, the Priory, to Mr. Harlakenden's children where the Lord wrought mightily upon his eldest son, Mr. Richard (now dwelling there), and afterward on Mr. Roger, who came over with me to New England and died here, Satan then began to rage, and the commissaries, registers, and others began to pursue me and to threaten me, as thinking I was a nonconformable man (when for the most of that time I was not resolved either way, but was dark in those things). Yet the Lord, having work to do in this place, kept me, a poor, ignorant thing, against them all until such time as my work was done. By strange and wonderful means, notwithstanding all the malice of the ministers round about me, the Lord had one way or other to deliver me. The course I took in my preaching was (1) to show the people their misery; (2) the remedy, Christ Jesus; (3) how they should walk answerable to this mercy, being redeemed by Christ. And so I found the Lord putting forth his strength in my extreme weakness and not forsaking of me when I was so foolish as I have wondered since why the Lord hath done any good to me and by me.

So the time of three years being expired, the people would not let me go but gathered about £40 yearly for me. And so I was intended to stay there if the Lord would, and prevailed to set up the lecture in the town of Towcester where I was born, as knowing no greater love I could express to my poor friends than thus. And so Mr. Stone (Dr. Wilson giving way thereto) had the lecture and went to Towcester with it where the Lord was with him. And thus I saw the Lord's mercy following me to make me a poor instrument of sending the gospel to the place of my nativity.

So when I had preached awhile at Earle's Colne about half a year the Lord saw me unfit and unworthy to continue me there any longer, and so the Bishop of London, Mountain,[22] being removed to York and Bishop Laud (now Archbishop) coming in his place, a fierce enemy to all righteousness and a man fitted of God to be a scourge to his people, he presently (having been not long in the place) but sent for me up to London and there, never asking me whether I would subscribe (as I remember) but what I had to do to preach in his diocese, chiding also Dr. Wilson for setting up this lecture in his diocese, after many railing speeches against me, forbade me to preach, and not only so, but if I went to preach anywhere else his hand would reach me.[23] And so God put me to silence there which did somewhat humble me, for I did think it was for my sins the Lord set him thus against me. Yet when I was thus

22. George Mountaigne (or Mountain) (1569–1628), successively Bishop of Lincoln, London, and Durham, 1617–28, was a staunch ally of Laud's High-Church party. His term as Archbishop of York was cut short after less than four months by his death.
23. The following passage is reprinted with spelling and punctuation modernized from Thomas Prince, *A Chronological History of New England, in the form of Annals . . .*, new ed. (Boston, 1826), pp. 338–39. "I have by me," Prince wrote, "a manuscript of Mr. Shepard's, written with his own hand, in which are these words."

> December 16, 1630. I was inhibited from preaching in the diocese of London by Dr. Laud, bishop of that diocese. As soon as I came in the morning, about eight of the clock, falling into a fit of rage, he asked me what degree I had taken in the University. I answered him, I was a Master of Arts. He asked me, Of what College? I answered, Of Emmanuel. He asked how long I had lived in his diocese. I answered, Three years and upwards. He asked who maintained me all this while, charging me to deal plainly with him, adding withal that he had been more cheated and equivocated with by some of my malignant faction than ever was man by Jesuit, at the speaking of which words he looked as though blood would have gushed out of his face and did shake as if he had been haunted with an ague fit, to my apprehension by reason of his extreme malice and secret venom. I desired him to excuse me. He fell then to threaten me and withal to bitter railing, calling me all to naught, saying, You prating coxcomb! Do you think all the learning is in your brain? He pronounced his sentence thus: I charge you that you neither preach, read, marry, bury, or exercise any ministerial function in any part of my diocese, for if you do, and I hear of it, I will be upon your back and follow you wherever you go, in any part of the kingdom, and so everlastingly disenable you. I besought him not to deal so, in regard of a poor town. Here he stopped me in what I was going on to say. A poor town! You have made a company of seditious, factious Bedlams, and what do you prate to me of a poor town? I prayed him to suffer me to catechise in the Sabbath days in the afternoon. He replied, Spare your breath; I will have no such fellows prate in my diocese. Get you gone, and now make your complaints to whom you will! So away I went, and blessed be God that I may go to him.

silenced the Lord stirred me up friends. The house of the Harlakendens were so many fathers and mothers to me, and they and the people would have me live there though I did nothing but stay in the place. But remaining about half a year after this silencing among them, the Lord let me see into the evil of the English ceremonies, cross, surplice, and kneeling, and the Bishop of London, *viz.,* Laud, coming down to visit, he cited me to appear before him at the Court at Reldon[24] where, I appearing, he asked me what I did in the place, and I told him I studied; he asked me what—I told him the fathers; he replied I might thank him for that, yet charged me to depart the place. I asked him whither should I go. To the University, said he. I told him I had no means to subsist there, yet he charged me to depart the place. Now about this time I had great desire to change my estate by marriage, and I had been praying three year before that the Lord would carry me to such a place where I might have a meet yoke fellow. And I had a call at this time to go to Yorkshire to preach there in a gentleman's house, but I did not desire to stir till the Bishop fired me out of this place. For the Bishop having thus charged me to depart, and being two days after to visit at Dunmow in Essex, Mr. Weld, Mr. Daniel Rogers, Mr. Ward, Mr. Marshall, Mr. Wharton[25] consulted together whether it was best to let such a swine to root up God's plants in Essex and not to give him some check. Whereupon it was agreed upon privately at Braintree that some should speak to him and give him a check. So Mr. Weld and I traveling together had some thoughts of going to New England, but we did think it best to go first unto Ireland and preach there, and to go by Scotland thither. But when we came to the church Mr. Weld stood and heard without (being excommunicated by him); I, being more free, went within. And after sermon Mr. Weld went up to hear the Bishop's speech and being seen to follow the Bishop the first thing he did was to examine Mr. Weld what he did to follow him and to stand

24. Perhaps Peldon, near Colchester, Essex.

25. Daniel Rogers: son of Richard Rogers; lecturer at Wethersfield, Essex. Mr. Ward: probably Nathaniel Ward (1578–1653), then rector of Stondon Massey, Essex; later pastor at Ipswich in Massachusetts; author of *The Simple Cobler of Agawam.* Mr. Marshall: Stephen Marshall, vicar of Finchingfield, Essex. Mr. Wharton: Samuel Wharton, vicar of Felsted, Essex.

upon holy ground. Thereupon he was committed to the pursuivant and bound over to answer it at the High Commission. But when Mr. Weld was pleading for himself, and that it was ignorance that made him come in, the Bishop asked him whither he intended to go, whether to New England, and if so whether I would go with him. While he was thus speaking I came into the crowd and heard the words. Others bid me go away, but neglecting to do it, a godly man pulled me away with violence out of the crowd. And as soon as ever I was gone the apparitor calls for Mr. Shepard, and the pursuivant was sent presently after to find me out. But he that pulled me away (Mr. Holbeach[26] by name, a schoolmaster at Felsted in Essex) hastened our horses and away we rid as fast as we could. And so the Lord delivered me out of the hand of that lion a third time. And now I perceived I could not stay in Colne without danger, and hereupon receiving a letter from Mr. Ezekiel Rogers,[27] then living at Rowley in Yorkshire, to encourage me to come to the knight's house, called Sir Richard Darley, dwelling at a town called Buttercrambe, and the knight's two sons, viz., Mr. Henry and Mr. Richard Darley, promising me £20 a year for their part, and the knight promising me my table, and the letters sent to me crying with that voice of the man of Macedonia, Come and help us. Hereupon I resolved to follow the Lord to so remote and strange a place, the rather because I might be far from the hearing of the malicious Bishop Laud who had threatened me if I preached anywhere. So when I was determined to go, the gentlemen sent a man to me to be my guide in my journey, who coming with me, with much grief of heart I forsook Essex and Earle's Colne and they me, going, as it were, now I knew not whither.

So as we traveled (which was five or six days together near unto winter) the Lord sent much rain and ill weather insomuch as the floods were up when we came near Yorkshire, and hardly passable. At last we came to a town called Ferry-brig where the waters were up and ran over the bridge for half a mile together and more. So we hired a guide to lead us, but when he had gone a little way the

26. Martin Holbeach, headmaster of Felsted School, where a number of prominent Puritans were educated.

27. Ezekiel Rogers (1590–1661), son of Richard; at that time rector of Rowley St. Peter, Yorkshire; pastor at Rowley in Massachusetts, 1639–60.

violence of the water was such that he first fell in and after him another man who was near drowning before my eyes, whereupon my heart was so smitten with fear of the danger and my head so dizzied with the running of the water that, had not the Lord immediately upheld me and my horse also and so guided it, I had certainly perished that bout. But the Lord was strong in my weakness. And we went on by some little direction upon the bridge, and at last I fell in, yet in a place where the waters were not so violent, but I sat upon my horse, which, being a very good horse, clambered up upon the bridge again, but Mr. Darley's man, for fear of me, fell in also but came out safe again. And so we came to the dry land where we had a house and shifted ourselves and went to prayer and blessed God for this wonderful preservation of us. And the Lord made me then to profess that I looked now upon my life as a new life given unto me, which I saw good reason to give up unto him and his service. And truly about this time the Lord that had dealt only gently with me before began to afflict me and to let me taste how good it was to be under his tutoring. So I came to York late upon Saturday night, and, having refreshed ourselves there, I came to Buttercrambe to Sir Richard's house that night very wet and late, which is about seven miles off from York.

Now as soon as I came into the house I found diverse of them at dice and tables. Mr. Richard Darley, one of the brothers, being to return to London the Monday after and being desirous to hear me preach, sent me speedily to my lodging (the best in the house), and so I preached the day after once, and then he departed, the day after, having carefully desired my comfortable abode there. But I do remember I never was so low sunk in my spirit as about this time, for (1) I was now far from all friends; (2) I was, I saw, in a profane house, not any sincerely good; (3) I was in a vile wicked town and country; (4) I was unknown and exposed to all wrongs; (5) I was unsufficient to do any work, and my sins were upon me, etc. And hereupon I was very low and sunk deep, yet the Lord did not leave me comfortless. For though the lady was churlish, yet Sir Richard was ingenious, and I found in the house three servants, *viz.,* Thomas Fugill, Mistress Margaret Touteville, the knight's kinswoman that was afterward my wife, and Ruth Bushell (now married to Edward Michelson),[28] very careful of me, which somewhat refreshed me. But it happened that when I had been there a little while there was a marriage of one Mr. Allured, a most profane young gentleman, to Sir Richard's daughter, and I was desired to preach at their marriage, at which sermon the Lord first touched the heart of Mistress Margaret with very great terrors for sin and her Christless estate, whereupon others began to look about them, especially the gentlewoman lately married, Mistress Allured, and the Lord brake both their hearts very kindly. Then others in the family, *viz.,* Mr. Allured, he fell to fasting and prayer and great reformation. Others also were reformed and their hearts changed—the whole family brought to external duties—but I remember none in the town or about it brought home. And thus the Lord was with me and gave me favor and friends and respect of all in the family, and the Lord taught me much of his goodness and sweetness. And when he had fitted a wife for me, he then gave me her who was a most sweet humble woman, full of Christ, and a very discerning Christian, a wife who was most incomparably loving to me and every way amiable and holy and endued with a very sweet spirit of prayer. And thus the Lord answered my desires: when my adversaries intended most hurt to me, the Lord was then best unto me and used me the more kindly in every place. For the Lord turned all the sons and Sir Richard and Mr. Allured so unto me that they not only gave her freely to be my wife but enlarged her portion also. And thus I did marry the best and fittest woman in the world unto me after I had preached in this place about a twelvemonth, for which mercy to me in my exiled condition in a strange place I did promise the Lord that this mercy should knit my heart the nearer to him and that his love should constrain me. But I have ill requited the Lord since that time and forgot myself and my promise also.

But now when we were married in the year 1632,[29] she was unwilling to stay at Buttercrambe, and I saw no means or likelihood

28. Thomas Fugill later went to the New Haven colony; the Michelsons settled in Cambridge, Massachusetts.
29. July 23, 1632.

of abode there, for Bishop Neile[30] coming up to York, no friends could procure my liberty of him without subscription. And hereupon the Lord gave me a call to Northumberland, to a town called Heddon, five mile beyond Newcastle, which, when I had considered of and saw no place but that to go unto and saw the people very desirous of it and that I might preach there in peace, being far from any bishops, I did resolve to depart thither, and so, being accompanied with Mr. Allured to the place, I came not without many fears of enemies, and my poor wife full of fears it was not a place of subsistence with any comfort to me there. But the good Lord who all my life followed me made this place the fittest for me, and I found many sweet friends and Christian acquaintance, Mistress Sherbourne maintaining me and Mistress Fenwick lending us the use of her house, and so God comforted us in our solitary and yet married condition many ways.

Now when I was here the Lord blessed my poor labors both to the saints and to sundry others about and in Newcastle, and I came here to read and know more of the ceremonies, church government and estate, and the unlawful standing of bishops than in any other place. I lived at Mistress Fenwick's house for a time, about a twelvemonth or half a year, and then we went and dwelt alone in a town near Heddon, called [*blank*], in a house which we found haunted with the devil, as we conceived, for when we came into it a known witch went out of it. And being troubled with noises four or five nights together, we sought God by prayer to remove so sore a trial, and the Lord heard and blessed us there and removed the trouble. But after we were settled the Bishop put in a priest who would not suffer me to preach publicly anymore. Hereupon means was made to the Bishop of Durham, Bishop Morton,[31] and he professed he durst not give me liberty because Laud had taken notice of me. So I preached up and down in the country and at last privately in Mr. Fenwick's house, and there I stayed till Mr. Cotton,

30. Richard Neile (1562–1640), successively Bishop of Durham, Rochester, Lichfield, Lincoln, and Winchester was translated to the See of York in 1631. He was a prominent Laudean and a vigorous exponent of the royal prerogative and the divine right of episcopacy.

31. Thomas Morton (1564–1659), successively Bishop of Chester, Lichfield, and Durham, the last from 1632 to 1659, was a man of Low Church sympathies who took no active part in Laud's campaign for uniformity.

Mr. Hooker, Stone, Weld went to New England,[32] and hereupon most of the godly in England were awakened and intended much to go to New England. And I having a call by diverse friends in New England to come over and many in old England desiring me to go over and promising to go with me, I did thereupon resolve to go thither, especially considering the season. And thus the Lord blessed me in this dark country and gave me a son called Thomas, anno 1633, my poor wife being in sore extremities four days by reason she had an unskillful midwife. But as the affliction was very bitter, so the Lord did teach me much by it, and I had need of it, for I began to grow secretly proud and full of sensuality, delighting my soul in my dear wife more than in my God, whom I had promised better unto, and my spirit grew fierce in some things and secretly mindless of the souls of the people. But the Lord by this affliction of my wife learnt me to desire to fear him more and to keep his dread in my heart. And so, seeing I had been tossed from the south to the north of England and now could go no farther, I then began to listen to a call to New England.

The reasons which swayed me to come to New England were many. (1) I saw no call to any other place in old England nor way of subsistence in peace and comfort to me and my family. (2) Diverse people in old England of my dear friends desired me to go to New England, there to live together, and some went before and writ to me of providing a place for a company of us, one of which was John Bridge,[33] and I saw diverse families of my Christian friends who were resolved thither to go with me. (3) I saw the Lord departing from England when Mr. Hooker and Mr. Cotton were gone, and I saw the hearts of most of the godly set and bent that way, and I did think I should feel many miseries if I stayed behind. (4) My judgment was then convinced not only of the evil of ceremonies but of mixed communion and joining with such in sacraments, though I ever judged it lawful to join with them in preaching. (5) I saw it my duty to desire the fruition of all God's or-

32. John Cotton (1585–1652), vicar of St. Botolph's in Boston, Lincolnshire, settled in Boston in New England in 1633. Hooker and Stone left England the same year. Weld had gone the year before.

33. John Bridge preceded Hooker to Newtown and remained there when Hooker's congregation left. He served as deacon, selectman, and deputy to the General Court.

dinances which I could not enjoy in old England. (6) My dear wife did much long to see me settled there in peace and so put me on to it. (7) Although it was true I should stay and suffer for Christ, yet I saw no rule for it now the Lord had opened a door of escape. Otherwise I did incline much to stay and suffer, especially after our sea storms. (8) Though my ends were mixed and I looked much to my own quiet, yet the Lord let me see the glory of those liberties in New England and made me purpose, if ever I should come over, to live among God's people as one come out from the dead, to his praise, though since I have seen as the Lord's goodness, so my own exceeding weakness to be as good as I thought to have been. And although they did desire me to stay in the north and preach privately, yet (1) I saw that this time could not be long without trouble from King Charles; (2) I saw no reason to spend my time privately when I might possibly exercise my talent publicly in New England; (3) I did hope my going over might make them to follow me; (4) I considered how sad a thing it would be for me to leave my wife and child (if I should die) in that rude place of the north where was nothing but barbarous wickedness generally, and how sweet it would be to leave them among God's people, though poor; (5) My liberty in private was daily threatened, and I thought it wisdom to depart before the pursuivants came out, for so I might depart with more peace and less trouble and danger to me and my friends. And I knew not whether God would have me to hazard my person and comfort of me and all mine for a disorderly manner of preaching privately (as it was reputed) in those parts. So after I had preached my farewell sermon at Newcastle I departed from the north in a ship laden with coals for Ipswich, about the beginning of June, after I had been about a year in the north, the Lord having blessed some few sermons and notes to divers in Newcastle from whom I parted filled with their love. And so the Lord gave us a speedy voyage from thence to Ipswich in old England, whither I came in a disguised manner with my wife and child and maid, and stayed a while at Mr. Russell's house, another while at Mr. Collins his house, and then went down to Essex to the town where I had preached, *viz.,* Earle's Colne, to Mr. Richard Harlakenden's house where I lived privately but with much love from them all, as also from Mr. Joseph Cooke, and also with friends at

London and Northamptonshire.[34] And truly I found this time of my life wherein I was so tossed up and down and had no place of settling, but kept secret in regard of the bishops, the most uncomfortable and fruitless time to my own soul especially that ever I had in my life. And therefore I did long to be in New England as soon as might be, and the rather because my wife, having weaned her first son Thomas, had conceived again and was breeding, and I knew no place in England where she could lie in without discovery of myself, danger to myself and all my friends that should receive me, and where we could not but give offense to many if I should have my child not baptized. And therefore, there being divers godly Christians resolved to go toward the latter end of the year if I would go, I did therefore resolve to go that year, the end of that summer I came from the north. And the time appointed for the ship to go out was about a month or fortnight before Michaelmas (as they there call it); the ship was called the *Hope of Ipswich;* the master of it (a very able seaman) was Mr. Gurling who professed much love to me, who had got this ship of 400 ton from the Danes, and as some report, it was by some fraud. But he denied it, and, being a man very loving and full of fair promises of going at the time appointed and an able seaman, hence we resolved to adventure that time, though dangerous in regard of the approaching winter.

Now here the Lord's wonderful terror and mercy to us did appear. For being come to Ipswich with my family at the time appointed, the ship was not ready, and we stayed six or eight weeks longer than the time promised for her going. And so it was very late in the year and very dangerous to go to sea, and indeed if we had gone, doubtless we had all perished upon the seas, it being so extreme cold and tempestuous winter, but yet we could not go back when we had gone so far. And the Lord saw it good to chastise us for rushing onward too soon and hazarding ourselves in that manner, and I had many fears, and much darkness (I remember) overspread my soul, doubting of our way, yet I say we could not now go back. Only I learnt from that time never to go about a

34. John Russell and Joseph Cooke crossed with Shepard in 1635. Edward Collins settled in Cambridge in the same year or the next; his confession and that of his wife, Martha, are printed below.

sad business in the dark, unless God's call within as well as that without be very strong and clear and comfortable.

So that in the year 1634, about the beginning of the winter, we set sail from Harwich, and, having gone some few leagues onto the sea, the wind stopped us that night, and so we cast anchor in a dangerous place. And on the morning the wind grew fierce and rough against us full, and drave us toward the sands, but the vessel, being laden too heavy at the head, would not stir for all that which the seamen could do, but drave us full upon the sands near Harwich harbor. And the ship did grate upon the sands and was in great danger, but the Lord directed one man to cut some cable or rope in the ship, and so she was turned about and was beaten quite backward toward Yarmouth, quite out of our way. But while the ship was in this great danger a wonderful, miraculous providence did appear to us, for one of the seamen, that he might save the vessel, fell in when it was in that danger and so was carried out a mile or more from the ship and given for dead and gone. The ship was then in such danger that none could attend to follow him, and when it was out of danger it was a very great hazard to the lives of any that should take the skiff to seek to find him. Yet it pleased the Lord that, being discerned afar off floating upon the waters, three of the seamen adventured out upon the rough waters, and at last, about an hour after he fell into the sea (as we conjectured), they came and found him floating upon the waters, never able to swim but supported by a divine hand all this while. When the men came to him they were glad to find him, but concluded he was dead, and so got him into the skiff, and when he was there tumbled him down as one dead. Yet one of them said to the rest, Let us use what means we can if there be life to preserve it, and thereupon turned his head downward for the water to run out, and having done so the fellow began to gasp and breathe. Then they applied other means they had, and so he began at last to move and then to speak, and by that time he came to the ship he was pretty well and able to walk. And so the Lord showed us his great power, whereupon a godly man in the ship then said: This man's danger and deliverance is a type of ours, for he did fear dangers were near unto us, and that yet the Lord's power should be shown in saving of us. For so indeed it was. For the wind did drive us quite backward out of our way and gave us no place to anchor at until we came unto Yarmouth Roads, an open place at sea yet fit for anchorage, but otherwise a very dangerous place. And so we came thither through many uncomfortable hazards within thirty hours and cast anchor in Yarmouth Roads, which when we had done upon a Saturday morning the Lord sent a most dreadful and terrible storm of wind from the west, so dreadful that to this day the seamen call it Windy Saturday, that it also scattered many ships in diverse coasts at that time, and diverse ships were cast away. One among the rest, which was the seamen's ship who came with us from Newcastle, was cast away, and he and all his men perished. But when the wind thus arose, the master cast all his anchors, but the storm was so terrible that the anchors broke and the ship drave toward the sands where we could not but be cast away, whereupon the master cries out that we were dead men, and thereupon the whole company go to prayer. But the vessel still drave so near to the sands that the master shot off two pieces of ordnance to the town for help to save the passengers. The town perceived it and thousands came upon the walls of Yarmouth and looked upon us, hearing we were New England men [this word doubtful], and pitied much and gave us for gone because they saw other ships perishing near unto us at that time, but could not send any help unto us though much money was offered by some to hazard themselves for us. So the master not knowing what to do, it pleased the Lord that there was one Mr. Cock, a drunken fellow but no seaman yet one that had been at sea often and would come in a humor unto New England with us; whether it was to see the country or no I cannot tell, but sure I am God intended it for good unto us to make him an instrument to save all our lives. For he persuaded the master to cut down his mainmast. The master was unwilling to it and besotted, not sensible of ours and his own loss. At last this Cock calls for hatchets, tells the master, If you be a man, save the lives of your passengers, cut down your mainmast. Hereupon he encouraged all the company who were forlorn and hopeless of life, and the seamen presently cut down the mast aboard, just at that very time wherein we all gave ourselves for gone to see neither old nor New England nor faces of friends anymore, there being near upon 200 passengers in the ship. And so when the mast was down, the master had one little anchor left and cast it out, but the ship was driven away toward the sands still, and the seamen came to us and bid us look (pointing to the place) where our graves should shortly be, conceiving also that the wind had broke off this anchor also. So the master professed he had done what he could and therefore now desired us to go to prayer. So Mr. Norton[35] in one place and myself in another part of the ship, he with the passengers, and myself with the mariners above decks, went to prayer and committed our souls and bodies unto the Lord that gave them. Immediately after prayer the wind began to abate, and the ship stayed, for the last anchor was not broke (as we conceived) but only rent up with the wind, and so drave and was drawn along plowing the sands with the violence of the wind, which abating after prayer (though still very terrible) the ship was stopped just when it was ready to be swallowed up of the sands, a very little way off from it. And so we rid it out, yet not without fear of our lives though the anchor stopped the ship, because the cable was let out so far that a little rope held the cable, and the cable the little anchor, and the little anchor the great ship in this great storm. But when one of the company perceived that we were so strangely preserved, had these words, That thread we hang by will save us, for so we accounted of the rope fastened to the anchor, in comparison of the fierce storm. And so indeed it did, the Lord showing his dreadful power toward us and yet his unspeakable rich mercy to us who in depths of mercy heard, nay helped, us where we could not cry through the disconsolate fears we had out of these depths of seas and miseries. This deliverance was so great that I then did think if ever the Lord did bring me to shore again I should live like one come and risen from the dead. This is one of those living mercies the Lord hath shown me, a mercy to myself, to my wife and child then living, and to my second son Thomas who was in this storm but in the womb of his dear mother who might then have perished and been cut off from all hope of means and mercy, and unto my dear friends then with me, *viz.,* brother Champney, Frost, Goffe,[36] and diverse others,

35. John Norton (1606–63), curate at Bishop's Stortford, Hertfordshire; pastor at Ipswich in Massachusetts, 1636–53, and at Boston, 1653–63.

36. Richard Champney crossed with Shepard in the *Defense* in 1635; Edmund Frost and Edward Goffe came the same year in another ship. All three settled in Cambridge where they held high posts in town and church.

most dear saints, and also to all with me. And how would the name of the Lord suffered if we had so perished; that the Lord Jesus should have respect to me so vile and one at that time full of many temptations and weaknesses, amazed much and deeply afraid of God's terror, yet supported. I desire this mercy may be remembered of my children and their children's children when I am dead and cannot praise the Lord in the land of the living anymore. And so we continued that night, many sick, many weak and discouraged, many sad hearts. Yet upon the Sabbath morning we departed and went out of the ship—I fear a little soon, for we should have spent that day in praising of him. Yet we were afraid of neglecting a season of providence in going out while we had a calm, and many sick folk were unfit for that work and had need of refreshing at shore.

So upon the Sabbath-day morning boats came to our vessel from the town, and so my dear wife and child went in the first boat. But here the Lord saw that these waters were not sufficient to wash away my filth and sinfulness, and therefore he cast me into the fire as soon as ever I was upon the sea in the boat, for there my first-born child, very precious to my soul and dearly beloved of me, was smitten with sickness; the Lord sent a vomiting upon it whereby it grew faint, and nothing that we could use could stop its vomiting, although we had many helps at Yarmouth, and this was a very bitter affliction to me. And the Lord now showed me my weak faith, want of fear, pride, carnal content, immoderate love of creatures and of my child especially, and begot in me some desires and purposes to fear his name. But yet the Lord would not be entreated for the life of it, and after a fortnight's sickness at last it gave up the ghost when its mother had given it up to the Lord, and was buried at Yarmouth where I durst not be present lest the pursuivants should apprehend me and I should be discovered, which was a great affliction and very bitter to me and my dear wife. And hereby I saw the Lord did come near to me, and I did verily fear the Lord would take away my wife also, if not myself not long after. And these afflictions, together with the Lord's crossing us and being so directly against our voyage, made me secretly willing to stay and suffer in England, and my heart was not so much toward New England. Yet this satisfied me, that seeing there was a door opened of escape, why should I suffer? And I considered how unfit

I was to go to such a good land with such an unmortified, hard, dark, formal, hypocritical heart, and therefore no wonder if the Lord did thus cross me. And the Lord made me fear my affliction came in part for running too far in a way of separation from the mixed assemblies in England, though I bless God I have ever believed that there are true churches in many parishes in England where the Lord sets up able men and ministers of his gospel, and I have abhorred to refuse to hear any able ministers in England.

So that now I having buried my first born and being in great sadness and not knowing where to go nor what to do, the Lord sent Mr. Roger Harlakenden and my brother Samuel Shepard[37] to visit me after they had heard of our escape at sea, who much refreshed us and clave to me in my sorrows. And being casting about where to go and live, Mr. Bridge,[38] then minister in Norwich, sent for me to come and live with him, and being come, one Mistress Corbet who lived five miles off Norwich, an aged, eminent, godly gentlewoman, hearing of my coming and that by being with Mr. Bridge might hazard his liberty by countenancing of me, she did therefore freely offer to me a great house of hers standing empty at a town called Bastwick, and there the Lord stirred up her heart to show all love to me, which did much lighten and sweeten my sorrows. And I saw the Lord Jesus' care herein to me and saw cause of trusting him in times of straits, who set me in such a place where I lived for half a year, all the winter long, among and with my friends (Mr. Harlakenden dwelling with me and bearing all the charge of housekeeping) and far from the notice of my enemies, where we enjoyed sweet fellowship one with another and also with God, in a house which was fit to entertain any prince for fairness and greatness and pleasantness. Here the Lord hid us all the winter long, and when it was fit to travel in the spring we went up to London, Mr. Harlakenden not forsaking me all this while, for he was a father and mother to me. And when we came to London to Mistress Sherborne, not knowing what to do nor where to live privately, the Lord provided a very private place for us where my wife was brought to bed and delivered of my second son Thomas, and

37. Samuel Shepard went with his brother in the *Defense,* listed as servant to Roger Harlakenden.

38. William Bridge, a Cambridge graduate.

none but our friends did know of it. And so by this means my son was not baptized until we came to New England the winter following, being born in London, April 5, 1635. One remarkable deliverance my wife had when we were coming up to London. Mr. Burrows, the minister, kindly entertained us about a fortnight in the way, and when my wife was there, being great with child, she fell down from the top of a pair of stairs to the bottom, yet the Lord kept her and the child also safe from that deadly danger. When we had been also at London for a time and began to be known in the place, my wife was brought to bed. The Lord put it into our hearts to remove to another place in Mr. Eldred's house in London which stood empty, and the very night we were all come away then came the pursuivants and others to search after us, but the Lord delivered us out of their hands. And so, when the Lord had recovered my wife, we began to prepare for a removal once again to New England.

And the Lord seemed to make our way plain (1) because I had no other call to any place in England; (2) many more of God's people resolved to go with me, as Mr. Roger Harlakenden and Mr. Champney, etc.; (3) the Lord saw our unfitness and the unfitness of our going the year before, and therefore giving us good friends to accompany us and good company in the ship, we set forward, about the tenth of August, 1635, with myself, wife, and my little son Thomas, and other precious friends, having tasted much of God's mercy in England and lamenting the loss of our native country when we took our last view of it. In our voyage upon the sea the Lord was very tender of me and kept me from the violence of seasickness. In our coming we were refreshed with the society of Mr. Wilson,[39] Mr. Jones,[40] by their faith and prayers and preaching. The ship we came in was very rotten and unfit for such a voyage, and therefore the first storm we had, we had a very great leak which did much appall and affect us. Yet the Lord discovered it unto us, when we were thinking of returning back again, and much comforted our hearts. We had many storms, in one of which

39. John Wilson (1588?–1667), pastor of the church at Boston, had crossed with Winthrop in 1630. He was returning in 1635 from his second visit to England.

40. John Jones (1593–1665), pastor at Concord, 1635–44, and Fairfield, Connecticut, 1644–65.

my dear wife took such a cold and got such weakness as that she fell into a consumption of which she afterward died. And also the Lord preserved her with the child in her arms from imminent and apparent death, for by the shaking of the ship in a violent storm her head was pitched against an iron bolt, and the Lord miraculously preserved the child and recovered my wife. This was a great affliction to me and was a cause of many sad thoughts in the ship how to behave myself when I came to New England. My resolutions I have written down in my little book. And so the Lord after many sad storms and wearisome days and many longings to see the shore, the Lord brought us to the sight of it upon October 2, anno 1635, and upon October the third we arrived with my wife, child, brother Samuel, Mr. Harlakenden, Mr. Cooke, etc., at Boston with rejoicing in our God after a longsome voyage, my dear wife's great desire being now fulfilled, which was to leave me in safety from the hand of my enemies and among God's people, and also the child under God's precious ordinances.

Now when we came upon shore we were kindly saluted and entertained by many friends and were the first three days in the house of Mr. Coddington, being treasurer at that time, and that with much love.[41]

When we had been here two days, upon the Monday, October 5, we came (being sent for by friends at Newtown) to them to my brother Mr. Stone's house. And that congregation being upon their removal to Hartford at Connecticut, myself and those that came with me found many houses empty and many persons willing to sell, and hence our company bought off their houses to dwell in until we should see another place fit to remove unto. But having been here some time, divers of our brethren did desire to sit still and not to remove further, partly because of the fellowship of the churches, partly because they thought their lives were short and removals to new plantations full of troubles, partly because they found sufficient for themselves and their company. Hereupon

41. William Coddington (1601–1678), a leading citizen of Boston from 1630 to 1638 when, having supported Anne Hutchinson, he removed to Aquidneck where he helped found Newport and served as governor both of Aquidneck and later of the united plantations of Rhode Island and Providence. He was a successful merchant; late in life he became a Quaker.

there was a purpose to enter into church fellowship, which we did the year after about the end of the winter,[42] a fortnight after which my dear wife Margaret died, being first received into church fellowship which, as she much longed for, so the Lord did so sweeten it unto her that she was hereby exceedingly cheered and comforted with the sense of God's love, which continued until her last gasp.

No sooner were we thus set down and entered into church fellowship but the Lord exercised us and the whole country with the opinions of Familists, begun by Mistress Hutchinson, raised up to a great height by Mr. Vane[43] too suddenly chosen governor, and maintained too obscurely by Mr. Cotton, and propagated too boldly by the members of Boston and some in other churches, by means of which division by these opinions the ancient and received truth came to be darkened, God's name to be blasphemed, the churches' glory diminished, many godly grieved, many wretches hardened, deceiving and being deceived, growing worse and worse. The principal opinion and seed of all the rest was this, *viz.*, that a Christian should not take any evidence of God's special grace and love toward him by the sight of any graces or conditional evangelical promises to faith or sanctification, in way of ratiocination (for this was evidence and so a way of works), but it must be without the sight of any grace, faith, holiness, or special change in himself, by immediate revelation in an absolute promise. And because that the whole scriptures do give such clear, plain, and notable evidences of favor to persons called and sanctified, hence they said that a second evidence might be taken from hence but no first evidence. But from hence it arose that, as all error is fruitful, so this opinion did gender about a hundred monstrous opinions in the country, which the elders perceiving, having used all private brotherly means with Mr. Cotton first and yet no healing hereupon, they publicly preached both against opinions publicly and privately maintained, and I account it no small mercy to myself that the Lord kept me from that contagion and gave me any heart or light to see through those devices of men's heads, although I found it a

42. Winthrop's *Journal* has an account of the ceremonies under date of February 1, 1636.
43. Sir Henry Vane (1613–62) was defeated by John Winthrop in March, 1637, after one term as governor of the Bay Colony. His departure from Massachusetts in August of the same year deprived the Hutchinsonians of their principal lay supporter.

most uncomfortable time to live in contention. And the Lord was graciously pleased by giving witness against them to keep this poor church spotless and clear from them. This division in the church began to trouble the commonwealth. Mr. Wheelwright, a man of a bold and stiff conceit of his own worth and light, preached (as the Court judged) a seditious sermon,[44] stirring up all sorts against those that preached a covenant of works, meaning all the elders in the country that preached justification by faith and assurance of it by sight of faith and sanctification, being enabled thereto by the spirit. The troubles thus increasing and all means used for crushing and curing these sorts, a synod was thought of and called from the example, Acts 15, wherein by the help of all the elders joined together those errors through the grace and power of Christ were discovered, the defenders of them convinced and ashamed, the truth established, and the consciences of the saints settled, there being a most wonderful presence of Christ's spirit in that assembly, held at Cambridge, anno 1637, about August, and continued a month together in public agitations, for the issue of this synod was this:

(1)The Pequot Indians were fully discomfited, for as the opinions arose, wars did arise, and when these began to be crushed by the ministry of the elders and by opposing Mr. Vane and casting him and others from being magistrates, the enemies began to be crushed and were perfectly subdued by the end of the synod.

(2) The magistrates took courage and exiled Mr. Wheelwright, Mistress Hutchinson, and diverse Islanders,[45] whom the Lord did strangely discover, giving most of them over to all manner of filthy opinions, until many that held with them before were ashamed of them, and so the Lord within one year wrought a great change among us.

At this time I cannot omit the goodness of God as to myself, so to all the country, in delivering us from the Pequot furies. These Indians were the stoutest, proudest, and most successful in their wars of all the Indians. Their chief sachem was Sassacus, a proud, cruel, unhappy, and headstrong prince who, not willing to be

44. John Wheelwright (1594–1679), later pastor at Hampton, New Hampshire, and Salisbury, Massachusetts, preached the Fast Day sermon, January 19, 1636/37.

45. The Islanders were the inhabitants of Aquidneck, many of whom were Hutchinsonian exiles.

guided by the persuasions of his fellow, an aged sachem, Momanattuck, nor fearing the revenge of the English, having first sucked the blood of Captain Stone and Mr. Oldham, found it so sweet and his proceedings for one whole winter so successful that, having beseiged and killed about four men that kept Saybrook fort, he adventured to fall upon the English up the river at Wethersfield where he slew nine or ten men, women, and children at unawares and took two maids prisoners, carrying them away captive to the Pequot country. Hereupon those upon the river first gathered about seventy men and sent them into Pequot country to make that the seat of war and to revenge the death of those innocents whom they barbarously and most unnaturally slew. These men marched two days and nights from the way of the Narragansett unto Pequot, being guided by those Indians, then the ancient enemies of the Pequots. They intended to assault Sassacus' fort, but falling short of it the second night, the providence of God guided them to another nearer, full of stout men, and their best soldiers being, as it were, cooped up there to the number of three or four hundred in all for the divine slaughter by the hand of the English. These therefore being all night making merry and singing the death of the English the next day, toward break of the day being very heavy with sleep, the English drew near within the sight of the fort, very weary with travail and want of sleep, at which time 500 Narragansetts fled for fear and only two of the company stood to it to conduct them to the fort and the door and entrance thereof. The English, being come to it, awakened the fort with a peal of muskets directed into the midst of their wigwams, and after this, some undertaking to compass the fort without, some adventured into the fort upon the very faces of the enemy standing ready with their arrows ready bent to shoot whoever should adventure. But the English, casting by their pieces, took their swords in their hands (the Lord doubling their strength and courage) and fell upon the Indians where a hot fight continued about the space of an hour. At last, by the direction of one Captain Mason,[46] their wigwams were set

46. John Mason (c. 1600–1672), soldier and colonial magistrate, saw service in the Low Countries before coming to New England, c. 1633. In addition to his military exploits, he founded the towns of Windsor and Norwich, handled Indian affairs for Connecticut and for the Confederation of New England, and held prominent offices in the government of Connecticut.

on fire, which, being dry and contiguous one to another, was most dreadful to the Indians, some burning, some bleeding to death by the sword, some resisting till they were cut off, some flying were beat down by the men without, until the Lord had utterly consumed the whole company except four or five girls they took prisoners and dealt with them at Saybrook as they dealt with ours at Wethersfield, and 'tis verily thought scarce one man escaped unless one or two to carry forth tidings of the lamentable end of their fellows, and of the English not one man was killed but one by the musket of an Englishman (as was conceived); some were wounded much but all recovered and restored again.

Thus the Lord having delivered the country from war with Indians and Familists (who arose and fell together), he was pleased to direct the hearts of the magistrates (then keeping court ordinarily in our town because of the stirs at Boston) to think of erecting a school or college, and that speedily, to be a nursery of knowledge in these deserts and supply for posterity. And because this town (then called Newtown) was through God's great care and goodness kept spotless from the contagion of the opinions, therefore at the desire of some of our town the deputies of the Court, having got Mr. Eaton to attend the school, the Court for that and sundry other reasons determined to erect the college here, which was no sooner done but the chief of the magistrates and elders sent to England to desire help to forward this work. But they all neglecting us (in a manner), the Lord put it into the heart of one Mr. Harvard,[47] who died worth £1600, to give half his estate to the erecting of the school. The man was a scholar and pious in his life and enlarged toward the country and the good of it in life and death. But no sooner was this given but Mr. Eaton (professing eminently yet falsely and most deceitfully the fear of God) did lavish out a great part of it, and being for his cruelty to his scholars, especially to one Briscoe, as also for some other wantonness in life not so notoriously known, driven [from] the country, the Lord about a year after gra-

47. John Harvard (1607–1638), a graduate of Emmanuel College, settled in Charlestown in 1637 where he served as elder of the church. In addition to the money, his legacy to Harvard College included some 400 books. The College was named for him by an appreciative General Court in 1639. As a regular lecturer at Charlestown, Shepard would have known Harvard well; his influence may be apparent in the bequest to the College.

ciously made up the breach by one Mr. Dunster,[48] a man pious, painful, and fit to teach, and very fit to lay the foundations of the domestical affairs of the college, whom God hath much honored and blessed.

The sin of Mr. Eaton was at first not so clearly discerned by me, yet after more full information I saw his sin great and my ignorance and want of wisdom and watchfulness over him very great, for which I desire to mourn all my life, and for the breach of his family.

But thus the Lord hath been very good unto me in planting the place I lived in with such a mercy to myself, such a blessing to my children and the country, such an opportunity of doing good to many by doing good to students, as the school is.

After this I fell sick after Mr. Harlakenden's death, my most dear friend and most precious servant of Jesus Christ. And when I was very low and my blood much corrupted, the Lord revived me and after that took pleasure in me to bless my labors that I was not altogether useless nor fruitless.

And not only to speak by me to his people but likewise to print my notes upon the nine principles I intended to proceed on with in Yorkshire but never intended them or imagined they should be for the press. Yet six of them being finished in old England and printed,[49] and the other three desired, I finished (the Lord helping) those at Cambridge and so sent them to England where they also are printed,[50] which I do not glory in (for I know my weakness) that my name is up by this means, but that the Lord may be pleased to do some good by them there in my absence, for I have seen the Lord making improvement of my weak abilities as far as they could reach and of myself to the utmost, which I desire to bless his name forever for.

The year after those wars in the country, God having taken away my first wife, the Lord gave me a second, the eldest daughter of Mr. Hooker,[51] a blessed stock. And the Lord hath made her a

48. Henry Dunster (1609–1659), president of Harvard College, 1640–1654.
49. *The Sincere Convert* (London, 1640).
50. *The Sound Believer* (London, 1645).
51. Joanna Hooker.

great blessing to me to carry on matters in the family with much care and wisdom, and to seek the Lord God of her father.

The first child I had by her (being a son) died (through the weakness of the midwife) before it saw the sun, even in the very birth. The second (whom the Lord I bless hath hitherto spared), viz., my little Samuel, is yet living. The third son, viz., my son John, after sixteen weeks departed on the Sabbath-day morning, a day of rest, to the bosom of rest to him who gave it, which was no small affliction and heartbreaking to me that I should provoke the Lord to strike at my innocent children for my sake.

The Lord thus afflicting yet continued peace to the country, that amazing mercy, when all England and Europe are in a flame. The Lord hath set me and my children aside from the flames of the fires in Yorkshire and Northumberland whence if we had not been delivered I had been in great afflictions and temptations, very weak and unfit to be tossed up and down and to bear violent persecution. The Lord therefore hath showed his tenderness to me and mine in carrying me to a land of peace, though a place of trial, where the Lord hath made the savage Indians who conspired the death of all the English by Miantonomo upon a sudden, if Uncas could have been cut off first who stood in their way, and determined an open war upon us by the privy suggestions of some neutral English on the Island, to seek for peace from us upon our own terms without bloodshed, August 26, 1645.

But the Lord hath not been wont to let me live long without some affliction or other, and yet ever mixed with some mercy, and therefore, April the second, 1646, as he gave me another son, John, so he took away my most dear, precious, meek and loving wife in childbed after three weeks lying in, having left behind her two hopeful branches, my dear children Samuel and John. This affliction was very heavy to me, for in it the Lord seemed to withdraw his tender care for me and mine which he graciously manifested by my dear wife; also refused to hear prayer when I did think he would have harkened and let me see his beauty in the land of the living in restoring her to health again; also in taking her away in the prime of her life when she might have lived to have glorified the Lord long; also in threatening me to proceed in rooting out my family, and that he would not stop, having begun here, as in Eli for not being zealous enough against the sins of his son. And

I saw that if I had profited by former afflictions of this nature I should not have had this scourge. But I am the Lord's, and he may do with me what he will. He did teach me to prize a little grace gained by a cross as a sufficient recompense for all outward losses. But this loss was very great. She was a woman of incomparable meekness of spirit, toward myself especially, and very loving, of great prudence to take care for and order my family affairs, bring neither too lavish nor sordid in anything, so that I knew not what was under her hands. She had an excellency to reprove for sin and discerned the evils of men. She loved God's people dearly and studious to profit by their fellowship, and therefore loved their company. She loved God's word exceedingly and hence was glad she could read my notes which she had to muse on every week. She had a spirit of prayer beyond ordinary of her time and experience. She was fit to die long before she did die, even after the death of her first-born, which was a great affliction to her, but her work not being done then, she lived almost nine years with me and was the comfort of my life to me, and the last sacrament before her lying in seemed to be full of Christ and thereby fitted for heaven. She did oft say she should not outlive this child, and when her fever first began (by taking some cold) she told me so, that we should love exceedingly together because we should not live long together. Her fever took away her sleep; want of sleep wrought much distemper in her head and filled it with fantasies and distractions, but without raging. The night before she died she had about six hours unquiet sleep, but that so cooled and settled her head that when she knew none else so as to speak to them, yet she knew Jesus Christ and could speak to him, and therefore as soon as she awakened out of sleep she brake out into a most heavenly, heartbreaking prayer after Christ, her dear redeemer, for the spirit of life, and so continued praying until the last hour of her death—Lord, though I unworthy; Lord, one word, one word, etc.—and so gave up the ghost. Thus God hath visited and scourged me for my sins and sought to wean me from this world, but I have ever found it a difficult thing to profit even but a little by the sorest and sharpest afflictions.

[The following material consists of notes written by Shepard in the manuscript of the autobiography.]

Anno 1639

The good things I have received of the Lord:

(1) He is the God of my being who might have made me a worm.

(2) He is the God of my life and length of days, with health which I have enjoyed long.

(3) He is the God who took me up when my own mother died, who loved me, and when my stepmother cared not for me, and when lastly my father also died and forsook me, when I was young and little and could take no care for myself.

(4) He is the God that brought me out of Egypt, that profane and wicked town where I was born and bred, under the care of one of my own brethren, and that gave me time and will to desire learning, where if I had lived I had sinned and been forever damned.

(5) He is the God that brought me, the least and most despised of my father's house, to the University of Cambridge and strangely made way for me there, after many prayers for it and promises (when I was young) to be the Lord's if he should do that for me, though it were by spending all the portion my father left me, which accordingly was done.

(6) He is the God that began to strive with me there as soon almost as I came thither, by Mr. Dickinson and Dr. Chaderton's sermons. And although I oft resisted the Lord and neglected secret prayer and care of his ways a long time and followed my bowling, loose company until I came to that height of pride that for their sakes I was once or twice dead drunk and lived in unnatural uncleanesses not to be named and in speculative wantonness and filthiness with all sorts of persons which pleased my eye (yet still restrained from the gross act of whoredom which some of my own familiars were to their horror and shame overtaken with), yet at this very time of being worst and under wrath the Lord dealt most graciously with me and made my last act of drunkenness the beginning of more serious thoughts of making my peace with God.

(7) He is the God that when I was thus in this place made me acquainted with many godly friends whose lives and examples were or might have been patterns to me, Mr. Stone, Mr. Simonds,[52]

52. Joseph Simonds, a fellow-student at Emmanuel, subsequently silenced for nonconformity.

whose speeches God always blessed to me, especially when they described God's wrath by the fireside, so the intolerable torment of the fire, and when in walking with one I heard him set out men's misery that all they did was sin without Christ. And he blessed also their counsel to me by setting me to read *The Practice of Christianity,* which did much affect me, and to hear Dr. Preston.

(8) He is the God that sent, I think, the best ministers in the world to call me, Dr. Preston and Mr. Goodwin. The words of the first at the first sermon he made when he came into the College as Master of it and divers that he preached at that time did open my heart and convince me of my unbelief and of a total emptiness of all and enmity against all good. And the Lord made me honor him highly and love him dearly, although many godly men spake against him.

(9) He is the God that set me not only to attend upon the word publicly, but to private meditation and prayer in which I seldom sought but found the Lord, taking me out of the world when I was scoffed at for what I did. And I so found him in meditation that I was constrained to carry my book into the fields to write down what God poured in.

(10) In these ordinances he is the God that convinced me of my guilt and filth of sin, especially self-seeking and love of honor of men in all I did, and humbled me under both so as to set a higher price on Christ and grace, and to loathe myself the more, and so I was eased of a world of discouragements. He also showed me the worth of Christ and made my soul satisfied with him and cleave to him because God had made him righteousness, etc., I Corinthians 1:30, and here also revealed his free justification and gave me support and rest upon and in his promises made to them that receive him as as [*sic*] Lord and King, which I found my heart unwilling to long, which was the ground or rather occasion of many horrid temptations of atheism, Judaism, Familism, Popery, despair as having sinned the impardonable sin. But yet the Lord at last made me yield up myself to his condemning will as good, which gave me great peace and quietness of heart through the blood and pity of Christ. I have met with all kinds of temptations but after my conversion was never tempted to Arminianism, my own experience so sensibly confuting the freedom of will.

(11) He is the God which melted my heart after a relapse from

the glorious condition I had in Cambridge, by taking a journey into the country with a carnal professor, and this the Lord did when I never sought nor regarded him.

(12) He is the God that made me a poor means of scattering the knowledge of Christ, and setting up days of fasting and times of holy conference, and conscientious Sabbath keeping. I was weak every way, and young among the scholars where I lived, and to study what to do for the Lord.

(13) He is the God that carried me into Essex from Cambridge and gave me the most sweet society of so many godly ministers, as Mr. Hooker and Mr. Wells [Weld] and Mr. Wharton, Mr. Beadle,[53] and Mr. Burrows, etc., although I could do no good among them.

(14) He is the God that sent me by all these ministers to obey the voice of God in the call of the people of Earle's Colne, a most profane place, where the Lord blessed my poor labors to Mr. Harlakenden and his family and to many others in the town and country. And here the Lord kept me from troubles three years and a half until the bishop Laud put me to silence and would not let me live in the town, and this he did when I looked to be made a shame and confusion to all.

Mr. Cotton repents not, but is hid only. (1) When Mistress Hutchinson was convented he commended her for all that she did before her confinement and so gave her a light to escape through the crowd with honor. (2) Being asked whether all revelations were lost because all revelations were either to complete Scripture or for the infancy of the weak church, he answered that they were all ceased about particular events, unless to weak Christians, and seemed to confirm it now; whereas in the sermon it was to the weak church under the old testament, he did extend it to weak Christians also under the new. (3) He doth stiffly hold the revelation of our good estate still, without any sight of word or work.

(1) Law: that the magistrate kiss the church's feet, that he meddle not beyond his bounds,

(2) that all churches give obedience unto him,

53. John Beadle, M. A. Cambridge, 1620, rector of Little Leighs, Essex; submitted to Laud in 1633.

(3) that none be elected magistrate but such a one as is member *ecclesiae,* yet if after he prove bad, he be not cast off from his office till condition broken,

(4) that there be an universal reformation of extreme wages and selling, etc.

Q: is it fit that any law should be before divulged?

(2) Church businesses not yet settled.

My life: Lord Jesus, pardon every day.

(1) I seek not the Lord in prayer till I find him. Hence [1] I manifest contempt of Christ, can live without him; [2] contempt of this great privilege who may have all I seek for of him; [3] provoke Christ who loves my company and is angry with me for not keeping it.

(2) Then I go from prayer and follow my calling but not for the Lord; am not holy in all manner of conversation; and hence I lose what I got in prayer, nay, forget what I gained, and so make no progress nor increase in a Christian course. And so either there is no life of Christ, which is most sad, or if there be any I crucify it and disfigure it and put it to open shame, which is most sad also.

(3) I maintain not a will and firm resolution when I see[k] to avoid these practices. Remember, my soul, to wait all the day long upon the Lord to plant it in thee, for my soul will not bear it nor bring it forth.

(4) I would fain have notice of the work of grace in my heart, that so I might be comforted in the midst of my sins which I am not resolved to leave.

April 4, 1639: preparation for a fast

May not I be the cause of the church's sorrows which are renewed upon us, for what have the sheep done?

For (1) my heart lying long out from the Lord, the Lord [1] sent a terrible storm at sea to awaken me, and the deliverance from it was so sweet that I could not but think my life should after that be only heavenly, as being pulled from an apparent death to live a new life. [2] Immediately upon this my child was taken from me, my firstborn, which made me remember how bitter it was to cross the Lord's love. [3] Set my face toward New England where considering the liberties of God's house I resolved and thought it fit to be wholly for the Lord in all manner of holiness, at bed, at board. [4] Then the Lord took my dear wife from me, and this made me resolve to delight no more in creatures but in the Lord and to seek him. [5] Then the Lord threatened blindness to my child, and this made God's will afflicting sweet to me, but much more commanding and promising, and that I would do his will and leave these things to himself. But oh, how is my gold become dim, etc. How little have I answered the Lord, considering also my ship resolutions which I have writ down. I have wanted both remembrance, heart, strength, or will to do any of these things, and therefore have not cause to blame the Lord, for he hath persuaded my heart to this, but my own concupiscence and vileness which, Lord, that I may mourn for, that thou mayst restore comforts to me. Apostacy from God is grievous, though but in a little degree: to serve Satan without promise, to forsake the Lord against promise. What evil have I found in the Lord's? This brings more disgrace upon the Lord than if there had never been any coming to him. This is a sin against more love Lord might never have drawn.

(2) The people being committed to me [1] not pitied so much, [2] nor prayed for, [3] nor visited, [4] nor have I shown so much love unto.

(3) The family I have not edified nor instructed nor taking all occasion of speech with them.

(4) The gospel I have preached [1] not seen in the glory, [2] not believed, [3] not affected at, [4] not seeking to Christ for supply, that all hath been dead work and fruit of pride.

(5) Walking daily without Christ and approving myself unto him, and hence, though I do his work, yet I do not mind him in it, his command and his presence, nor yet any endeavor to grow somewhat every day.

(6) My not lamenting the falls of professors and condition of the country, who are not indeed the glory of God in the world nor the holy people.

Is it not hence?

(1) That many pillars in this church have fallen as if the Lord would not betrust such precious vessels to my care, and hath not the sorrow lain upon me?

(2) Hence universal mortality: when Hezekiah's heart was lifted up, then wrath came not only on him but on all the rest.

(3) Hence I have had this long sickness, as if the Lord would delight no more in me to use me.

Oh my God, who shall be like to thee in pardoning and subduing mine iniquities?

A Roman, being asked how he lived so long, answered, *Intus melle, foris oleo. Quid loquacior vanitate, ait Augustinus.*[54]

54. On the inside, honey; on the outside, oil. Which babbled more of vanity? said Augustine.

THE JOURNAL

THE INSIDE of the front cover of the *Journal* bears the following inscription in the hand of Ezra Stiles:

This book belongs to the Second Congregational Church Newport

1771.
Given by Major Jonathan Otis
Received by Ezra Stiles
Pastor

Two leaves precede the text of the *Journal*. On the first, recto and verso, appears the following in Shepard's hand:

1. My son Thomas was born in old England in London, anno 1635, April 5, and about a twelve-month after brought over the sea and baptised in New England by Mr. Hooker.

2. My son Samuel was born October 18, 1641.

3. My son John was born March 9, 1643 (according to the account of old England who begin their year March 25) but the first month by New England accounts, and so 1644. But he died the same year, July 14, on the Sabbath-day morning. As for man, his days are as grass, and as the flower of the field so he flourisheth, but the wind passeth over it and it is not. Psalm 103.

4. My second son John was born April 2, 1646, to whom I gave this name because the Lord seemed to make up the breach and repair the loss of my first John, and it may be hath and will hear all the prayers for the first in the second.

My son Jeremiah was born August 11, 1648.[1]

At the top of the second leaf, recto, Shepard wrote:

1. Three of Shepard's sons, Thomas (1635–77), Samuel (1641–68), and Jeremiah (1648–1720), graduated from Harvard College into the ministry. Thomas served at Charlestown (1659–77), Samuel at Rowley (1665–68), and Jeremiah at Rowley (1673–78), Essex (1679–80), and Lynn (1680–1720).

This book I leave with my son Thomas
Try all things and hold fast that which is good.

Below, in an unknown hand:

> This book was wrote by the Rev. Mr. Thos. Shepard, pastor of the first church in Cambridge in New England. His son Thomas was pastor of the church of Charlestown.

The same leaf, verso, has a note by Stiles:

Memo. by Ezra Stiles
In 1747 the Rev. Tho. Prince of
Boston printed this Diary from
Nov. 25, 1640, to Dec. 27, 1641.

1640

November 25. I found my heart and mouth straitened on the lecture day and for want of enlargement much troubled. Hence I resolved to humble my soul before God, which the Lord helped me to do in this manner:

(1) I saw the vanity of honor, and therefore why should I be troubled for the loss of it by the want of enlargements [1] because it was but a conceit in men's minds of itself; [2] because it was naturally most dear and so stood between me and Christ?

(2) I saw how fit it was that the will of Christ should be done, as well in denying as in giving enlargements, though he should strip me naked of them and all other things.

(3) When my heart objected, Can you be content that Christ should lose his honor and his ordinance blemished by your straitening? I then saw that I was to be content to want them in regard of my own unworthiness, and so [1] to be vile in my own eyes for my sin that moves the Lord to deny; [2] to mourn that he should not glorify himself by me; [3] then to pray the more earnestly to glorify himself by doing all for me by his own hand. [4] Hence I saw wherefor I should leave myself with the Lord for that end, forever with him who had all and only did all.

November 29. [In] prayer I saw my heart very vile, filled with nothing but evil, nay, mind and mouth and life, and void of God. Hence I prayed to the Lord to possess me again (1) because he only was good; (2) because he only was worthy.

December 1. A small thing troubled me. Hence I saw that though the Lord had made me that night attain to that part of humiliation, that I deserved nothing but misery, yet I fell short in this other part, viz., to submit to God in any crossing providence or command, but [had] a spirit soon touched and provoked. I saw also that the Lord let sin and Satan prevail there, that I might see my sin and be more humbled by it and so get strength against it.

December 16. I saw myself very miserable (1) because by my sin I had separated myself from God and turned my face from him; (2) that he was turned in his face from me: [1] I had no sense of his majesty, power, mercy, being; [2] no sense of his love, (3) I saw sin had shut him from me, and my unbelief when he came to me shut him out of me. Hence I saw a need of a mediator between us and mourned.

I had a glimpse of the fullness of grace in Christ, in meditation on John 1:14: like a fountain overflowing and above all my conceiving to poor sinners which come to him. And hence my heart began to be filled with lively hope and assurance.

December 26. In reading of the 12 of Hebrews that things shaken and made must be removed, that things unmovable may stand, I saw hence two [*sic:* three] things: (1) that only Christ and his word shall remain and stand unshaken; (2) that it's sweet hence to forsake all creatures and there to abide as the stone on the foundation: [1] 'tis borne up with it; [2] it rests there. (3) I saw how good it was to depart out of this world and to be with God, perfectly near him where no more shaking is or shall be.

December 28. I desiring to be led by the truth, it was objected, Follow it in your practice and prize it dearly, and I will go before you and lead you into all truth. But I saw how little I loved the truth and ways of God, either practical or speculative truth.

I saw on this morning how all my mercies came from Christ: (1)

he had plotted them, (2) purposed them. (3) promised them, (4) effected them. And my heart was drawn near to the Lord with these thoughts.

1641

January 6. I saw I could have no grace at death that I should go to Christ unless I did intend to do Christ's work while I lived. Hereupon I considered, If I love him my soul will seek him. So I considered that I must keep alive my love to him in my heart for this end. And why should I love him? Because none was good or could do me good but him. Myself, sins, child could do me nor themselves any good but only him. Then I considered, Shall I love him only because he is only good to me? I then reflected upon myself and saw my own vileness and how fit it was the Lord should never regard me. Yet I resolved to seek him.

On this morning in meditation and prayer I was tempted to think no promise, no, nor command, to seek the Lord or submit to him was spoken to me, but rather he had in justice forsaken me and so let me do what I please. But when I considered the scriptures, how that they did but manifest that acting will of a living God, revealing that secret will which is ever so set as the word reveals, my soul was quieted and I loved the scriptures the more.

January 9. As I was walking in my study musing on my sermon in Q. 10, that God's mercy was as near as his justice also was, the one to men that come to Christ, and that are out of Christ, the other. Hence I considered when I come to Christ there is no wrath, justice to devour, but sweet love. Wrath there is for refusing him, not else. It was then objected, But is it not to the elect only? The Lord let me then see I had nothing to do with that but to look on his truth which is to them that come to him, that he would stand as a rock between that scorching sun and their souls. Hence my heart was sweetly ravished and began to long to die and think of being with him. And my heart said, Remember to comfort yourself thus when you lie on your sick-bed, to lie under this rock as in a hot day. If one saw a rock in a hot day and should say, That rock will cool [me only] if I be elected and God hath purposed it, and so keep off in fears; no, God hath purposed that one and the other shall be thus to all that come to them and are drawn by his love.

January 30. When I was in meditation I saw when Christ was present, all blessings were present, as when any without Christ were present, there sorrows were. Hence I saw how little of Christ was present in me. I saw I did not cease to be and live that Christ might be and live in me. I saw Christ was to pray, do, counsel, and that I should be wholly careless of myself and careful for this. Hence I blessed Christ for showing this, mourned for want of this.

At the same time I saw his will, how that it was my sin so to pray as to bring the Lord's will to mine, with a secret murmuring or thinking 'tis in vain to seek if he doth not so, for what is this but pride and to command and to be above Christ and to be wiser than Christ, but to bring my will to his. And this gave me much light and set my heart in a sweet frame. And hence I understood that place,[1] Whatever you ask according to his will he hears us, and this is not only when we pray according to his will of precept and promise, but when we have done, by bringing our wills to his secret sovereign will, let him do with us what he please, which is his will of sovereignty.

Now in the time of prayer I considered why the Lord should command me to ask pardon, peace, light, brokenness, etc. And I considered that it must needs be that he might give me the thing promised (1) because his commanding will is ever attended with a promise; (2) because it was for his glory that I should ask, as well as my good, and hence he would give certainly when I did ask, especially being set on by his command. Hence my heart was much moved and melted to consider of my unbelief past and how much I had dishonored Christ thus to think of him and to maintain hard thoughts of him, that he will not hear. And so I began that day of fast to believe.

February 8. When I was on my bed in Monday morning the Lord let me see I was nothing else but a mass of sin and that all I did

1. Cf. Matt. 7:7, 21:22; John 14:13, 15:16, 16:23.

was very vile, which when my heart was somewhat touched with, immediately the Lord revealed himself to me in his fullness of goodness with much sweet affection. The Lord suddenly appeared and let me see there was strength in him to succor me, wisdom to guide, mercy in him to pity, spirit to quicken, Christ to satisfy, and so I saw all my good was there, as all evil was in myself. Hereupon I began to entertain thoughts of the glory of this mercy if the Lord would become mine, so that I should be strong with God's strength and live by God's life and be guided by God's wisdom, etc., and so I become his, for him to take care for me and love me, and I to pitch my thought and heart on him. I considered this would be an exchange of wonderful love for me to have God and not myself, and God to have me and give me himself.

I arose with these thoughts and some purposes to consider more of them. And on Monday night the same day in prayer and meditation these thoughts came in from the experience which I found then, viz.,

(1) I saw all fullness in God of all the good I did need, and so all my good, or what might be good for me there, and so considered that the first thing the Lord reveals to draw the soul to himself is the fullness of grace in himself.

(2) Being doubting, Is this mine or no?, I then considered that the Lord did invite me to come to him because I saw that his word did not bid me depart from him, and methought in considering this, the Lord's word, Come, poor creature, was so sweet to me that I came to him.

(3) Being thus come, I considered I must cleave to him and be knit to him, and then the remembrance of this, that all my good, ALL was in him, made me so to do in some measure with dear affections.

(4) Cleaving thus to him, I considered whether he was become mine now, and I his. And here I stuck a while as being loath to fancy such a thing and because God did not cleave to me as I could feel. But the Lord returned the night after this answer: [1] that he had applied himself to me because he had drawn me to himself who else could never have come, and hence if he so pitied me when far from him, much more being now near to him; [2] because of the riches and fullness of his tender grace: hence being

come, he would let it out; [3] because of his promise, He that comes I'll not cast away,[2] and Hosea 14:4,5.

February 9. I considered when I could not bring Christ's will to mine I was to bring mine unto his, but then it must be thus: (1) that if he ever gives my desire, it will be infinite mercy, and so his will is good; (2) if he doth not, yet that I deserve to be crossed and to feel nothing but extremity.

February 15. I was in prayer, and in the beginning of it that promise came in, Seek me and you shall live, Amos 5:6. Hereupon I saw I had cause to seek him alway because there was nothing else good and because he was alway good. And my heart made choice of God alone, and he was a sweet portion to me. And I began to see how well I could be without all other things, with him and to learn to live by faith. Only it came in, Why did I desire to live with him alone in heaven? And I saw my heart very apt to comfort itself in other things beside him.

March 11. In prayer I was cast down with the sight of our worthiness in this church to be utterly wasted. But the Lord filled my heart with a spirit of prayer not only to desire small things but with a holy boldness to desire great things for God's people here and for myself, viz., that I might live to see *all breaches made up* and the glory of the Lord upon us and that I might not die but live to show forth God's glory to this and the children of the next generation. And so I arose from prayer with some confidence of answer (1) because I saw Christ put it into my heart to ask; (2) because I saw the cry of the humble.[3]

March 18. I saw if my mind acted it spun nothing but deceit and delusion; if my will and affections acted, nothing but dead works. Oh, how do I need Christ to live in me! Yet I saw if a man hath eyes and life he will not lean on another to lead him and carry him as when he wants both; so here. I saw the Lord made me live by

2. John 6:37; see also Lev. 27:44, Isa. 41:9.
3. Cf. Ps. 34:18.

faith by making me feel a want of both, to distrust myself and trust more unto the Lord.

March 19. After day of fast as I saw in the day that I had cause to weep exceedingly for my sin because it did lie so heavy not only on the Father but upon the Lord Jesus that they were so wroth with me that they hid their faces, and hence I saw that sin lay heavy on their hearts and that therefore they were not only angry but left me to my sin—which caused some sorrow. So after the day I saw and said, As pride was my sin, shame should be my portion, and many fears I had of Eli's punishment for not reproving sin in Mr. E.[4] when I saw it, and that sharply. And here I considered that the Lord may and doth make sometimes some one godly man a terror and dreadful example of outward miseries that all others may fear that be godly lest his commands should be slighted, as he did Eli. And so I saw the Lord justly might never let my sins be purged away with sacrifice.

April 2 and 3. I was earnest in prayer for God's favor and love, and doubting of it for myself and for others (because I looked to God's secret decree). At last I saw it was God's decree in the gospel and his will that whoever come to Christ[5] should have life and favor and so answer to all prayer for himself and others—which gave me some sweet assurance.

After this I saw the Lord might deny all prayers for outward things for us. I begged therefore for mercy, and that being granted I had an end of all my suits and requests for myself and others, and there my heart stayed.

April 4 and 5. On Sabbath morning I saw the Lord frowning on me in several providences: (1) that he was hid from me whose face else would shine brighter on me than 10,000 suns; (2) that he was angry and had been and is still with my prayers. (3) Nothing I did,

4. Probably Nathaniel Eaton, first master of Harvard College; his confession is printed below. Shepard's failure to detect and reprove the malfeasance in office for which the General Court fired Eaton in 1639 caused him much retrospective anguish, as the journal and the autobiography testify. For Shepard's part in the unhappy business, see Hosmer, ed., *Winthrop's Journal,* I, 310–14.

5. In the margin Shepard gives the text, John 10.

nay, none under my shadow, did prosper. (4) I saw I wanted wisdom for my place to guide others. (5) I saw I did want a spirit of life within to make me exemplary without. (6) I saw I did want the power of the Holy Ghost and was not mighty in word and spirit in my administrations. (7) I saw a secret eye I had to my name in all I did, for which I judged myself worthy of death, and saw good reason to glory in nothing which I had or did. And I saw that in this latter point of humiliation under God's hand I had failed long, for I saw myself worthy of death but I did not grow weaned from all created glory of honor, wisdom, esteem of others, etc.

April 5. I saw I did not remember the sins of my youth, nay, the sins of one day I forgot the next day and so spent my time.

I was on my bed praying this morning, and the Lord helped me to pour out my heart before him. And I saw that I could plead nothing in myself in regard of any worthiness or grace or anything in regard of God['s] providence or promise, but only his good pleasure. I saw it was not if I willed but if he will, then I should see and believe and live. And here I hung, pleading how good, how pitiful and tender, how free this will was. I saw it stood immovable till it moved itself toward me. I saw God's will was that I should come, but I was afraid of my own activity and working and hence pleaded, Lord, turn me, draw me, and I shall come. And so I begged for my child, friends, wife, church, with earnestness that the Lord would give us but mercy and not suffer his name to be polluted by us and by our debts, though he should not honor himself by us, and then if mercy would make us poor and vile, blessed be it, and if it would lead us and carry us to some other place and there cover and overshadow us, blessed be it. And I had secret hints that these prayers from our wants were but preparations for future mercies and that we should see his glory in the land of the living. Then I began to arise after prayer without faith, leaving all to his grace. But the Lord showed me how he had come to me and stirred up prayers (1) according to his own will, (2) for his own ends, for though I sought myself, yet seeing this, I entreated the Lord to glorify himself and make us like unto his. And then I saw how great a sin it was to make feeling the ground and cause of my faith, and I also thought how exceedingly I should honor Jesus

Christ if I did believe before I felt, how I should honor the truth of Christ who hath said he is one that hears prayers.

I saw also a secret distemper of my heart, how I grew faint in prayer contrary to the rule, Luke 18, viz., not only by discouragement, but also by encouragement and enlargement and affections in prayer.

April 10. I had many thoughts which came in [to] press me to give up myself unto Christ Jesus which was the dearest thing I had. And I saw if when I gave myself to Christ he should give himself to me again, that it would be a wonderful change, to have the bottomless fountain of all good communicated to me. Thus two or three days I was exercised about this, and at last (which was the day before I fell sick on the Sabbath) in my study I was put to a double question—(1) whether Christ would take me if I gave myself to him; (2) whether I might take him again upon it—and so resolved to seek an answer to both from God in meditation. So after dinner on the Saturday, April 11, I gave up myself to the Lord thus:

(1) I acknowledged all I had or was, was his own (as David spake of their offerings), and so I acknowledged him the owner.

(2) I resigned not only my goods [and] estate but child, wife, church, and self unto the Lord out of love, as things the best and dearest things which I have.

(3) I prized it as greatest mercy if the Lord would take them, and so desired the Lord to do it.

(4) I desired him to take all for a threefold end: [1] to do with me what he would; [2] to love me; [3] to honor himself by me and by all mine.

(5) Because there is a secret resignation that the Lord shall do all and the soul gives itself to the Lord, but 'tis that God may please his will and love me, and if he doth not then the heart dies. Hence I gave up my will also into the Lord's hand to do with it what he please.

(6) Many whorish lusts, but that he would take me.[6]

Thus I gave myself to the Lord, but then I questioned, Will the

6. In the margin Shepard adds: "(7) that he would keep me also from all sin and evil."

Lord take me? Answer: (1) I saw that the Lord desired and commanded me to give him my heart. (2) I saw that this was pleasing to him, as *e contra* displeasing. (3) I saw that it was fit for him to take me to do what he would with me.

April 13. I questioned whether the Lord could pardon some sins or would. And I was made to cast my eye upon the gospel, Romans 3:25: whom God hath set out to be a propitiation to them that believe in his blood. This faith I saw to be nothing else but receiving God's kindness, special favor with my whole heart, and so was quite opposite to doing. And herein methought the exceeding riches of God's grace appeared, that he should now, after all wrongs done against him, offer special love and require me only to take it and possession of it, and so I felt my heart receive it with my whole spirit, with all my heart. Only I questioned, Will the Lord receive me again with his hand when I receive it? And I saw (1) that the Lord had bound himself by promise to me so to do; (2) I prayed God he would do so to me.

April 15. When I looked over the day I saw how I fell short of God and Christ, and how I had spent one hour unprofitably. And why? Because though the thing I did was good, yet because I intended not my God in it as my last end, set not my rule before me, and so set myself to please God, therefore I was unprofitable and so desired to be humbled for it, and so I saw the nature of fruitfulness.

I observed my heart in walking according to rule but I saw it fell off, and this I learned, that when a man sets himself to walk by rule, he will either say, I cannot, or else, Will not, but hates the same.

April 25. I saw God would accept me for Christ's sake but I feared much I might not take Christ aright. Hence this came to my mind, that to take Christ because he commands me so to do is no presumption (1) because this honors him; (2) because he that will submit to one command thus, will submit to all; (3) because I saw that he that lets in Christ's command into his heart receives Christ, and he that receives one command thus, receives all Christ and all the commands of Christ.

May 5. I saw how I was without all sense as well as sight of God, estranged from the life of God, for I saw that I respected man more than God, to please him rather than God. And why so? Because I was sensible of the presence of man. So if I had committed any sin against man I should be ashamed of it, but I blush not before God. I was not sensible of his glory, love, beauty, majesty. And hence I had no sense of sin because I had no sense of God. And hence I saw with sadness my widow-like separation and disunion from my Husband and my God, and that we two were now parted that had been nearer together once. And I saw (though not deeply) what my iniquities are, to prefer the creature above the Creator blessed forever, and that as the life is, the sense is.

May 6. The Lord Jesus revealed himself thus to me, viz., that as he was mercy and love to all meek, humbled, believing sinners that came to him, so he was fire and wrath against all obstinate sinners that would not bow to him but go on in their sin. And so I satisfied that doubt when my heart said, Why shall I be troubled for sin, seeing God in Christ takes it not much to heart but forgives, bears, and pardons, and he was all love and no wrath in him? I replied again, He is so to all meek ones that stop and yield, but he takes the least sin exceedingly to heart and very ill when men go on in it. My heart was much comforted with the knowledge of this and wrought to some more fear and love to him, and resolved to give up myself to him.

I saw also the greatness of sin to strike him by it who is the glory of heaven and earth and who takes it exceeding ill at my hands if I do so or especially persist in it.

The Lord also pressed my spirit to please Christ in everything, not in some things only, to be ever pleasing him.

I saw also that I was not in good earnest desirous that Christ should take away my sin by any loss of name or goods, etc.

May 7. On Saturday at night I saw union to God the greatest good, and my sin in not cleaving wholly to him with all my heart the height of all sin, from Hosea 10:2. Hence in prayer I saw sin my greatest evil (1) because it had separated me from the greatest good; (2) because it kept my heart with a secret love to it from returning again to him as my greatest good. (3) Nay, I saw that it made me make my death my life, viz., neglect of living and acting for God my very life, and my war (with God) my peace, and my damnation my salvation. Hence I mourned.

May 12. When I was stirred up to give thanks for mercy, I was put to a stand why not for evils as well, seeing both were from God's will. And the Lord put it into my heart to see because God's chiefest, dearest attribute is honored more that way. And so I saw I was not to be thankful because the blessings and mercy suited me, but because God's dearest and most beloved attribute of grace and mercy was glorified hereby.

I saw also how one sin begat another in this country, and we did not cease to increase therein. And hence I saw what just cause the Lord had to strike us with sore and great wants, yet how if sin was repented of by preaching against it, the Lord would return. So I saw it my duty to preach against them.

On the Sabbath, May 23, I came to a serious consideration what sins were between God and me that eclipsed his love. And I saw my evils and resolved with more care to walk with him and to be humbled for evils past. And I found my heart in looking upon those duties I was to do, how [I] should fail in the performance of them, and so I saw if I laid the evidence of my salvation upon my works that it would be various and uncertain as my gracious works were, and yet on the other side I saw that if I did not walk holily in all things before God I should not, I could not, have assurance of any good estate, so that here I was at some stand. And in musing thus the Psalm 25 came to mind, wherein God promiseth the meek and humble to show them his covenant, and so I saw the Lord at that time revealing his covenant unto me, on which I was to build by [*sic:* my] assurance, not on my performance on that covenant by my own strength or graces. Now God's covenant I saw thus:

(1) I saw him call me to himself that he might make good his everlasting covenant; so I came.

(2) I saw that his covenant was that he would pardon, heal, and work all my works of his people.

(3) I saw that he would do all this for me if I would by faith depend and rest upon the grace of his covenant so to do.

(4) This dependence on him to fulfill his covenant, sanctify,

quicken, humble me, etc., I took to be my evidence of love though I should fail in duties or God should leave me justly to my sins, etc.

May 29. I was musing on the witness of the spirit and I considered that as men had their voice, so the spirit his voice by which he spake, whose voice is most sweet.

June 8. I saw it my duty to be and live in every place as Christ in this world, to do that which he would do and live and walk as he would walk if here present. And so I saw, 1 John 2:4, [I] ought to walk as he walked, especially (1) in love, (2) in meekness. And my heart was much affected with this truth. And my heart secretly relented to think that, seeing Christ is not known, (1) what glory would this be to Christ, (2) what a presence of Christ there would then be in this place, (3) what sweet peace it would yield me when I came to die if I should live thus, or seek so to do. Oh Lord, imprint this image upon me and give the spirit of this thy Son to me!

June 26. On Sabbath when I came home I saw the hypocrisy of my heart that in my ministry I sought to comfort others and quicken others that the glory might reflect on me as well as on God. Hereupon I considered how ill the Lord took this and how averse he was from this self-seeking, by the sight of which I labored to be averse from it myself and purposed to carry it in my mind as one strong means to help against it for time to come.

July 2. I saw I was no debtor to the flesh to serve it, either (1) for any good it ever did me, (2) or in regard of any power by divine justice (satisfied in Christ) over me.

I saw it my duty not only to pray but to live by prayer and begging, for I observed how some of God's people did go. Hence I saw I was not to live by providence only, but by prayer (1) for myself, body, soul; (2) for my children and family, at home and abroad; (3) for the churches. Hereupon I asked the question, Would the Lord have me live by prayer thus? And I saw that he would have me because he gave me a heart framable to his will therein. And it did much refresh me to think that the Lord should desire me to live thus as if he took delight in my sinful prayers.

July 8. I was tempted to fear that I had been out of my way in occasioning any to come to this wilderness among so many snares. Yet considering that now by God's providence we were fallen here, I saw and purposed that it should be my duty and work to do all the good I could and to be the more earnest with God in prayer, and to *fingere fortunam,*[7] making all things better because they were vile.

I saw also some godly men and friends who, though they were sincere, yet were very weak and could not go through the present temptations of the place, of wants, etc., with that contentedness and sweetness of spirit as was meet. And when I saw it might possibly not come from want of grace but from weakness of it only, my bowels yearned toward Christ's weak ones, and I was secretly raised up with hopes that the Lord Jesus would pity them because they were weak and faint and would lead those gently who were with young. And it was a special ground of prayer and faith for them.

July 9. I saw that in preaching duties of obedience to the saints I should be careful how I set them a measure, and that I set not them to do them either to pacify anger by them, or to do them by their own strength, or to make doing of them an evidence of grace without inserting, Or unless they go to Christ and rely on him for his grace enabling them whereunto, and to preach them to them only as duties of thankfulness, to others as handwritings of death.

On the evening of this day before the sacrament I saw it my duty to sequester myself from all other things for the Lord the next day. And (1) I saw I was to pitch upon the right end; (2) on the means, all things to lead me to that end. I saw my ends were [to] procure honor, pleasure, gain to myself and not the Lord, and I saw how impossible it was for me to attain those ends I should, viz., to seek the Lord for himself, to lay up all my honor, pleasure, etc., in him, or if I did, it was for myself because good unto me. So the Lord helped me there (1) to see if honor, pleasure was good, oh how good was he that gave them, who could have cut me short of them! And so my heart was raised up a little unto God. (2) I saw my blessedness did not lie in receiving good and comfort from God

7. To improve the opportunity (redeem the time).

and in God, but in holding forth the glory of God and his virtues, for 'tis (I saw) an amazing glorious object to see God in a creature, God speak, God act, the deity not being the creature and turned into it but filling of it, shining through it, to be covered with God as with a cloud, or as with a glass lantern to have his beams penetrate through it. Nothing is good but God, and I am no farther good than as I hold forth God. The Devil overcame Eve to damn herself by telling her she should be like God. Oh, that is a glorious thing, and should not I be holy and so be like him?

Hereupon I found my heart drawn more sweetly to close with God thus as my end and to place my happiness in it, and also I saw it was my misery to hold forth sin and Satan and self in my course. And I saw one of these two things I must do. Now because my soul wanted pleasure I purposed thus to hold forth God and did hope it should be my pleasure so to do as it would be my pain to do otherwise.

July 23. At Boston lecture when Mr. Cotton was giving thanks for the safe arrival of the passengers lately come over, my heart questioned the thing, why I should be so thankful for them, and I considered if it were my own case I would have thanks so given for me and glad of it. Then I considered that (1) they were dear to Christ and beloved of him, and hence my heart began to love them dearly, and hence I rejoiced and was thankful; (2) that the Lord should so reveal his glory upon them in preserving of them.

July 24. At Charlestown lecture I hearing out of John 17:21 that disunion and sitting loose from Christ and his people was a means to hide and did, as it were, deny that Christ was come and was sent of the Father, my heart was hence much affected with shame and secret sorrow, with purpose to cleave closer to Christ that only Christ might be seen in me.

As I was writing the sermon that day my heart began to be much disquieted by seeing almost all men's souls and estates out of order, and many evils in men's lives, hearts, courses. Hereupon my heart began to withdraw itself from my brethren and others, but I had it secretly suggested unto me that Christ, when he saw evils in any, he sought to amend them, did not presently withdraw from them, nor was not perplexed and vexed only with them. And so I considered if I had Christ's spirit in me I should do so. And when I saw that thus the Lord had overcome my reasonings and visited me, I blessed his name.

I saw also the night before this that a child of God in his solitariness did wrestle against temptations and so overcome his discontent, pride, and passions. Another did reason and so wrestle for his temptation of discontent and so was overcome. Jonah indeed did reason for his passion for a time, but the Lord overcame his spirit.

August 13. I saw that I was worthy to be left to myself and in my misery and sin, (1) not only because I had sinned, but (2) because of my very desires to come out of it. For I saw that they did arise from pride, that when I saw how God did not prosper me nor any that came under my shadow and that he left me in the dark and hid his face and secrets from me, then when God had cast me down I would take hold on the Lord and seek to climb upon him that he might exalt me and that I might be exalted by being lifted up by him. Whereas I saw it was my duty when I was low [1] to be afflicted and mourn and learn the bitterness of sin and my own unworthiness, James 4; [2] to be desirous to come out only in regard of the Lord, that he may be exalted in me and by me. And I did think the Lord set my heart in such a frame at that time. I saw my vile heart also, that I could be troubled for sin [only] when it was cross to me.

August 15. This day in musing I saw that when I saw God angry I thought to pacify him by abstaining from all sin for time to come, but then I remembered (1) that my righteousness could not satisfy and that this was resting on my own righteousness. (2) I saw I could not do it. (3) I saw Christ's righteousness ready made and already finished, fit only for that purpose. And I saw that God's afflicting me for sin was not that I should go and satisfy by reforming, but only be humbled and afflicted for and separated from sin, being reconciled and made right by faith on Christ, which I saw a little of that night.

This day also I found my heart very untoward and sad and heavy, by musing on many evils to come. But I saw if I carried four things in my mind alway I should be comforted, as (1) that in myself I am a dying, condemned wretch, but by Christ reconciled and live; (2) in myself and in all creatures finding insufficiency and no rest, but God all-efficient and enough to me; (3) feeble and unable to do anything myself, but in Christ able to be efficient and do all things; (4) though I enjoyed all these but in part in this world yet I should have them all perfectly shortly in heaven, where God will show himself fully reconciled, be alone sufficient and efficient, and abolish all sin and live in me perfectly.

August 28. When I came from preaching I saw my own weakness (1) of body to speak, (2) of light and affection within and enlargement there, and that my weak mind, heart, and tongue moved without God's special help. (3) I saw my weakness to bless what I did. Hereupon I questioned whether the Lord would ever bless one so impotent that did my work without his power and sinned so much with such dead, heartless, blind works. And I feared he would not. But then I considered (1) that God doth show his power by the much ado of our weakness to do anything. God works not by strong but weak things, 1 Corinthians 1:21 [*sic:* 27,28]. He makes foolish things and weak things and things which are not to do his work that no flesh might glory. (2) I saw that if he did so, then the more weak I, the more fit I to be used, and that he could bless his own ordinance by me, 2 Corinthians 12:9. His power pitcheth his tents in weakness. (3) I saw that the Lord (as weak as I am) had blessed my poor labors, and if he should do it still, oh, how should I give the glory to him! So my heart was much affected and did give the glory of all was ever done by me to God, and I thought I did now begin to do that which I should do forever in heaven. And (4) seeing that by this way God should be glorified, I began to rejoice (with Paul) in my infirmities, and my heart began to be raised up from sinking under them, because I thought I was bound to rejoice in God that by my weakness he would glorify himself, and I began to see how good it was to acknowledge and not be ashamed of my weaknesses before others, that they might see the more clearly that glory of God, nor to be ashamed or discouraged with them before or after my work. Yet here was left one scruple, how that the Apostles were filled with the spirit of power and strength in their work and so God blessed, as 1 Thessalonians 1:4. I thought the Apostles were weak before their work, but were they in their work? Did the Lord by weak work in and upon them do any good? So I mourned, for a little before this time I observed weakness to do Christ's work and shame ever went together and that weakness of body and neglect of duty went together. So I prayed that evening immediately that the Lord would accept me in Christ's righteousness and make me strong and zealous for him and his name, nay, that Christ himself would be zealous to get himself a name by me who was but a worthless instrument in his hand, and so rested with some hope he would. And I resolved to walk in sense of my weakness and vileness daily before him.

September 8. I saw the reason why I did walk no more humbly, holily, was because I did make the creature something and did not make God all things, God all, for he that possesseth him possesseth something. So long as the creature is something in mine eye, that something will stand between God and me, that I shall not walk only in his sight. This is magnifying of God.

September 13. In my meditations at night I found my heart desirous to live in this world and do good here and not to die. Hence I asked my heart the reason why I should not be desirous to die. And in musing on it I saw that Christ was ascended up to heaven that not here, but there, all his elect might one day behold his glory and love him and glorify him forever. And I saw that this was God's main plot and the end of all, to make Christ very glorious and so beloved in heaven forever, where that which I desired most in this world (viz., that Christ might not only be precious but very dear and precious) should be perfectly accomplished. And hereupon I secretly desired this mercy and desired it for my children and brethren and all the churches, that though we were blind here and knew him not, loved him little, yet that this might be our portion at last. And I did feel my desires stirred up after this out of a secret love to Christ Jesus. It would do me good if he might be at last magnified thus. Then I inquired, What is the great thing I should desire in this world? And I saw that it was the beginning of that which shall be perfected in heaven, viz., (1) to see and know

Christ, though obscurely; (2) to take Christ and receive him and possess him; (3) to love him; (4) to bless him in my heart, with my mouth, by my life. And in this last clause I saw that I should study and stand for discipline and all the ways of worship, out of love to Christ, viz., to show my thankfulness.

October 6. I saw in prayer that my great sin was my continual separation, disunion, distance from God, not so much this or that particular sin, lying out with a loose spirit from God. Hereupon I saw Jesus Christ near me, next unto me—next unto me because he comes in as mediator between God and my soul, as one in a pit, a mid-man, holds both him below and him above. I saw that none could come into the chasm sin made, but him that satisfied justice, which is this mediator. Hereupon my heart was stirred up with thankfulness to lay hold upon this mediator, Christ Jesus, the object of faith being so near unto me and being of such worth as to fill up the chasm, and such love as to come so near unto me. I considered also that Christ was most near unto me by his word and the voice of that: Christ between God and me that were distant; the word between Christ and me; so faith closing with the word between the word and me, the word on Christ's part, faith on our part. The word is nigh thee, Romans 10, which is the word of faith. And hence oppose the word, you oppose the Lord where he is and wherein he is most near. Hence receive the word, you receive the Lord wherein he is most near.

October 9. On Saturday morning I was much affected for my life that I might live still to seek that so I might see God and make known God before my death. And then I saw if there was such thankfulness for deliverance from misery, would it not be greater mercy to be delivered and redeemed from sin? And I saw that this was a greater mercy, and hence I saw the love of Christ in afflicting and trying me with wants, because by these trials I came to see my sin and to have a heart severed from my sin. And so I saw there was no anger, but love, nay, the greatest love in this, viz., his redeeming love from my sin. Hereupon I learned three things. (1) That soul which felt sin the greatest evil, he would be willing, nay, glad, if the Lord would redeem him out of it by any misery, wants, poverty, temptations. (2) When he was delivered he would be as much thankful as for redeeming him out of hell. (3) He would account this the highest testimony of God's love, by redeeming him out of the greatest woe. And hence they that take sanctification as no sign never felt the evil truly of sin.

While I was thus musing in prayer I saw that then my soul was severed between sin indeed when Christ Jesus came to be in my soul in the room of my sin, when he was dear as sin was dear, when he did rule as sin did once rule me. And I thought this was sweet if [the] Lord would be so, and reasonable also that it should be so, and I began to make the Lord so indeed unto me. And so I learned this rule, viz., that if ever I would have any sin subdued, do not labor to get the sin removed only as a contrary grace in the room of it firstly, but first get Christ to come in the room of it, that his sweetness may be there, power there, life there, and so seek then for the contrary grace from Christ. For (1) it may be long before Christ will come and give the grace, and so the soul may lie miserable, but Christ may be then had. (2) At vocation Christ is given first and then sanctification; so in the renewed conversions of the saints, 'tis to be so again. (3) Else I seek for Christ's virtue without Christ. And cursed be that soul that is loath to have Christ to be in the room of a base lust, to make Christ that to him which a vile lust once was.

October 18. On Monday morning my child was born, and when my wife was in travail the Lord made me pray that she might be delivered and the child given in mercy, having had some sense of mercy the day before at the sacrament, and the Lord stayed my heart there. And I began to think, What if it should not be so and her pains long and [the] Lord remember my sin? And I began to imagine and trouble my heart with fear of the worst. And I understood at that time that my child had been born and my wife delivered in mercy already. Hereupon I saw the Lord's mercy and my own folly, to disquiet my heart with fear of what never shall be nor will be, and not rather to submit unto the Lord's will and, come what can come, to be quiet there.

When it was born I was much affected and my heart clave to the Lord that gave it, and thoughts came in that this was the beginning of more mercy for time to come. But I questioned, Will the

Lord provide for it? And I saw the Lord had made man to great glory, to praise him, and hence would take care for him though sometime the Lord seemed to make all men for naught, Psalm 89, which place I thus understood: God hath made man for glory of himself and hence to great glory, yet he made man for naught, especially the church, and their posterity for glory. And if God did not glorify them, then he seemed indeed to make all men for naught, and that when men are not made instruments of glory, 'tis for naught. And I saw God had blessings for all my children, and hence I turned them over to God.

November 4. On the end of the fast I (1) went to God and rested on him as sufficient; (2) waited on him as efficient, and said, Now, Lord, do for thy churches and help in mercy!

In the beginning of this day I began to consider whether all the country did not fare the worse for my sins, and I saw it was so, and this was an humbling thought to me. And I thought if everyone in particular thought so and was humbled, it would do well.

November 18. As I was going down my stairs I thought if Paul did so desire the good of the Israelites, his countrymen, his enemies that opposed him, that he could wish himself anathema for them, much more should I desire their souls good earnestly who under God had committed themselves to my care and charge. And so I left them to God's free grace to provide for them. And at night I had doubts whether the Lord would regard them or not, though I did resign them up to him. But it came to my mind that if God was an idol god, then I might give them to him in vain, but it was not so. And hence I had very sweet persuasion that night that my work herein was not despised of the Lord.

November 24. I felt overnight much darkness and unbelief, and saw that if Satan once had made us begin to doubt, he would hold us with doubts continually about the being of God and truth of scriptures. And I saw the next morning this error, viz., that I did believe what the Lord spake because I saw it agreeable to my reason and so made that my last resolution of all doubts. And I began to think how it should be otherwise. So I saw I was indeed to see the things God spake in the reality of them and in their agreement with reason, but not to make this the last resolution of doubts, though a resolution, but that when I had seen things so agreeable to reason, yet to look upon God's testimony of them in the scriptures as the last and chief light and ground of settlement, and to believe these things are true because I see they are true, but to believe the Lord sees them more clearly than I, and he knowing them to be so, I see them so and believe them upon his testimony much more. For if I believe anything to be true because I see it, so much more because God saith it who sees it better and whose word stakes me down and confirms me in it.

December 4. I felt a wonderful cloud of darkness and atheism over my head, and unbelief, and my weakness to see or believe God. But I saw that the Lord's ends might be these three: (1) by withdrawing the spirit of light, to give me a greater measure of it than ever I have had before, to give me a greater fullness by praying for more; (2) to humble me for my confidence in my light and knowledge past and in speaking so much with so little light, who knew so little; (3) to heal this wound, which was but skinned over before, of secret atheism and unbelief.

I saw all this was infinite love and mercy. Yet I saw this condition was a deep and deadly misery, and I saw I should be vile indeed if I did not mourn bitterly under it. For if I was but only under misery of evils, the Lord would be displeased and account himself neglected if I did not cry, much more if I should not under the power of my sins. This was on Saturday night.

I also saw a vast difference between knowing things by reason and discourse, and by faith or the spirit of faith. For by discourse (1) I saw that a thing was so; (2) by light of faith I saw the thing that was so.

A man's discourse about spiritual things is like philosophical discourse about the inward forms of things which they see not, yet see that they be. But by the light of the spirit of faith I see the thing presented as it is. I have seen a God by reason and never been amazed at God. I have seen God himself and have been ravished to behold him.

December 9. On Thursday morning in my bed after my Wednesday sermon I saw the pride of my heart acting thus, that when I had done public work, my heart would presently look out and inquire wherein it had done well or ill. And I saw I rejoiced in that as well done which pleased man, and that as done amiss which might not be so glorious in the eyes of man. Hereupon I saw [(1)] my vileness to make men's opinions my rule, but then saw my rule to be this, viz., to see what good I had done and give the Lord the glory, and to consider what sin I had committed and to mourn for that. (2) Here I saw a deceit, viz., to preach and pray to stir up spiritual affections because I saw it did beget commendations, hence preached terror and comfort (though false) to beget affection. I saw also upon enlargements I was apt to be somewhat in my own eyes, whereas my rule is to be more vile than any man in my eyes, and that daily.

December 10. I began to be troubled for my sin of passion, but I saw my heart did work thus: (1) it was troubled for the same and horror of sin, (2) purposed, (3) went to Christ for strength to do so no more and so was quieted. Whereas I saw it was my duty (1) to get my soul deeply loaden with the sin, as sin; (2) to come unto Christ and get his blood to give some peace unspeakable. Now in musing on this I saw how little repentance there was in the world and how many sins I had still to repent of. For I saw that most men had their peace after sin either by forgetfulness of it wholly, and so had their sorrows now and then, or else they did but skin over their wound with some general hope of mercy and grace, without sweet peace in Christ's blood. And hence my heart was very glad for this light in seeing this general wound.

I saw here also that the reason why men given to passion are so frequently overcome by it, because of all other sins they have many secret excuses and extenuations for it, as The suddenness of it, and 'Tis that I delight not in, and My heart is sad for it afterward, and Godly men may fall into it.

I saw also there was all reason why I should cleave to the Lord: (1) because all my good was from him in times of peace; (2) because he was my only support in time of trouble; (3) he alone was sufficient when all trouble, after life, should end. (4) I began to see how good his will was in all, and it crossing me should please me.

I also began to see, nay, feel, God in fire, meat, every providence, and that his many providences and creatures are but God's hands and fingers whereby he takes hold of me, etc.

December 11. Question: whether when a Christian feels a want of the light and life and faith of the spirit he should only humble himself for the want of them and do nothing in way of meditation or stirring up his heart to see and do, or stir up that ability he had to see and live and do? For I saw this, that when a man finds a loss of God, either he is wholly in the dark and cannot see him, or else Satan and his own natural abilities will be working and casting in light that so a man might be contented with that and seek no farther for the spirit's light nor feel such a need of it. Satan and nature by their work will prevent the Lord's.

Answer: to this I saw [1] that the scripture bids me meditate and use all means for the spirit and therefore not to confine myself to one means only of being humbled for want of the spirit; [2] that the rule here was, Use all means but trust only to the spirit to give thee blessing by them; depend only and wait only for the light of God in the use of them.

(2) Question: whether it was a duty or an error to pray and look for the fullness of the spirit in me without coming by faith out of myself and so finding and feeling the fullness of the spirit out of me in Christ, and whether I might not be mistaken and think I was empty of the spirit because I did not feel it in me, when haply when I am most empty I might be most full by faith in Christ, and whether the fullness of the spirit in the Apostles was not chiefly a power of the spirit giving them a subsistence out of themselves in Christ, in whom their life, joy was, seeing that Paul oft complains of his sin and insufficiency and inability to think or speak?

Answer: here I saw these things:

[1] that Christ had all fullness and so all fullness of the spirit;

[2] that all that fullness which I did want in myself was in Christ for his people, not for himself. He had perfect knowledge and grace and righteousness not only that by it he might virtually make me see and be righteous, but that it might be mine.

[3] I saw it my duty, therefore, out of sense of my emptiness to go unto Christ and possess and enjoy all that fullness that is in him as mine own, and to be as much filled with that and to rejoice as

much in that as if I had it in myself, because it is for me in Christ and my own there.

[4] I saw when I did thus, then I was full of the spirit, and that I was now as a fish that is got from the shore to the sea where it hath all fullness of waters to move in. And so I saw faith did first fill me and should first fill me. When I was most empty, then by faith I was most full.

[5] I saw this was the way to be filled with the spirit to my feeling within me—Stephen was full of faith and then of the Holy Ghost—(1) because this made me most empty and so most fit for the spirit to work in; (2) because this finding of the treasure of all grace in this field of Christ did beget strength, joy, glory, and so made graces alive; (3) because I should glory more in what I receive from Christ than in that fullness which is in Christ, the fountain of all his glory and my good and glory, if I should first receive the spirit from him without finding and filling and drinking in of that spirit which is in him.

[6] I saw a need for the Lord (to this end) to do two things: (1) to stablish me in Christ and settle me there and give me a being there; (2) to give me a certainty that all this was mine, for I saw this only would fill my heart and soul.

The conclusion of all was, I was resolved to pray for the spirit and not to give the Lord over for it.

December 21. I saw that man was an infinite kind of evil when he is crossed, as in hell, there he blasphemes because crossed, and hence men's sins lie hid because not crossed.

I saw also the deceit of man's heart which when it is very bad then it begins to seek to be very good. If it have and feel any good, it grows full and lifted up and loose.

December 28 and December 26. I felt my heart in this frame, viz., that though it had some light and affections, yet they hang together as sand. There was not an inward, ever-flowing, overflowing spring of them, as in winter, which runs with continuity of one part with another. And I saw I had not a spring of confession and sorrow and petition and thanksgiving.

Now I remembered Christ's promise, John 4:14: it shall be a spring of water, which Christ would give to all them that did deserve it, that gift of God. And hereupon the Lord exercised my thoughts with three things:

(1) that if I did desire this gift, the Lord would give it me, John 4:10, because 'tis more difficult for the Lord to work in me a desire after the spirit than for him to give the spirit, because the Lord finds resistance in the one but none in the other.

(2) I saw it was not any long continued spirit of prayer which should procure this spirit but look as if the woman had then asked,[8] the Lord would not have refused to give, such was the sweetness of his nature. So now the Lord will give at first asking. Though the spirit shall not be given till Christ be glorified, yet he will resolve to give then. This I conceived when I went a miry, wearisome journey to Charlestown to a ministers' fast.

(3) I saw that I was to believe certainly the accomplishment of this promise if I would have it made good, for I saw my usual manner was to pray for the spirit but not to believe an answer until he gave feeling. Now I saw I was to believe verily the Lord will give it [1] because this is the door at which the Lord gives out the good of the promise at, for he could give it if I came to mercy for it, but he saith, Then come to the door for it, of my promise; [2] because it makes the soul cleave unto the Lord more closely when it's persuaded he shall have it, and so receive it sooner; [3] because a man honors God more thus, viz., not only his mercy but his truth and faithfulness, as Abram in believing: when a Christian [one word illegible] upon the Lord's word, now the Lord's honor is much engaged; [4] because the very believing of it fills with the spirit of life and joy in pardon. Those were Sabbath thoughts.

1642

January 1. When I was sick overnight and in my bed on the morning I saw my life a vapor and bubble, a vanity, and all my righ-

8. John 4:7–29.

teousness the flower that fades. And I saw if it was not so, yet I was sinning and provoking God in every action, even in best duties, affections. And I saw this continuance in sin came from the first Adam. Hereupon I saw God's deep plot in perfecting the saints' salvation out of themselves in Christ, and I saw in Christ there was righteousness and life reigning. Hence I saw what need I had of prizing above all other things to be found in Christ and to rejoice only in him.

January 2. In singing Psalm 132:12, 13, 14, 15 in the public, I was sweetly refreshed by seeing the reason why the Lord's people, if they keep his covenant, he would not leave them [when they are] in church fellowship, because the Lord desired to be with his people; he is loath to depart. In musing on which when I came home I saw a strong motive to have God our God (1) because he makes choice of his people in Sion above all places and persons in the world; (2) because when this is done he desires never to be parted by any sin again; (3) because when this is done he takes full content and is at rest when he enjoys his people; (4) because he promiseth upon this there he will dwell, not because of their good but because he delights in them.

January 11. When the church was receiving in of members I saw my poor labors in my ministry blessed in some measure to those that came in, in having a power going forth with them to draw some hearts unto Christ, which when I saw, the Lord did sweetly affect my heart and raised my drooping and discouraged heart which was full of fears that the Lord would not accept of me or anything which I did. And my heart was lifted sweetly up to heaven to see Christ who had thus remembered me to show me such favor, notwithstanding my sins. And then I blessed him and clave to him and saw good reason to be alway beholding of him and to see him in every other work of mercy or favor he shows me.

January 14. In my bed a little after I did awake I found my heart sad for the loss of some of my respect from one man whom I feared would be a scourge to many others. But the Lord put it into my heart to consider that love of respect was a sin I had been long warring against and yet it prevailed more than the rest. And when I had so thought, the Lord let me see what sweet love was showed unto me, viz., to chastize me for that and so take away that which I did desire so greatly and was apt to take content in, that so I might take no more content in it, follow this lover no more, and that I might seek the Lord and his name only, for I saw my heart (1) seek respect, (2) take secret content in that and love of people, (3) discouraged when I lost that. Now I saw love of God in wounding me there, that I might not perish with love secretly to it and that I might seek him and his name only. And here my heart broke out into wondering, thanksgiving, and melting to think what God is like this, what love is like this, what work like this!

I was also troubled that the Lord gave me no more peace and assurance and joy; only he let me see and seek more sin, blindness, unbelief, etc. And I fell to question which was the greatest mercy, for the Lord to reveal more of himself or more of my own self, and I saw the latter was best for me.

January 22. On this Saturday night I saw these sins:

(1) That I was so brutish, so unacquainted with God, such a stranger to communion with him, so deprived of use of common reason by my fall in Adam in the knowledge of divine things, that I did not see but doubt of the very being of God, whereby I did bury his glory.

(2) When I did see this God, yet I saw that not his word but my reason was the ground of my faith. I was so estranged from God as that I knew him not, heard him not speaking in the holy scriptures.

(3) I was so estranged from him as [1] I questioned the person of Christ, [2] my faith, whether my knowledge of him was by reason or faith, [3] light from above and my adherence to him, whether it was not my own will.

(4) Hereupon I saw myself unfit for my ministry and that [I] was so blind a guide, questioned my call to it (though the Lord secretly told me if he helped me when worse, should I now desert him when he began to purify and make me better?), and I also saw that in it I had [blank] [1] God, by my self-seeking, [2] some men by my sin of passion, [3] others by want of wisdom and prudence to

govern, [4] others by want of eminency in holiness, [5] others by want of love to them and visiting of them, [6] others by my want of exemplariness in my life and speeches, not always doing good, [7] all of them by want of prayers and fears for them, as being worse for me.

And here I saw that the Lord might justly not only cast me away but bring all evils upon me and mine also and all curses on whatever I did, for doing the Lord and his dear people such wrong. And I said if the Lord would have me to lay by all, his will by his grace should sway my soul.

These sins I saw (1) I must die eternally for them; (2) that God was now already departed and hid his face and did not appear in his love to me; (3) they [one word illegible] the Lord therefore exceedingly. And hence I began to prize Christ's blood and saw that my help was in him and faith in him, which I saw I had because I came to him and was sanctified also so as to love him and fear him and delight in him by faith, only going to Christ for these.

February 1. I saw in prayer the reason why the Lord did not give me those feelings I desired and presence of his spirit, for I saw if I had had them I should build my faith and assurance upon my feeling and not on God's promise which the Lord would have me do. This I saw evidently in myself.

February 8. I saw that God was far from us and therefore our weakness could not see him. But he had made himself near unto us in Christ, and yet there we cannot see him. Oh how great is our ignorance therefore of God, when we see so little of him in him who is so near unto us!

February 11. In reading Galatians 4 I thus thought if the Lord would surely cast me off if I sought righteousness by the Law or trusted to it in whole or in part. And I might believe this verily. Why then should I not verily believe that if I sought righteousness by the gospel in Christ and rested upon that but that the Lord would surely receive me, and why should I not have peace in this and joy in this? I saw that a Christian's trouble came two ways: either by seeking to quiet his conscience by Legal duties which cannot give peace, or by unbelief in mercy when Christ is received.

Either they question whether their faith be right or whether the promise be sure and certain.[9]

I saw also how Legal righteousness makes us servants and how faith makes us sons. The first thus: the Law saith, Wilt thou do this and that, thou shalt then live and have the inheritance. I will, saith a sinner, and he sets about it, but finds no strength, nay, finds more sin. For sin is irritated by the Law, i.e., not the Law in the publishing of it only, but in the practicing of it when a man comes indeed to hear it and so is under the greater power of it. And if by some duties he quiet his conscience, he is then under the stronger power of sin than before because he is now sheltered under the Law and thus still he is a servant and in bondage.

But faith makes us sons because faith, renouncing all doing for the inheritance, immediately receives Christ who is his inheritance and gives him the inheritance of the spirit now and glory afterward, and hence a son, even as sons have all by free gift. And now he is free from the power of sin (1) because he hath Christ's power against it, and (2) because he is hereby freed from all fears of God's love and favor which ever make a man sad, sunk, slavish, dead-hearted, whereas being freed, love, joy, delight in God and his will, as in a father's, succeeds.

February 15. I saw that there was great cause of seeking life and quieting my soul in that life and righteousness which is in Christ (not that which is from him only) because not only in my worse condition but in my best estate, when I have most affection and holiness, I am accursed for the best duty I do as 'tis in me.

February 20. As I was coming from the meetinghouse upon the Sabbath, thinking upon Ephesians 3:*ult.,* I thought Paul prayed for these churches and for me and every particular godly man, and so should we lay up prayers for many years.

March 5. In prayer I saw how I did break loose from God and break all his bonds, not only commands and mercies but inward graces of God's spirit, love, fear, faith, etc., when the Lord hath

9. In the margin of this paragraph Shepard writes: "And when the heart objected, You may not prize Christ sufficiently, I saw I did so when I was content with no measure of it."

wrought them in me. And therefore I saw this most vile to rend the spirit asunder and his graces asunder, and that it were just if the Lord should use me as a wild beast and tie me up and bind me with iron chains of affliction, to try what they will do.

March 7. On Sabbath morning I saw God far from me and others wanting his consolations, and I hence did learn this, that God was far from me that I might look upon myself and mourn over myself for my sins which were alway near unto me.

At night in prayer I saw God and Christ could never be anything in my eyes until I was nothing in my own, and I saw that this was wrought thus: (1) I saw myself worse than any other creature, the dust of the earth, which never sinned against God. (2) I saw that it was so vile I did not so much as mind or look upon that, and so was as nothing in my eyes.

I had also this temptation to think that the Lord did not desire my company to come to him, and that though he did outwardly do it in his word, yet therein he did desire reprobates to come and so did not inwardly desire it, but rather that I would run my course and fill up my sin because he had no need of me, had no reason to desire me but reason to shut me thus out. And I saw that this was the cause why many a one did not come unto him when he did externally call, and I saw that here did lie a deep temptation, viz., to forsake the scriptures and wait for a spirit to suggest immediately God's inmost thought toward me. But I saw my duty was this: (1) to mourn for those sins which made the Lord seem to me to cast me off; (2) to lie down humbled, confessing I am worthy of this woe, to be forsaken of him; (3) to rest upon his free grace, seeing he may inwardly desire me as well as not, and there to cast my soul.

March 9. At night in meditation in my chamber I began to think of Christ's fullness, but my unbelieving heart did question himself. And I saw my darkness and ignorance of the things of God. And here I began to examine what light it was by which faith is established. For I saw it was not the power of my own reasonings and discourse, [(1)] for if I doubted the being of God or the coming of Christ or the truth of the scriptures, I saw those reasons might set me at a stand, but yet could not clearly reveal nor persuade, but some doubts would still remain.

(2) I saw that if I did believe any divine truth because of reason, it was suitable to reason. Then I did not believe it because of a divine testimony which is a bare affirmation or negation of a thing: thus saith the Lord.

(3) I saw hence it was righteous and just for the Lord to entangle and leave all men in the dark that seek for the final determination of any part of his counsel by reason, and that hence the Lord in mercy did leave his people to great doubts, both of the scriptures and of their own estates, that rest only or lastly upon this and the power of this to persuade their hearts. I did therefore conceive that the spirit of God's enlightening was firstly and chiefly a plain intuitive revelation of the truth, and afterward reason comes in to clear up to others what it reveals. And yet I dare not bind the spirit thus to work because by reason, as by a means, the spirit may let in his light and clear up the truth, so that not to them that use reason but that trust to reason doth the spirit leave in darkness, confusion, that they may feel a need of him. The Lord therefore made me thus to conceive.

Before the spirit comes there is nothing but darkness and unbelief upon man's heart. I saw that sin did blind, and God also for sin, three ways:

(1) Sin blinds by driving God, the God of all wisdom, from the soul, and so there is nothing but darkness; a man sees no spiritual things.

(2) It spoils the understanding of all light also inherent in it that when the Lord opens the truth against it, cannot see it.

(3) The soul when it endeavors to conceive of spiritual things, it grows more blind two ways: [1] by running into error instead of truth; [2] conceiving of the truth (and so speaking the truth) after a false manner, not seeing any truth as it is and as the saints by the spirit see it.

Now I saw the spirit, when it comes, doth three things suitably:

(1) It clears up the truth. For Christ having abolished sin, the spirit hence comes and gives us evident knowledge of the truth, so that look as before the soul saw nothing at all but was in total darkness, the spirit of Christ makes it to see, i.e., to begin to see, all truth, and that with nothing but clearness. Nothing reveals a thing so clearly as the spirit, more clearly than by all reason, which is but weak and dim in respect of the spirit. And though it sees a truth at

first but by morning light, yet it ends in clearness, so that the spirit doth not leave the soul to conjectures it is so and to fears it may not be so, but it is a most clear evidence of truth, as tasting of honey is to the tongue, wherein without discourse the soul knows certainly honey is sweet. Hence David saith, Psalm 119, Give me good taste.

(2) The spirit gives an understanding to know these truths.

(3) The spirit reveals things as they be and shall be, the vanity of [the] world as it is, the glory of heaven as it is, the day of the resurrection as it is, Christ given as it is, and Christ in his glory as it is, which doth infinitely raise and gloriously enlarge the heart and also persuade the heart, for unbelief ariseth from darkness.

Now I saw the Lord, when he comes to give this spirit of truth, he makes a soul (1) feel his darkness; (2) when he endeavors to see, lets him see the power of this unbelief and conjectural knowledge of things; (3) hence makes him cry for the spirit, that it would teach and persuade. It brings him to see an end of all the perfection of his own reason that he may seek for the spirit to help, that God would bring light out of darkness. (4) As the spirit at first gives some light by the sense of these, so its increase of light is by a renewed sense of that which remains. And hence the saints at some time find such a power of darkness and unbelief as if they never had any at all, and hence the Apostle prays for the Ephesians, chapter 1, that they had a spirit of revelation and wisdom, even after they were sealed by the Holy Ghost.

Now because I saw that if any should look for a spirit without or beside the word, that they stood upon the precipice of all delusion, hence I saw this holy book of the scriptures is to be set before my eyes, and then the spirit prayed for to clear up the things of God's kingdom therein. And this I saw was evident, and I saw a wonderful wisdom in the Lord [(1)] that his spirit should not teach but by the word, (2) that his word could not teach but by the spirit, that so I might not wander from him therein.

March 10. I saw the Lord let me see my sin and feel it and feel it in power that so I might be sensible of the power of Christ in subduing it and say, This is the Lord's work, when this time came. For I saw a wonderful part of our blindness did lie there, viz., that we cannot feel the Lord's power nor acknowledge it without feeling the contrary power first.

March 13. On Saturday night reading 1 Thessalonians 2:13, that the Thessalonians received the gospel as the word of God, hereby I had a light let into my mind to see that then the word is received with joy as, 1 Thessalonians 1:6, when 'tis received as the word of God. To look upon it as the word of God when the Lord saith, Believe, breeds a receiving of it with gladness. And so in the application of it unto myself I did look upon the Lord's call in the gospel to come, repent, and be converted, that sins might be blotted out, Acts 3:19.

I saw one truth therein confirmed: (1) that a soul should return to Christ; (2) that when he cannot, yet if he suffer the Lord to convert him, his sins shall be blotted out when he cries, Lord, turn me, having none of his own to do it. But the Lord making me see that this was faith to come unto Christ and hearing Christ calling, Come out of the world which will bewitch thee and come and take me, my righteousness and life, self and all, my heart was much filled with sweet hopes and comfortable assurance of peace, of my being at last with Christ whenever death shall seize upon me. For his words were very sweet unto me: Oh come! And I saw it was peculiar to a David's spirit to whom the Lord's words were sweeter than honey.

April 10. At a sacrament, in preparation the day before thereunto, I did consider (1) Is there a God and a Christ? And somewhat of them both I saw, but yet saw need of living by faith upon God to reveal himself more evidently to me. (2) Is this God in Christ mine or no? For I knew it was my duty so to examine myself as to bring my thoughts unto an issue one way or other. And so I saw on the one side there were those things made me doubt most of my sonship.

(1) Sin was not my greatest evil and most bitter. I felt it not as it was in itself, and hence rushed boldly upon it. Yet on the other side, the Lord let me see [1] that I had and did go to Christ to make it heavy; [2] that it was sometime most bitter when I considered that by sin I strike God and by punishment he only strikes me, and that he accounts it so and feels it so and knows it better than I, and that I was most vile and the Lord most glorious and better than I and therefore worse than any evil against me. [3] I did purpose to lay hold on all things which might embitter it unto me.

(2) Because the Lord Jesus had not revealed his electing love absolutely: I love thee; but many doubts and fears still remaining, for I considered, May not this be *vox spiritus* only so saying? But here I saw [1] that the Lord had revealed it by his word: Those that come to him, he will not cast away, viz., for [*sic:* from] himself, and that they that know and ask for the gift of God shall have it, and that the Lord had made me many and many a time ask for it. [2] I saw I did wait for the Lord's more special and immediate witness unto me. [3] I conceived that that testimony of electing love without showing [or] coming in God's call might be a delusion, but this could not, because it was God's plain word and spirit in it testifying.

(3) Because I had so little acquaintance with Christ, hence is he mine, there being so much distance between him and me after such means of knowledge of him? But here I saw [1] this should be more of mourning to me; [2] that the Lord did know me, and my faith was to look and did look to that.

(4) Because I felt my soul carried so much by my own principles for my own ends and not like the Apostles whose hearts were mighty with God and labored without weariness. I was soon faint. Yet here I saw [1] that my desires were to live to Christ; [2] my heart lamented this, [3] purposed to live for his ends, because I am vile but he is most worthy of honor, glory, life, and praise. I saw it odious to serve a lust rather than Christ.

I saw also my unfruitful walking, want of love in not taking all men's cases and necessities, especially of the saints and my dear friends, to heart. I saw my unbelief deep and my unwillingness to be stripped of all, to give away all, and become poor. I saw I did not turn all God's providences for humbling prayer or praise or holiness.

I asked my soul after all this if it would not enter into covenant with God and renew it. And my heart answered, If the Lord will renew his covenant of life and peace with me, I shall be glad of it and gladly accept it. And here I saw that God's covenant was to do all for me if I would believe and receive him for that end. I saw the Lord required this faith (1) because by that means he works it, and (2) those that are in Christ are made able to believe and to receive Christ. And so my soul was drawn to Christ in sacrament in some measure.

April 13. The day before a general fast[10] I was at prayer, and while I was desiring the Lord to subdue my sin and then I should be well, I thought the Lord did jog me and say, Suppose thou hadst power, yet thou art as miserable and I am as far from being pleased as before. And thereby I saw the Lord desirous that I would come for righteousness to his Son and seek it in him.

Toward the evening I saw Christ an infinite and an eternal good, and that therefore I should live only unto him in this world, all other things being so vile in comparison of him. And if I did not, I did make him more vile than any other things. Whereby I saw the greatness of my sin, and not only of sin in myself, but in all others.

I saw also these four things by my sin:

(1) My own soul was worse by it, by darkness, death, distance from God and God from me, and filling up daily my sins.

(2) The church was worse for them, for had not I them, the Lord would have been so near me that all that came under my shadow should be blessed, and the wisdom of God in me and his grace should have prevented many evils. But hence they came to be desolate and poor and sinful.

(3) All the country is the worse for them [1] as having a hand in drawing upon us general evils of want, etc. [2] If I had prayed more for it and been more holy, it may be one man might have done much. And here I saw all other vexations, sinkings of heart, all the withdrawings from God, were vile and from me. [3] Had I been more holy, my example might have spread.

(4) That my child and family and posterity were the worse for my sin.

Now hence I saw how bitter my sins were unto God that they were thus bitter to me.

April 27. I looking on my child and affectionately, secretly desiring the Lord to bless his meat unto him, perceiving he did not desire a blessing for it himself, hence I came to consider and think of Christ's blessing of his people and children, and had a light let in to see what it was, viz., that he did desire of the father that everything might be blessed to his people because he loves them. And I saw

10. On April 14, 1642, John Winthrop noted that "a general fast was kept for our native country and Ireland and our own occasions" (*Journal,* II, 57).

that (1) he desired a blessing upon everything to his; (2) that his blessing was as himself was, viz., spiritual; that as carnal parents desire a carnal blessing so Christ doth spiritual, and that by all carnal things that they might lead unto God. (3) I saw what Christ desires is done by him, even when we do not seek a blessing ourselves, but he turns all to blessing and so in blessing blesseth.

May 8. On Sabbath coming from sermon I preached about God's wrath. And so I was very desirous that the Lord would make it effectual to convert some, and I saw my soul did secretly command the Lord and put him and enjoin him to a necessity to do it, because this made so much for his glory. But I saw it was my duty, as to pray for blessing, so to leave all success to God's free will and good pleasure, and so to do in all the changes of my life.

May 19. In my bed I saw the reason why the Lord did not take away all sin in the hearts of the faithful presently. It was because he was so fully pleased in the righteousness of his Son. And as he would never have suffered the elect to fall had not he looked upon his Son, he would now not suffer them to sin but that he eyes him. Hence our sins do not displease him eternally. Hence also we have but little life and much sin to humble us.

June 13. On Sabbath morning I saw that if I did fix my eyes upon the Lord as upon my last end, then every sermon I did preach, making as a means for that end, would not be vile in my eyes, no more than the end, and that then my soul would not be discouraged for loss of my own glory by my own feebleness, and that then I would be carried full sail toward the Lord. And I was stirred up thus to fix my eyes from something in prayer the precedent night, viz., that the Lord being jealous of his own glory, it was wonderful that he could stand by and see my thought for myself and not strike me dead.

I went about this time to Hartford where I met the Lord many times and felt him exceeding sweet, especially in a sacrament where he appeared to me and refreshed me (July 10).

This glorious glimpse of Christ consisted (1) in seeing afresh

God's great plot [1] that Christ should do all for his people, [2] suffer all in their room, [3] to work all in his people.

(2) The Lord stirred up desires after Christ according to my wants of wisdom, life, faith.

(3) When the sacrament came, my heart not feeling the presence of the Lord, I began to mourn inwardly for my sins as standing between God and my soul. But the Lord put it then into my heart to see that here Christ was offered and given for remission of those sins and as having already suffered all for them.

(4) I saw that this grace and favor was mine own [1] because I did thirst and ask for water of life, came to Christ, was pleased he should help. [2] I saw the sacrament a seal of this, for I saw that the Lord did not give empty signs, but it was as if Christ was present, and though I felt no life for the present yet I considered that life and strength is to be felt afterward in time of trial, as patience when crossed. There was no cross at a sacrament, and hence no need of feeling it, etc. And I did believe that the Lord would help and assure in his time.

(5) Hereupon my soul was exceedingly refreshed, enlarged, and lifted up in some sweet assurance, though mixed with some scruples, and in special that the Lord would be with me in my place. And when I came home I observed the very same day Satan was busy in the church to lift up private men's [one word illegible].

(6) Hereupon my heart began to be thankful for these sweet looks, and I did covenant by his grace to be only for him and to be tender of his name and glory above my own life, considering that in time past I had not been so, as also not to let into my heart anything to be sweet but only Christ.

I saw when sin was unpardoned Christ did not appear but only sin, but when it is and is to be pardoned then Christ appears only and sin is hid. When this sun ariseth, the wild beasts go to their dens.

The sins I saw before I came to this sacrament: (1) ignorance: I did not know spiritual things, and that light I had went soon out; (2) unbelief: [1] want of assurance, conscience dark; [2] of dependence, sitting loose from Christ; [3] historical faith,[11] which I saw

11. Rational knowledge of holy things.

must be misused; atheism also; (3) sensuality: I saw I took content in pleasure of sin and refused secretly to abate in my carnal joy; (4) ambition, profit; (5) I saw not weakness but enmity against the ways of the Lord made me forsake them. (6) I saw I would serve Christ but it should be where and when and in what manner and as much as I would, so far and so much, secretly in me.

In my journey I saw that if a man have a noetical opinion and not follow it, it will wound his spirit; so much more, practical.

We fear and fly from nothing so much in God as his anger, and love nothing more than his love, and shall I be angry and unlike God in that wherein he is most lovely?

I saw public persons, if not public blessings, were public and common woes and miseries to the places where they live, and I was afraid of myself.

I saw Christ's frowns would damp all joys.

July 30. On Sabbath-day morning in prayer I earnestly sought God for Christ and his presence, feeling myself bound up, and I was discouraged in prayer as looking upon the immovableness of God's secret will that it may be he would not if he had decreed not to help. But I saw again after prayer how foolish and unreasonable my heart was to trouble itself about God's secret will which I cannot find out nor see immediately, rather than to believe God's revealed will who saith he will hear every prayer we make. And this refreshed me and healed me of that old sore of carnal objecting and of unbelief.

August 13. Upon Saturday morning the Lord enlarged my heart to be seriously desirous of Christ and spirit and conquest of my darkness and unbelief, etc., and to rest upon free grace and mercy for it. And when I had done prayer, I could not but be persuaded but that grace on which the Lord caused me to trust, to which he had caused me to look, for which he had caused me to pray, but that the Lord would pity me, and that grace, being rich and free, could not send me daily away, and that such was the sweet welcome grace gave to a soul that rests upon it that the soul cannot but believe it will help when 'tis serious indeed. So the Lord filled me with much grief and sorrow for joy grace should be so sweet and that the Lord should look to me.

I saw also the Lord makes the condition of his people mixed, mixeth wants with abundance and trouble with peace, else no mercy but would clog us, 'tis so sweet, and that therefore I should not wonder to meet with many sad things. Wisdom mingles all her wines, and the Lord all his blessings.

I also felt my heart mourn for my sin because God's frowns appeared in withholding the spirit of light, life, and faith from me. And I saw it a hard thing to walk in a midway between deep disconsolations for the Lord's desertions of me and extreme slighting of them. A midway of patience is best.

August 15. Being told of some heat in my speeches which were not seeming, and the Lord letting me see the evil of them, I resolved then to speak little or nothing in opposition to my betters upon these grounds no more: (1) because of my own darkness and unbelief and vileness which I was privy to, whatever others did think of me; (2) because they saw more and were nearer God than I and better than I, and therefore I would sit down under them; (3) because I saw this good to take a revenge on myself for my former too much forwardness in speech; (4) because I saw Christ made himself of no reputation. He did not make himself somebody by speech but of no repute with men that he might make God great and of repute.

August 29. I found it a great sin in myself that I was weary of prayer by enlargements in it, and that my prayers were not alway alive and running but short and soon out. So I saw it was my duty to make stretched-out prayers, so that the prayers this day should be lengthened out with some fresh affection or argument the next day after. And so I saw I had reason to do so because the Lord came not and his anger therefore continued and sin grieved. I considered also why prayer stretched out brings the blessing, not because but the Lord is moved with one prayer as with a thousand, but because we are brought near unto the Lord by such desires. For many times we pray but we do not pray ourselves near enough unto God. Now the Lord doth so love his people that he would have them near him, and hence he denies until they be near unto him and very near to him so as to abide in him. And then the Lord gives, John 15: abide in him and then whatever you ask you have.

By prayer we come to him, but we soon depart. But when we abide with him, when the Lord saith, Stay!, and the heart doth so, 'tis a sign of answer to prayers, as a father will give his child a thing he asks but, Come near me then, saith he. When he is near him and within the reach of it, now he hath it.

September 26 and 27. At evening prayer the Lord let me feel my lusts of pleasure, profit, honor rising up against me so as I was unwilling to part with them, and by wrestling against them I felt some strength. And so I saw that not a general hatred but a real wrestling with sin in a pitched field, as it were, doth deliver and doth give some strength against sin. That which gave me strength was this, that Christ being first and last and middle was sufficient portion without any of these things. For I saw that seeing he was God, all was from him, and hence I should magnify him.

October 24. Walking in my garden I saw suddenly how my own ends in a business put life to me, but not the Lord's ends only. And I saw this was one reason, because I was sensible of my own good, not the Lord's. For what good had the Lord by my doing his will? Yet I saw though I was not sensible of any good, yet when I did the duty, the Lord was sensible of it, and I should also have the sense of it in time, and comfort of it also.

October 25. It came to my thoughts in my bed that every Christian hath some one special request above all others which he could have, Psalm 27:4. And when I came to examine what mine was I found it manifold, as (1) for the special presence of the spirit in grace and power; (2) for the students in the College that they might be Christ's; (3) for this whole country, that it might be supplied and by that means their hearts opened to acknowledge God's tender mercy here; (4) for my children, that they might be in covenant.

December 3. On Saturday night reading Psalm 30, I saw the end of our life was to declare God's truth in this life and our experience of it. And in meditation I saw (1) we should bring forth experience of the truth and faithfulness, (2) of the comfort in the promise as fulfilled. And I asked how one might know when the Lord hath given a promise before he feels it. Answer: if by viewing God's goodness to make such a promise the Lord himself be therefore very sweet to us. His disposition is very sweet; his affection to make such a promise to vile man is sweet to us. If God be sweet before the thing come and it be sweet, it's certain I have that sweetness which is better than that in the thing and then shall have and taste the other also in time. God is also more glorified when himself is very sweet for making such a promise, rather than when the soul tastes the sweetness of the thing.

I saw also that whatever grace the Lord hath wrought in me, 'tis not only against my weakness but against the grain of my heart and course which hath resisted God, and therefore and thereby I knew this grace is of God and he shall have this glory of it, as of whatever he shall work for time to come which I cannot attain to now.

December 7. On lecture morning this came into my thoughts, that the greatest part of a Christian's grace lies in mourning for the want of it. I say the greatest part because there is some life and feeling withal. And hence (1) I saw that he who hath his grace lying and appearing chiefly in feeling of it is a pharisee and proud, if there be high-flown expressions and the least part is mourning for want or equally mourning for want; (2) that a poor Christian lamenting his wants is the most sincere; (3) that the Lord when he shows mercy to any of his, it is in withholding much spiritual life and letting them feel much corruption.

December 26. It came suddenly into my heart to see the errors of many Christians that would have and like well to have joy and peace alway but think their condition woeful if they be left to temptations, fears, and wrestlings and prayers, which I looked then upon as good as the other. And I thought this was like as if one should desire alway to have the harvest last but would have no seedtime, would be reaping only, without sowing in fears.

December 28. When I was sick and weak I felt and saw my extreme ignorance of all things and my unbelief in all, but the Lord by it made me eye Christ by faith. And then I thought, It is no matter though I am foolish if my head be wise, if I be miserable yet the Lord merciful. And I thought my chief life was out of myself, enjoyed by faith, not in feeling.

1643

January 25. I saw (1) my weakness: how blind and unbelieving I was and thence unfit to teach others. (2) I saw my boldness that I had taken upon me at first a bigger and greater work than I was well able to go through with, viz., ministry and profession of Christianity, for I saw if I neglected my work in either, others would be offended; if I did anything, I could not but act without life. (3) I saw my vileness that I had polluted and blasphemed God's name by my foolish and weak and sinful walking in my place, whereby I was justly slight[ed] and God's work not carried on with success and authority. (4) I saw my misery that God, Christ, spirit, grace, mercy had forsaken me and mine to mourn and lie down and look up still to all-able and all-working mercy, and that I should be humbled by all this more than any and not lift up myself and render all my little.

February 4. On Saturday night I felt nothing but death, darkness in me, and hence saw all my actions were works of darkness and dead works like the principle whence they came. And I saw my woeful unbelief and that I had no help left but in free mercy to take away these sins and heal me of them. Now two or three days before, the Lord let me see that though I had no certainty the Lord would pity me, yet that resting on it as on the *primo principio*[12] and last end immovably, that this was faith. Yet I did somewhat doubt of God's purpose to help me because I saw all my life did hang on God's good pleasure. Now I felt the Lord persuading my heart that it was his good pleasure to have mercy upon me and so his eternal purpose, upon these meditations, which came in as light by degrees into me:

12. First principle.

(1) I saw this good pleasure was a merciful and gracious good pleasure, inclining him to pity;

(2) that it was hence ready to forgive, not slow, because his grace and mercy was abundant.

(3) I saw the Lord had let me see my unbelief and desire the removal of it. Now hence I considered, Why hath the Lord let me see my unbelief and come for strength against it and pray for mercy, if the Lord had no purpose to help me? Why would he let me feel want of the spirit and pray for it if he intended not to succor and give it me? For I saw promises to them that ask, pray, and come, especially such that did it for the Lord's name sake.

(4) I saw the reason why I felt so much blasphemous unbelief, that it might be of God only to try my faith. And the 32 Psalm refreshed me, and thus I saw the Lord by not giving immediate testimony stablished me the more in faith by acquainting me with himself and his sweet nature. Yet I thought that when the spirit comes it gives [1] great comfort, [2] strength, [3] opening of the scriptures.

February 12. Upon this day overnight in preparation for the sacrament, this came to my mind, viz., whether faith was any act of the affections or no, and whether love and desire were in it, for if they were, then faith is made up of works and hath somewhat to boast of, and therefore whether faith was not only our fiat and testimony to God's truth. I had no full answer to my own spirit but saw that they that did fly to Christ by desire should have him and that the merchant sold away all for his pearl.

I was put to question whether faith was not an assurance that Christ and all the good in him was mine, for I saw the gospel (1) revealed this is Christ; (2) commanded to believe this is he; (3) that all our good is in this Messiah; (4) to expect all good from him and desire all that good in him; (5) what is more, to be persuaded all this is mine. And for the grounds of this persuasion, 'tis the command of Christ in the gospel who saith, If thou believest this is he and that he is thine and then come and rely upon him, he shall be thine. If thou canst believe that he is thine, he shall be thine. But I could not issue this. Only I found that my faith, formerly closing with Christ by affection, was battered and shaken as if I had sought the righteousness of Christ by my own works, and that these shakings came in after the Lord gave me some secret and sweet persuasion that Jesus was the Christ partly by considering his miracles, partly considering the testimony of so many Apostles. And after the sacrament the Lord gave me some sweet sense of his love, for seeing that if I did pray to Christ for light, life, mercy, I saw I was bound to believe I should have what I prayed for, John 4:10; 1 John 5:14, 15. And I saw, having a promise, the sacrament did really exhibit what the word did promise, and so I saw, being God's institution, it was no empty but a real thing and that Christ was mine. And Christ crucified and broken being mine, I saw I was to believe that God was fully pacified with me in his Son. And this revived me, and seeing myself condemned stirred me up to live with Christ.

February 17. In my garden the Lord checked me for going on in secret sins without fear, care, or sorrow, and so told me I made no conscience of sin, which did smite my heart much in that if I made not a conscience of every sin I made conscience of none, and that in time of trouble such a course would be bitter. And so I saw the Lord called in upon me to be very holy in all my ways (1) because by this I was like to him, (2) answered the end of Christ's death. Else I made it to be shed in vain.

The next day my sad sorrows of spirit increased, and I saw or feared that I had no faith neither, and that I had mistaken faith, which made me search the more and seek to God.

February 21. On a day of private fast by myself I saw that as the Law did set out man's sin, so the gospel God's love, viz., grace and righteousness toward man. And as the gospel set out God's love chiefly, so the Law man's hatred of God chiefly. Now here I saw that in every sin I hated God, Proverbs 8: *ult.,* which did not a little affect my heart with sin.

March 11. I was very heavy and sad in my spirit by seeing my own vileness and unfitness to know, believe, or do anything, and that hereby I stood between the good of God's people and the Lord. And hence I resolved (1) never to quarrel with any man; (2) to loathe myself and depend on the Lord for all. And seeing some men against me and the elders in our work, and finding my heart ready to rise against them, I then considered (1) that it was not them but the wrath of the Lord in them against me. And so I saw that all the risings of people in the churches was from that ground and that the holy God saw some other sin with which he had a quarrel. And hence I resolved to fall down before God, to be vile in my own eyes, to seek his face, and then to leave the doing and governing of the church and men's unruly spirits unto him, and did believe he would do it himself after that I was humbled before him.

April 21. At Charlestown lecture when the receiving of the word was sweet, I thought thus: if the receiving in of God's glory be sweet, should not the putting forth of his glory be as sweet in acting for God?

I also felt some good that sermon, as the sweetness of Christ, that if it were not for him God's wrath would seize upon and consume all the Christians in the world in a moment. Hence I considered that everything in a sermon is not for every Christian, but for various, and that if Christians in their conference would lay together their flowers, it would [be] the sweetest way of communicating, etc.

As I was riding home I considered that all the times of patience God called for no account, but after death that time came and so judgment. Hereupon I saw that whenever any affliction befalls us, then there is a little day of judgment (and hence called judgment) and that then the Lord calls us to give an account of some sinful course or other.

May 21. On Sabbath-day morning in prayer it was a trouble to me that God did not give some absolute promise as the first ground of my faith. And I was tempted to think that to receive a promise from the sense of any work was to build on an uncertain ground, e.g., to believe God will hear because I know I have prayed for an answer. But the Lord cast this into my mind: that though the Lord doth not present me with an absolute promise of grace, yet if he doth present me with a special work of his grace and so show me my interest in the promise, this is all grace and a fairer and fuller manifestation of God's grace. I know sometimes I cannot pray, yet I see 'tis God's work to enable me. Here is grace to work, and grace then to promise.

May 30. After I had some sense of God's love and doubted of it again by reason of my sin, I saw this truth: that those that think themselves cast out of God's favor because of every little relapse into sin, they do think by their duties and obedience to procure God's favor.

Hereupon I saw as I did not procure favor by any obedience, so I did not lose it by disobedience and sin, but I procure favor by faith in Christ. Hence I will never conclude I am cast out of favor till I have cast away my faith, which God commands me not to do, Hebrews 10:36 [*sic:* 10:35], and that I will not do. But yet as by obedience I come to the sense of favor, so by disobedience I lose only the sense of it.

June 3. On Saturday night I did much desire that the Lord would speak immediately to me as to the prophets, that so I might certainly feel and know this living God. But I saw when I came down from my study that the difference between our knowledge of God and the prophets' is that they received the word immediately from God, but we are to look for it and so to hear it mediately by man, yet with the expectation of the same spirit that taught them, to instruct us.

June 11. On Sabbath day I found my soul restless till it had such a measure of grace, and that it would be at rest and so grow full with it if it had it. And I also found that my conscience was troubled with questioning God's love while I did want it, but would be quieted when I had it. Now this I saw erroneous and that it was a kind of pharisaical course (1) because I should aim at a perfection, not a measure; (2) to be full of a measure was pride; (3) that when God gives never so much, yet I should alway want and cry out, Oh Lord, how far short do I fall! (4) Hence I should not be assured from any measure received, but rather from sense of Christ's fullness, my own want, and my desire after perfection. I saw that I should mourn for falling short not only of my measure but of perfection itself. And I saw that this was true poverty and the Christ-like life of all the saints, feeling and complaining of want alway as if they had nothing until they have perfection, yet believing God's good will to them in that 'tis thus (as it should be) with them.

June 25. On the Sabbath I saw my unbelief kept me from prayer and deadened my heart in it (1) because I did believe that I could not seek so as to find and to be any whit the better; (2) because if I did, yet God would not hear nor give, because of his absolute will to show mercy to whom he will, which I found did usually dash my faith; (3) because I felt not my own wants, so I did not see by faith the infinite glory of the good I did want, hence did not seek.

For answer hereunto I found this of use especially to the first: that it was mere mercy that did save and that could give a heart to seek, not of him that willeth or runneth. I saw to rest on mercy, being utterly undone, was safe and sure.

I saw also this day that in myself I was a clod of earth, weakness, wickedness, and rottenness, and consequently all glory and all my good was in Jesus Christ, as also that hence I should not desire, or be unwilling to part with, any good which made for the good of myself, for what was I? And here I understood that the way to save myself was to seek for or not to care for the ruin of myself. But I found this hard, and yet God cast in this thought, that when I found any good I was unwilling to part withal, as plenty for poverty, etc., I should consider three things: (1) what my self was: a clod of filthy earth; for if I loved anything for myself as last end, then love not myself, I shall not love other things; (2) what the creature was: most vile and perishing as flower of the field; (3) what Christ himself and his will was, and how precious, for whose sake I should forsake these things.

July 8. In morning prayer after I was alone I considered what little reason I had to doubt of God's love after afflictions or because of afflictions, though never so bitter. For I thought: Was not God's love seen as much in taking from [me] what I desired, that he might humble me (whether inward or outward refreshings), as well as in giving what I desired, to rejoice and comfort me?

I also saw how apt my heart was to be like the sea, troubled and unquieted with cares, with griefs, with thoughts of future events, with men, with God. Now I saw that God's spirit delighteth to dwell in a quiet still heart. And hence I resolved to be troubled at nothing but what troubles my God, and desired and purposed to turn all crosses to cheerfulness.

August 1. I saw that the little which a godly man doth for Christ is ever more than he thinks he doth, as, *e contra,* the sin is more vile than they think 'tis. One word that a godly man speaks for [?] an ordinance or to encourage a minister hath a recompense according to all the fruits of it.

Fickleness of spirit is like a sea wave or froth: it's blown with any wind. If a good wind comes, it goes that way, and *e contra.* If God's spirit breathes, it follows that; if Satan, he follows that. But a godly man resists the one and co-works with the other.

September 21. In riding on my horse and seeing myself kept every moment from dangers in my way, I saw that I did step every hour upon the neck of death through the redemption of Christ.

September 23. I saw that I should not pray for my own ends, and hence when I would have a blessing that nearly concerns myself and therefore apt to ask for myself, let me not so much seek after that thing as after my last end, God and his favor, and bring my soul to a renewed esteem of them, though I want the thing, and then I shall have it.

I was much troubled with sense of my own inability to think of anything fit to be preached. And I saw God withdrew, which I looked upon (1) because of my own sins; (2) as a token and fruit of wrath against the people—and this made me mourn—arising from reprobation toward some. It was well if it was but anger, if not reprobation and a fruit of God's sore displeasure.

I saw also that I did question the main principles; hence I learned when God did shake anything it was to make me look to their standing, and this was great mercy to do thus for this end.

I was also this day thinking, Why should I press the people to some one small duty? And I saw the reason, because if I did not make conscience of one, I made conscience of none; if of any one, then of all; so that I saw all duties and all God's glory is concerned in preaching for and practicing some one thing.

October 2. On Monday morning in my bed I saw that my spirit did make the fruits of God's love, as power against sin, etc., the motives to move God to love, for I could believe if I felt sin removed, if I could remove that which did provoke. Now I did hope the Lord would be moved to love when as I did not believe, when I did rest upon free mercy to move, which was a far greater mover than my duty. And here I saw that one cause of my want of peace of conscience was making my duties motives to move love, for if I made mercy rested on the only moving cause, why did I not then believe before I felt these fruits? Why did I not believe the Lord would love me when I rested upon the only motive and cause of love rather than when I felt the fruits of it, considering what an ill method of believing 'tis to think the Lord loves me only when I feel fruits given and not when I see and feel the cause given and fountain of all love the Lord hath brought me to? Blessed are they that trust in his mercy. This did sweetly affect me.

November 13. On Sabbath after sermon I saw that as in old England men's wickedness put forth itself against saints in hating them, so here against ordinances, some against one, others against all.

November 22. I was seeking the Lord with fears for his favor, and I saw one reason why I staggered so much by unbelief was because I did think the removal of sin did move God to favor, when as it was a fruit and an effect of his favor. And hence I saw that resting upon free mercy for mercy sake and Christ's sake to accept and love me and to remove my sins from me, that remain constant, my peace would remain constant also. And here I saw that there was no such effectual motive to favor as mercy itself. And I thought if I would believe mercy by removing sin, then much more by moving God by his own mercy.

December 10. I saw an effectual offer was a gift: when God did effectually offer Christ, he gave Christ. In this sacrament I was much troubled about the ground of my faith because I wanted an immediate absolute testimony of special mercy. Yet I looked unto the word and saw (1) if those that look up to Christ for all from him, (2) if those that come to him and seek for supply of all wants from him, (3) if those that receive Christ by election of him above all (as by refusing of the will he is shut out), (4) if receiving of him as my own because called by the gospel to come up to possess him, and so trusting to him—if this or these were faith, that I [had] some cause of being assured that the Lord had forgiven my sins, and the sacrament was a full assurance to me.

I had some glimpsings that this was faith (1) because else I saw I must forsake the word for the guiding of my estate; (2) because I saw trusting to works and Christ were opposite, as therefore those that trusted to works (*opere*[)], though with some fears, for life thereto, Romans 9, so those that trusted to Christ can thus rest upon him with absolute certainty, so resting, and say, Who shall condemn? (3) because I saw the Lord had caused me to trust not my own self, because I had a heart given me to bless him dearly, and to see that he had let me see Christ, who once saw him not. He had let me desire Christ and taste Christ and roll myself upon Christ, forcing me thereto by sense of want of all.

1644

January 7. When I had ended sermon in the afternoon I saw my heart looking out of myself upon what I had done and what effect it took, but Christ suggested to me: Now return unto me and turn thyself so to me and come so in me as to see nothing else but me! And I did so and there fell down in his presence, confessing my sins and seeking for favor.

January 20. I saw my vile heart did not take notice of many sins lest I should be troubled about my estate for them, when as now I saw I should take notice of them all because all were little enough to carry my soul out of myself to Christ by humbling of me. For I considered that by feeling the evil of sin my soul only could be carried out effectually to Jesus Christ, that good. The soul will fall short of esteem and longing after Christ if it feels not misery to purpose. And so I saw one special reason of humiliation to precede faith.

I saw also the Thursday upon my bed in the morning before this Sabbath that coming by faith to mercy I should believe certainly that Christ was mine and God pacified. And hereupon I should not think that my sin casts me now out of favor nor my duties bring me into favor, but I should love Christ and out of love hate my sin, not out of fear of wrath, and there hold.

February 5. At night in meditation I saw (1) that this whole world and the churches in general were up in arms against God. (2) Hence I saw the Lord did come forth in arms, fire, and sword and blood against them. (3) The principal cause I saw was the crossing of God's will in that he did principally command, and that was faith and obedience to his son Christ who though he be not seen yet is exalted to be prince and savior, and hath all creatures put into his hand, and being preached is to be believed in and received of all princes and people as savior, prince, and husband, so that hence (4) not to receive Christ as preached by man is the great sin of the world for which God doth fill it with war and blood, Daniel 9: Not obeyed voice of his servants.

February 9. In my bed on Friday morning I saw the glory of having a part in the satisfaction of Christ. (1) This would make me mourn for sin bitterly as having crucified Christ. (2) This would make me glory and joy only in Christ's cross. (3) This would make me love Christ dearly. (4) This would make me believe my sins should die in me in time. (5) This would make me come with boldness to God's grace and presence. (6) This would make me act only out of love, not in thinking that I should move God to love me by my prayers or praises, but only as out of love. For I saw so long as I did think my sins did anger God against me, so long I did and should think the removal of my sin would move him to be pleased with me. I saw therefore that I should see sin provoking God, but by laying it on Christ, the Father pacified.

February 10. At night I saw two things should make Christ sweet: (1) my wants, because I saw how precious he was in whom was supply of such evils. Usually my wants cause me to prize his grace less because I felt not supply, but now I saw there was the more reason to prize him the more as more sweet. And here I saw how sin was sanctified and made a blessing, because it made Christ more sweet. (2) By believing what I see of God in his word, for look on God in himself I could see nothing but infinite good, but yet saw it not. Now in his word I saw it dropped in so many expressions as I could drink in at a time.

March 6. In the day of fast I remember my heart was raised up to heaven to see and call upon the name of the Lord Jesus as if I was present with him. I did lie by him and lie at him all that day. And hence my prayers were not to one afar off, but every word in confession and petition did affect me much. And here I saw that it was not because Christ was afar off but because I was afar off from him that he was so to me. And I also saw what the meaning of that scripture[13] was that faith enters within the veil and that through his flesh we go into the holy of holies because though Christ was on earth yet now he is in heaven, and hence as if he was on earth I should so converse with him and see him as filling heaven with his glory, so being in heaven I should so come to him there and be with him there as filling the earth also and seeing my soul in special.

March 29. In my bed in the morning I saw the madness of the world and the evil of my own heart in not getting nearer to God by everything, nor yet endeavoring so to do my happiness. And I saw it my duty so to do and did purpose weakly so to do and to cast off that which did not lead me to him.

13. Heb. 6:19.

THE PEOPLE SPEAK: CONFESSIONS OF LAY MEN AND WOMEN

THE CHURCH OF Cambridge—the second in that village, the first having moved away to Connecticut—was organized in 1636, soon after Thomas Shepard arrived there.[1] The founding ceremony was a do-it-yourself affair. An initial handful of the settlement's leading men, in the presence of members of the community and representatives of the colony, bound themselves to one another by pledges of fidelity and fellowship, adopted a covenant, and chose a pastor—all of this after the manner, so they thought, of the very earliest Christians.[2] By common consent they based their church on principles of choice and consensus that the ceremony of creation itself enacted.

Membership in this church was not taken for granted, as in the parishes of England these people had left behind. Rather, affiliation was premised on axioms of willingness that made a church, in their eyes, truly a church and made its members true members, they believed, of the body of Christ. This body was highly selective; its spiritual legitimacy depended on getting the right people in and keeping the wrong people out. As Shepard noted, "matter fit to ruin a church is not fit to make a church."[3] Thus while all adults in early Puritan New England were compelled to attend sabbath services—the principle of choice did not apply to them—the circle of members embraced only a minority of inhabitants.

Members were admitted by a method peculiar to New England—one that most of the world's Christian communions would

Passages in this preface have been drawn or adapted with permission of the publisher from my article "The Church on the Square and the Church on the Common," *Bulletin of the Congregational Library,* XLII-XLIII (1991), pp. 4–14. Spelling and punctuation in the confessions have been modernized.

1. The town was then called Newtown. The name was changed to Cambridge in 1638.

2. The event was recorded by Governor John Winthrop, who was there. See James Kendall Hosmer, ed., *Winthrop's Journal, "History of New England," 1630–1649* (New York: Charles Scribner's Sons, 1908), I, 173–74.

3. Shepard, *The Parable of the Ten Virgins* (1660), in *Works,* ed. John A. Albro (Boston, 1853), II, 188.

have dismissed as improper or impolitic. The Cambridge participants confessed their faith, which was normal enough, but then went on to tell "what work of grace the Lord had wrought in them"—which was definitely unusual.[4] More than assenting to a creed or memorizing a catechism was needed to get into these new self-made fellowships. It took a credible report of an encounter with God—really, a sequence of encounters—that Puritans recognized as the experience of conversion and calling. New England's congregations were meant to be made up of saved souls—Puritans called them "saints"—and the sanctity of those saints had to be made "visible"—that is, manifest in their lives.

That was where the New England oddity came in. To demonstrate visible sainthood, applicants for admission publicly recounted, at appointed solemn times, the salient data of their spiritual experience. This ritual, with local variations, became a signature—critics would say a stigma—of New England's Puritan churches.[5]

This section of *God's Plot* presents personal narratives given in the 1630s and 1640s by aspirants to membership at Cambridge. We know what these people said because their pastor, Shepard, wrote it down. What they said is valuable as history because, while ministers made many tracks in print, lay people made far fewer, and for the most part ordinary folk made none at all. In Shepard's record, these ordinary folk have an afterlife: their words survive for us to read. Most of the narratives became available in print in 1981; the rest, in 1991. Shepard called them "confessions." The confessors were charged to "make known to the congregation the work of grace upon [their] souls."[6] The minister, scribbling fast, set down their words. If we cannot know what he may have left out, we can be pretty sure he got the main things in—and those things tell what it was like to be a Puritan at that time and place.[7]

Picture the scene at Cambridge at the moment we cut in. The church members—kinfolk, friends, and neighbors—pack the

4. Ibid., p. 173.
5. Edmund S. Morgan, *Visible Saints: The History of a Puritan Idea* (New York: New York University Press, 1963).
6. George Selement and Bruce Woolley, eds., *Thomas Shepard's Confessions,* Colonial Society of Massachusetts *Collections,* LVIII (Boston, 1981), p. 19.
7. Other confessions from early New England are noted ibid., p. 3.n.7.

benches of the small, plain meetinghouse. The minister sits at one side, quill pen poised. The candidate for admission stands, takes a breath, gets ready—no speaking had ever been so hard. We know these were not impromptu performances; they had been practiced at home, coached by the minister, and vetted by senior saints.[8] The confessors tell us, too, that they had sometimes shared their spiritual problems with other ministers, relatives, and friends. Still, for all this private rehearsing, it cannot have been comfortable for these folk to bare their souls. There were high expectations to be met, for they were speaking before God, from whom no secret could be hid, and in the presence of God's watchdog representatives. Under these pressures the Cambridge confessors showed remarkable fortitude. Only one broke down—a Mrs. Greene, who managed five sentences and then gave up. Shepard noted that others spoke on her behalf and got her in.[9]

Shepard provided a model by example—for his piety was well known—and also by precept. Do it right, he told them, and do not overdo it. If you relate a "long story of conversion," the chances are "one hundred to one" that "some lie" will "slip . . . out with it." The lie would always be self-serving: "the secret meaning is, I pray admire me"—admire me, above all, as a truly "broken-hearted Christian." This was tough teaching, and Shepard did not soften it. Do not spin out your recitals with "relations of this odd thing and the other," he told his pupils; do not "heap up all the particular passages of [your] lives wherein [you] have got any good"; do not parade your knowledge of the Bible or your recall of sermons (a caveat often disregarded). Instead, keep the story short and stay on track. Speak simply of things that "may be of special use unto the people of God, such things as tend to show, Thus was I humbled, then thus was I called, then thus I have walked, though with many weaknesses, since: and such special providences of God I have seen, temptations gone through, and thus the Lord hath delivered me, blessed be his name, etc."[10] Shepard's formula draws a design for communicative piety that was characteristically Puritan for that

8. The process is described ibid., pp. 18–21, drawing on Thomas Lechford's *Plain Dealing or News from New England* (1642) and other contemporary sources.
9. Selement and Woolley, eds., *Shepard's Confessions,* p. 118.
10. Shepard, *Ten Virgins,* II, 284–85, 631.

generation in New England. How well the people learned and applied the formula we may judge from the confessions themselves.

Puritans were notoriously a different sort of people, and New England Puritans, especially of the first generation, amply lived up to the reputation of their kind. It follows that the confessions should not be viewed as representing lay piety and clerical teaching for all times and all places where Puritans were ever found. For one thing, the confessors' religious sensibilities were screwed painfully tight by the stress of their experiences as refugees.[11] The practice of confession, a New England invention, reflected this heightened intensity. Moreover, at the very time that some of the early confessions were recorded, the infant colony of Massachusetts Bay was being shaken by a challenge to its power structure and morale—the so-called antinomian controversy of 1636–1638. Struggling with this crisis, the colony's magistrates and ministers, including Shepard, took steps to consolidate orthodoxy's authority and avert further threats. Given the timing, it seems plausible that the requirement of confessions, with their pervasive conformities, was initiated as one means among others to confirm control through consensus. Shepard had worked hard to keep his town clear of antinomian heresy. His people's response suggests that his teaching harmonized with their opinion, so that confession was seen from both angles as a valuable and appropriate exercise.[12]

Most of the confessors were between the ages of twenty-five and thirty-five. Nearly half were women. Whatever their age or sex, their stories trace broken life-lines through ordeals of dislocation—in England, in the sea passage, and in New England too, since Cambridge was not the first stopping place for many of them. Like their pastor, they had been people on the move—even on the run—and their emotional adjustment to their new land and life had not been easy. Several recall falling into deep depression after getting to

11. On the disruptions of crossing and settling see Virginia Dejohn Anderson, *New England's Generation* (Cambridge: Cambridge University Press, 1991), David Cressy, *Coming Over: Migration and Communication between England and New England in the Seventeenth Century* (Cambridge: Cambridge University Press, 1987), and Andrew Delbanco, *The Puritan Ordeal* (Cambridge: Harvard University Press, 1989).

12. Janice Knight explores these themes in *Orthodoxies in Massachusetts: Rereading American Puritanism* (Cambridge: Harvard University Press, 1994).

New England; their miseries illustrate the adage that it is better to travel hopefully than to arrive. The experience of their hearts, as of their lives, was rough and jagged.

Here is a woman, known to us only as Brother Crackbone's wife, who, after crossing the ocean with her children, "forgot the Lord as the Israelites did" after crossing their sea. New England is a great disappointment; she becomes despondent. "I had a new house," she says, but not a "new heart." Then her new house burns down; she gets the point and turns metaphoric: "my spirit was fiery so to burn all I had, and hence [I] prayed [the] Lord would send [the] fire of [his] word [and] baptize me with fire."

Trial by fire; trial by water: here is a man, William Andrews, a sea captain from Ipswich, England, who builds himself a ship and cannot keep his mind off it, even on the sabbath day. This fault worries him, but Providence solves his problem. God sends a storm; the storm sinks the ship, drowns most of the crew, and leaves the skipper and four sailors perched "naked upon the main topsail in very cold weather." Brought safe to shore, he recalls that "glad I was that I lost my ship and so lost my sin." (There is no mention of any feelings about the loss of the crew.)

Here is another man, Nicholas Wyeth, whose story does not please. The congregation know more about him than he tells. They go after him. "Are you not one unfruitful tree to be hewn down?" "Are you privy to any guile in your way?" "Have you not seen more into your heart and life?" "Why do you forget things, brother?" Prizing sincerity, scorning secrecy and hypocrisy, these people scrupulously narrow the entrance to their outpost of the kingdom of heaven. In their cross-examination of the unfortunate Wyeth we see how well they had mastered Shepard's formula and how ready they were to apply it critically.

Even for men and women with less to hide, the trial was strict. It has been suggested that Shepard let down the bars, that "ministerial compassion" made him "lax in his admissions standards."[13] But his people would assuredly have disagreed, and the suggestion is also belied by the fact that Shepard led in blocking the formation of a church at nearby Dorchester in 1636—at a time when the require-

13. Selement and Woolley, eds., *Shepard's Confessions*, pp. 20, 22.

ment of public confession was just beginning to be worked out in practice—because he thought the would-be founding members defective. Above all, any notion that this man was soft or pliable or complicit in sanctified fakery is disproved by the spiritual discipline he imposed on himself. Because he knew how easy it was to deceive oneself and others in matters of the spirit, he took great pains to ensure, by prior sifting, that the wrong people would not get as far as the public confession.

To get that far and even farther—into the church itself—each individual had to grapple with the question that controls the whole series of narratives: How can I know, and how can I show, that I am saved? How can I be sure that God has chosen me? The problem, as Shepard kept reminding them, was that no one could know for sure and that if you thought you did know, you were wrong—dead wrong. The blessing of absolute assurance belonged to no one, not even the most conspicuous of saints—not even, Shepard's journal tells us, to Shepard himself. Common experience confirmed Shepard's teaching on this point. Edward Hall speaks for all the confessors when he admits to "cleaving to Christ" only "by fits and starts." So do Elizabeth Olbon, whose spirit is often "dead and dull," and John Sill, who says he is too much "a hearer and not a doer," and Nathaniel Eaton, caught in a spiritual Catch-22: "to neglect duties [such as prayer and worship] I durst not, [but] to do [them] out of love I could not." Doubts pervade these stories; worries abound. The confessors have been running—are still running—a broken course that zigs and zags from anxiety to assurance and back again. Their anxieties stand out sharply; their pain is evident. Their assurance, by contrast, seems transient and incomplete—as indeed, in Shepard's spiritual calculus, it was supposed to be.

Puritans of Shepard's sort identified two classes of people as bad examples. On one side were foolish folk like Anne Hutchinson, the trouble-making Massachusetts antinomian, who claimed, in effect, to read God's mind: these folk *knew* they were saved; they had God's own word for it by a personal revelation that was positive and final. Orthodox believers called this claim a cover for immorality; they nodded knowingly when Jane Holmes told in her confession of the carnal solicitations of the shipboard antinomian preacher for whom faith licensed sin.

On the other side were equally deluded (and far more unhappy) people who took the undoubted truths of Calvinism—original sin, total depravity, limited atonement, eternal damnation, and so forth—so deeply to heart that they judged themselves condemned to hell. Like Elizabeth Olbon, they "fell down in discouragements" and stayed down. Spiritual depression appears, in these confessions, to have been a predominantly female affliction, though men, too, often experienced it.

Wise heads lumped together these two types—the cocksure and the forlorn—and charged them both with copping out. Too daring or too diffident, they missed the very point of religion. They did not understand that religion meant the life of faith. Instead, the former took a short cut to heaven, while the latter sat down and moped in their puddle of tears.

Authentic saints knew better. We get an inkling of what they knew—of their way of understanding their spiritual predicament—when we hear Barbary Cutter, a teenager, explain that the "Lord hath let me see more of himself as in doubtings." Why is that? we can imagine one of Barbary's tutors asking. Her answer is normative: the "Lord did leave saints doubting [so] as to remove lightness and frothiness, . . . and to cause [them to look] for fresh evidence, and by this means kept them from falling." I doubt, the girl is saying. Because I doubt, I know I care. Because I care, I take the trouble to look at what I am and what I do; I want to find out how I stand with God. Because I want to stand well, I try to be good and do right. My doubts remain, but though I cannot lose them, I can learn to use them.

Here was a primer for Puritans. Young Barbary Cutter has encountered the practical paradox that assurance can be inferred from its absence. She is learning that this inference takes time. Grace does not just happen, nor does it happen suddenly; instead, divine power works gradually upon the human material—slowly mending, shaping, schooling, refining. Conversion is thus not a lightning strike, but a carefully scripted process, with a part assigned even for ingenues. Barbary is learning, too, that God always leaves his work unfinished here and now, and she has found out why—so that true saints, being only dimly visible to themselves and to others, will go on asking the hard questions and trying to work out the answers in all the hours of their lives. To accept this lesson, as she accepts it, is to grasp the secret of saintliness.

Not surprisingly, then, the stories are unfinished: they often break off in mid-flow, on a point of doubt or of tremulous hope. We cannot be sure whether the speaker just ran out of fuel, stalled, and sat down or whether the scribe stopped writing because he had enough for a decision on admission. In any case, these frayed endings and subverted conclusions show, in a Puritan way, how God left saved souls rough-hewn. It followed that confessors received the benefit of the doubt—their own doubt most of all. Doubt, they were told, was instrumental to faith: these people were still in training for holiness. Their public confessions were thus part of the onflowing, never-ending process of regeneration, understood as a continual turning to God that gave depth, value, and direction to their lives. "Still I am doubting," said Robert Holmes, humbly and bravely, at the very end of his testimony, "but I know I shall know if I follow on. . . ."

Clearly, then, public certification of sainthood, for this first generation of Puritan New Englanders, did not bring about a tidy happy ending to spiritual stress. A confessor might pass the test, in the judgment of the saints, but human judgments were notoriously fallible, especially where God was the true judge. Moreover, such assurance as church membership conveyed could be undercut by the same old resurgent doubts, their edges now sharpened by the expectations and requirements of membership itself. So the faithful were bound to go on laboring to square their impression of God's unmerited favor with their own self-targeting sense of shame and justice. Theirs was undoubtedly a hard case; had it been easier, these people and their pastor would have felt themselves untrue to their better selves and to their God.

Scholars used to be impressed by the hardness of the procedure, the test in the testimony; such words as "trial," used above, reflect this emphasis, as do observations on the candidates' uneasiness and the congregation's readiness to pounce. Certainly, there is something to be said for it. The theme of confession as ordeal concurs with the Calvinist estimate of the radically unequal distribution of grace, in which each individual had only an outside chance. It also agreed with Puritan sensitivity to hypocrisy: even the most visible saints, Shepard explained, could live good lives and die expecting to go to heaven and never realize they were "counterfeit" till God brought them to the "strict and last examination" and sent them to hell.[14] It is true, too, that Cambridge folk knew well the common rubs and tugs of village life: the well-to-do Nathaniel Sparrowhawk was not the only confessor to complain about a "spirit of enmity" in New England. Furthermore, as Puritans, these folk (so their adversaries charged) had special temptations to feel holier-than-thou. They were thorough-going moralists with a strong sense of the strict opposition between right and wrong and between right people and wrong people. They were great fault-finders, and they would have had no lack of faults to find.

All this admitted, newer scholarship takes a more positive line. It highlights constructive aspects of Puritan character, New England community, and the church admission process. Recent studies revise the picture of New England's early villages as communities in crisis, dens of spiritual ferrets and moral moles, of gossips and snoops all busily getting the dirt on one another. Getting the dirt, or handing it out, was not the purpose of confession: the confessors were intended to pass, not fail, and it is a striking fact that almost every one did pass, even Nicholas Wyeth. New England's churches were meant to be exclusive clubs of bona fide saints, to be sure, but for those who knocked at the sanctuary's door, the principle of exclusivity was applied as inclusively as possible—in Shepard's own words, through "the judgment of charity which hopes for the best."[15] The sieve, in other words, was also a net. The unspoken but primary intent of the exercise was to create a support system for the practice of piety.

14. Shepard, *The Sincere Convert* (1646), in Albro, *Works*, I, 61.
15. Thomas Shepard and John Allin, *A Defense of the Answer . . . Made Unto the Nine Questions* (London, 1645), p. 190. See Baird Tipson, "Invisible Saints: The 'Judgment of Charity' in the Early New England Churches," *Church History*, XLIV (1975), pp. 460–71. But see also Shepard's caution "not to lavish your charity too far" in receiving members, with the graphic warning that it was a "sinful extreme to swallow down all flies that be in the cup . . ." (*Ten Virgins*, II, 189).

That was the church's purpose and function. Had conversion been finished and complete at the time of confession, Puritan churches would have lost their central reason to exist. That being so, conversion did not come to a sudden stop at the point of admission to membership. The church's need virtually required that the process extend well past that point. Accordingly, Shepard's judgment of charity measured promise far more than performance, for, as he knew only too well, most of the confessors were spiritual toddlers and all of them had a long way to go. In addition, acceptance into the body of Christ supplied strong incentives to continue the work of personal transformation, as minister and members united in pursuing holiness through disciplines of devotion designed to enable them, as they said and as they deeply hoped, to grow in grace and close with Christ.

Confession was the essential first step, and it had deeply affirmative connotations—both for individuals and for their community. One need not read far in the texts to see that the confessors were doing something that mattered and were behaving, indeed, as though they themselves mattered—in the sight of God and in the eyes of others. We may call them Shepard's people—and they would not have objected—yet they were far from being simple sheep. As they evaluated themselves, singly and altogether, these women and men were practicing the same skills that ministers commanded. In the moment of confession, they became public players in the greatest of plays, not supplanting their priests but supplementing them. The act of self-presentation may have been particularly validating for women, who had few opportunities in that patriarchal age to exercise such independence. Like their menfolk, when they stood up to speak in the meetinghouse, they affirmed their personal spiritual autonomy and agency.

Each in her or his own way, the godly folk of Cambridge were defining themselves, and the deepest definition was constructive. No matter how negative their self-judgments, the subtext is a positive sense of self. The affirmation of the self that chooses comes through powerfully, and not paradoxically, even as they denigrate themselves. After all, said Nathaniel Eaton, "it was not for nothing that God had spent so much pains upon me." Their conversion had been difficult for God; the hardness of the job proved their value to him and to themselves. They are the leading actors in their stories—bad actors by definition but central all the same as objects of God's interest and as subjects in their own right. Thus they are fashioning themselves in words—shaping a character, projecting a part, authorizing the scenario of their own lives, simultaneously producers and critics. The confessors are attempting, like Shepard himself, to make God's plot their own and to confirm, by an act of choice, their appointed roles in the divine scenario. These individual tales thus construct the collective persona of the Puritan saint.

In that undertaking, as regards assurance, the ritual itself had a steadying effect, despite the nervousness it roused. In confessing, these people ceased to be private individuals too shy or shamed (as some said of themselves) to speak to anyone about their plight. In this crucial moment of disclosure they came out of hiding, into the open, into the light. The release, the sheer relief, the unimagined sense of freedom—in a word, the happiness—topped anything that antinomians could ever offer. Behind their words there is thus a confidence that anxiety cannot quite conceal. Individuals who had thought themselves alone now found themselves companioned and supported, receiving assurance from the reassurance of others and giving it back again. Here they touched the concordant heart, the living inner principle, of religious consensus. Requiring confession, in this aspect, was far more than gatekeeping. It was one of the ways—perhaps, indeed, the most important way—by which New England's Puritans forged their community of values and purposes.

Think of the confessors, too, in their next role. Today, as applicants, they are speaking and asking; tomorrow, as members, they will be listening and deciding. As enfolded saints, they will continue to reenact the ritual time after time, year after year, choosing others in God's name. Again and again they will revisit their experience; they will see themselves in others' stories. Through this periodic reiteration of the entrance exam—this grooved continuity of discourse—their community will reaffirm its essential identity, validity, and stability; it will remind itself of its reason to be.[16]

16. On the positive value of ritual and the structuring of assurance, see David D. Hall, *Worlds of Wonder, Days of Judgment: Popular Religious Belief in Early New England* (New York: Alfred A. Knopf, 1989), chap. 3, and "On Common Ground: The Coherence of American Puritan Studies," *William and Mary Quarterly,* 3d Ser., XLIV (1987), pp. 218–21.

Thus the practice was full of promise. Yet it was also novel and different. This experimental application of the rules of choice and consensus carried no guarantee of success. How well would it work? How long could it last? There was no question that spiritual assurance could be institutionalized through such rituals as confession—but that, in fact, was just the problem. Was there not, from the beginning, a potential discrepancy between means and end? Could the practice be continued very long without subverting the very vitality it was meant to replenish? Becoming habitual with use, constrained to a standard form, would not the public confession become routine and decay into convention and cant, and would not God's people, when comfortably seated in the church, lose the urgency they had felt when they were still outside looking in? None of these questions would have startled Thomas Shepard, who had no faith in human expediencies and was quite used to finding failure in apparent success. Perennially problematic for salvationist Christianity, these issues were starting to emerge by the time Shepard's record stops. He died too soon to see the answers working out in the religious life of the village and the region.

Shepard and the Cambridge saints developed their spiritual support system in a place they sacralized by their own words and deeds, including the confessions. They were trying to open a space for holiness, and they had to start from scratch and use materials of their own making, just as they did in clearing pastures and garden plots. Their meetinghouse was bare of icons and incense; the graveyard needed more graves to become hallowed ground; never before had any of these people worshipped in a building their own hands had made from wood their own hands had cut—a room so necessarily expressive of rude human toil, so unendowed with the insignia of reverence. Their worship, too, was spare, stripped of the comforts of traditional ceremony by Protestant economy. Lacking the old forms and ways, then, they had to invent new ones—makeshift, no doubt, but all that could be managed then and there. Thus the rite of confession acquired for them an importance beyond itself; it became functionally joined with sermon and sacraments in their imagination of holiness. Such sanctity as human beings, acting for their God, could give a place was given by their speaking—the minister from the pulpit, the members from the pews at confession time.

Confession also had an extraecclesial function: it supported the sociability of saints outside the church as they set about to form and run their young village. First, they had to get to know each other. A few Cambridge folk were left over from Thomas Hooker's group. A few more had made the sea crossing with Shepard. Some had been in one of Shepard's English flocks; there was a nucleus of at least ten from Northumberland. But most came from here and there in England—all the way from Kent in the south to Yorkshire in the north; they were as new to one another as to the place they all found themselves. Consequently, there were personalities to be assessed, differences to be adjusted, ties to be knotted. As strangers and exiles, set down in this far place, these people were sorting themselves out and sizing each other up. Stitching together a social network, they had to know who was who, and who could do, and who was worth what.[17]

We also see a power center forming. Joining the church opened the way for adult men to become members of the body politic; this status, called freemanship, conveyed the right to vote and hold public office. Several of the confessors represented here—Sparrowhawk, Collins, Andrews, among others—served as town selectmen or deputies to the colony's General Court. They were supported by a second tier of men who performed a variety of essential lower-level public tasks as constables, road surveyors, fence menders, and the like. In February 1636, the town's leaders ordered that no house be built in town without the town's approval.[18] House-

17. The tension between the regional-cultural diversity of English emigrants and the need for conformity is underscored by David Grayson Allen, *In English Ways: The Movement of Societies and the Transferal of English Local Law and Custom to Massachusetts Bay in the Seventeenth Century* (Chapel Hill: University of North Carolina Press, 1981), pp. 8ff. On the forming of community around the church, with a strong sense of people, see Ola Elizabeth Winslow, *Meetinghouse Hill, 1630–1783* (1952; reprint, New York: W. W. Norton Co., 1972).

18. Clarified in April 1636 to specify consent by a majority of townsmen, the order's basic principle was reaffirmed in December and again in March the following year. Significantly, exceptions were made for would-be purchasers or tenants of houses already built who were members of the congregation (*The Records of the Town of Cambridge (Formerly Newtowne) Massachusetts, 1630–1703* [Cambridge, Mass., 1901], pp. 17, 22, 24, 32–33). On the economic power structure of early Massachusetts towns, see John Frederick Martin, *Profits in the Wilderness: Entrepreneurship and the Founding of New England Towns* (Chapel Hill: University of North Carolina Press, 1991). Cambridge is not included in Martin's sample.

holders who got through that screen are prominent among the confessors. Though church membership ran the gamut of the community, the circle of the elect included most, if not all, of Cambridge's principal persons. Confession, for men, was thus, not incidentally, a political act. It confirmed a correlation of position and power that underwrote the stability of church and town and colony as well. This correlation was a cultural commonplace: Shepard captured it in one crisp line: "Church members of public spirits are ever prosperous men."[19]

Church confessions advanced the work of creating the community and structuring the polity by sharing information about new neighbors: confession time was a great get-acquainted time when, quietly and effectively, the confessors and their audience were shaping a new society. Above all, public confession applied the binding power of religious commitment to the common interest, giving it the force of moral mutuality and focusing it in sacred space. Confession can thus be understood, and its value appreciated, not only as an expression of Puritan spirituality but as a communal act, a crossing-point of church and village. In this act, Puritans like Thomas Shepard and his people, forging new lives, new relations, and new selves, brought down God's plot to earth and home.

19. Shepard, *Ten Virgins* II, 22.

THE CONFESSIONS

Edward Hall

—only a mended man . . . cleaving to Christ by fits and starts

Edward Hall (1607–1680), a farmer, had lived in Surrey and Northumberland before coming to Cambridge in 1636, the year he made his confession. He served as local constable and performed such public services as mending fences and tending sheep on the town common.

The first means of his good was Mr. Glover's ministry,[1] whereby he saw his misery from Jeremiah 7—the temple of the Lord[2]—and that he was without Christ. But he went from thence to another place under the sense of an undone condition. But in that place he was deprived of the ordinances of God, and hence the scripture came oft to mind—what if a man win the world and lose his soul?[3] Hence he desired to come to that place again, but the minister was gone. But Mr. Jenner[4] came, and by him he saw more evil in himself. But Mr. S[hepard] came, and then the Lord did more clearly manifest himself to him from John 3 concerning the new birth. And here he saw more of his misery and that he had followed examples and duties and made them his Christ and lived without Christ. Hereby the Lord let him see he was Christless and built upon false foundations, and by this text he saw himself no new creature but only a mended man. Now when the Lord did humble him under this, he saw the want of Christ and that without him he must perish. And afterward, John 5:40 was opened—

1. Jose Glover (d. 1638), minister at Sutton, Surrey, 1628–1636.
2. Jer. 7:4.
3. Matt. 16:26; Mark 8:36; Luke 9:25.
4. Thomas Jenner (1607–c. 1676) preceded Shepard as preacher at Heddon, Northumberland; after 1636, minister at Roxbury, Massachusetts, and Saco in Maine; returned to England in 1650.

you will not come to me to have life. And here he saw how freely Christ was offered, and hereby the Lord did stay and comfort his spirit and so was stirred up with more vehemency to seek Christ. And then that promise was opened—the son of man came to seek that which was lost.[5] And he did not know but the Lord might seek him. And out of that text, Peter 2:8, that unto you that believe he is precious,[6] and here he saw his unbelief in cleaving to Christ by fits and starts. And since the Lord brought him to this place, he found his worldliness, and this bred many fears whether ever any work of Christ in him was in truth, and that he was one that might fall short of Christ and that he was humbled. But his heart was not deep enough, and hence he was put to more search whether ever he was humbled. Yet the Lord made it more clear from Ephraim's condition, Jeremiah 31:18, that the Lord had made him loathe himself, and this made him loathe himself. And here he hath found more enmity of his heart against the Lord than ever before. But hearing the Lord was willing to take away his enmity, he by Revelation 22:17 was brought nearer to the Lord.

Francis Moore

—security, sloth, and sleepiness

Francis Moore (1586–1671) came to Cambridge with his wife and two children in the 1630s. He was a tanner and perhaps a cooper. He served the town as constable, leather sealer, and fence surveyor. He became an elder of the church during the pastorate of Shepard's successor, Jonathan Mitchell.

The Lord revealed his estate to him that he was miserable. And then he found the flesh resisting and contradicting the Lord, and the Lord showed him that without repentance none could be saved and that there must be sorrow for and hatred of sin. Now when

5. Matt. 18:11; Luke 19:10.
6. Correctly, 1 Pet. 2:7.

the Lord had gone thus far with him, he questioned whether his repentance was right or no, or whether no farther than the repentance of Cain and Judas.[1] But seeing that he did not only leave the evil but cleave to the contrary good, hence he concluded it was no feigned work. But having many doubts afterward, the Lord did show him that Christ came to save those that were lost,[2] and so him, not only in general sinners, but himself. And hereby the Lord wrought farther humiliation and sorrow for sin past. And then applying that promise, those that mourn and hunger shall be comforted and satisfied,[3] here arose that question whether he did mourn under his misery truly or no. Now here the spirit of God did seal to his soul that he was truly humbled, not only broken for, but from, sin with detestation of it, and hence was a new creature and hence was received to mercy. Since that time the Lord hath made his estate more clear, yet many sins committed and so hath questioned whether ever this work was wrought or no, that after such infinite love he should depart from God. Yet the Lord set on that word, though he had such a heart to abase his grace, yet that the Lord was unchangeable in himself and so in his love, and that Christ being come to seek and save that which is lost. Yet after his relapse he conceived, though it was not possible the Lord should pity, yet hearing—to him that believes all things are possible[4]—and that, though he had backslid, yet returning to the Lord, here was rich love. This drew his heart to the Lord again because his love was unchangeable. His relapse was thus: (1) the Lord forsook him, and then fell from him to loose company and so to drunkenness. And then the Lord broke his soul the more for what he had done. But before the Lord forsook him, he fell to security, to profane the sabbath. Other relapses he finds, as security and sloth and sleepiness and contenting himself in ordinances without the good of them. Yet the Lord recalling him usually back again, he said he knew his mourning after his relapse to be genuine because it did more endear his heart to the Lord and to walk more humbly.

1. Gen. 4:13–14; Matt. 27:3–5.
2. Matt. 18:11; Luke 19:10.
3. Matt. 5:4, 6; Luke 6:21; Isa. 61:2.
4. Mark 9:23.

Elizabeth Olbon

—arise and be doing

Elizabeth Olbon, birth date unknown but probably in her mid-twenties when she made her confession, came from Derbyshire to Cambridge, where she married James Luxford. She appears in Shepard's record as "Goodman Luxford His Wife." After one child was born and with another on the way, it was discovered that James already had a wife in England. The marriage was declared void; Elizabeth later took a more satisfactory husband and lived into the 1660s.

From a speech of a sister who said she was going to means and I going from it, was stirred, and by her conversation mine was condemned, and hence she desired to live from her and to go to another place. And there she was troubled and desired to go and live again with her, whereby she saw more of her sin. And living under a minister at Bury, where the Lord, 2 Thessalonians 1:10, that Christ would come in fire to render vengeance to all that knew him not,[1] hence she saw her own condition. She knew him not, and so sin was heavy, and she saw no possibility how to get out of it. And he showing what sin a man must see before he could be humbled, and here did show many sins, especially the sin of pride. Yet burdened, and speaking with her, he pressed her rather to be fitted for comfort than to seek for comfort. And when the Lord had wrought upon one or two of her friends, she saw so few to be saved, two of a family, that she thought she should not. Then hearing, with God all things are possible,[2] this stayed her, but yet she went under many scoffs and scorns, which tempted her to look back. But thinking of that place—he that puts his hand to plow and looks back is not fit for the Kingdom of God[3]—and out of the place of the Proverbs—the prudent man foresees the evil and hides himself[4]—and there she saw what she never found before, which was the bitterness of sin we brought into the world. And

1. Correctly, 2 Thess. 1:7–8.
2. Matt. 19:26; Mark 10:27; Luke 18:27.
3. Luke 9:32.
4. Prov. 22:3; 27:12.

then he showed how we should see it. And then he showed what that hiding place was. But seeing her evil, she saw she had no right to it, which hiding place was Christ.

But hearing that a soul might be contented to lie under the punishment of his sin, and there he showed how all discontent did arise from pride. And then he preached, to him I look that is poor and humble and that trembles at my word.[5] But she felt so much evil in her own heart, she thought it impossible so poor a creature should be saved or received to mercy and so fell down in discouragements. And then hearing, arise and be doing and the Lord will be with you,[6] and this quickened her again. And then she saw the Lord could but knew not whether the Lord would help her or no. Hence the Lord gave her a heart earnestly to seek after him, and hearing, they that mourn should be comforted,[7] she felt she could not mourn. And then she saw how duties could not help her because a man in prison must be alway paying his debts. And hearing from 2 Corinthians 5:20—I beseech you, be reconciled to God—yet she felt her will contrary to this. But yet it stayed her heart for a time, and some comfort it gave, but it stayed not long. And then she heard, whoever is athirst, come and buy without money.[8] Now she saw she had no money, yet hearing [that] they that come to Christ might have comfort, then she felt fain she would have somewhat of Christ and something of her own. And that teaching—blessed are those that hunger and thirst after Christ[9]—she saw she longed after Christ to save and sanctify. And then she saw no unclean thing should enter into heaven, yet she saw she must come to a naked Christ, and that she found the hardest thing in the world to do. Yet by this scripture out of Isaiah and Matthew he let her feel his love.

Since she came hither, she hath found her heart more dead and dull, etc., and being in much sickness when she came first into the land, she saw how vain a thing it was to put confidence in any creature. But yet it wrought some discontent in her own spirit, but

5. Isa. 66:2.
6. 1 Chron. 22:16.
7. Matt. 5:4.
8. Isa. 55:1.
9. Matt. 5:6.

[she] hath since witnessed the Lord's love to her. Sometime a heart to run and sometime to sit still in the Lord's way.

George Willows

—the more he did strive, the more he was overcome

George Willows came to New England about 1630 and to Cambridge by 1636. He lived there till 1690. He had two wives (the first a widow with two children), two sons, and a small farm. The confession of his first wife, Jane Palfrey Willows, appears below.

It pleased the Lord to carry him on in a civil course a long time, but going to a friend's house, he brake the sabbath. And coming to hear a minister preach against that sin, he was terrified by it and so lay under the anger of God and sense of it and so saw nothing but hell due to him, but saw not all this while the evil of sin. But under sense of wrath was sick after Christ and longed after him and so after this was brought under more powerful ordinances. And that he rested in his duties and ordinances, and now he was as much terrified with corruption as before with wrath. And now he saw the deadness of his heart under ordinances, and the more he did strive against corruption, the more he was overcome by corruption. And then thought, oh, if I could but mourn under sin, then I should be happy, but he could not. But yet hearing Isaiah 40:ult.—he gives strength to them that have no strength[1]—and this gave him peace and support, and farther heard Isaiah 30:6–7—their strength is to sit still in his ordinances. And then hearing that Christ came to seek them that are lost,[2] then why may not the Lord save me? I thought if he would look upon me, a lost creature, how should I admire the Lord. And this promise did stay his heart: if he comes to seek the lost, why then not me? And so he was carried to long after Christ Jesus and heard, those are blessed that did hunger and thirst.[3] Yet he had no power to lay hold upon

1. Correctly, Isa. 40:29.
2. Matt. 18:11; Luke 19:10.
3. Matt. 5:6.

me, unless the Lord did draw his love to himself. Since this, the Lord hath revealed himself and drawn himself to him by his ordinances.

Since I came hither, that hath been my grief that I walked no more closely with God in the place where I came.

The Lord revealed Christ unto me by revealing the fullness of the riches of grace and help in Christ.[4]

John Sill

—a hearer, not a doer

Farmer John Sill, Joanna his wife, and their two children came to Cambridge from Northumberland about 1637. He died by 1652.

He was brought up in an ignorant place, yet God took away those that maintained him. Hence he went to some other place, and here he saw an alteration both in place, people, and means, and he thought that it was better with him there than elsewhere. So, approving of their ways, he fell to imitate them, and so by the ministry, 1 James 23, 24—be ye doers, not hearers only[1]—it pleased the Lord to point him out that he was the man to whom the minister did then speak. He had lived under means and been a hearer and not a doer, and so he saw himself lying under the wrath due to such, and this did work sadly upon him, and the more by keeping it secret. He saw no hope of help in that condition but must look out for another. Those directions and means in the ministry, the Lord did help him in some measure to use them. And now came in this temptation: such and such people whose example you imitate you think are God's people, but if they were the Lord's, he would prosper them and love them and let others know that they were the Lord's. And so [he] was staggered, but helped by Jeremiah 12:1 a little, and having got some help against that, another temptation followed. Those that are the Lord's people, they are people of parts and gifts and so and so qualified, but for his own part he did not

4. Eph. 2:7.
1. Correctly, Jas. 1:22–23.

find it so, and hence thought the Lord had no thoughts of him, and hence was cut off almost from looking for mercy from the Lord because he found himself not like them. And remaining thus, it pleased the Lord to give him scriptures against this from Matthew 11:25—I thank thee that thou hast hid these things from wise and prudent ones—and hence he thought the Lord might help him. Then after this came another temptation, *viz.,* whether Christ was the son of God or no. For then the Lord helped me to look after him, and this sat sadly; it was fearful to doubt, and yet he could not make it out that it was indeed so. Hence the Lord helped him with Matthew 17:5, 8—they heard a voice—for he thought if there was a Christ, there might be some else, but they saw none but Jesus. Then arose a fourth temptation: how could I prove this was scripture which said he was the son of God? And this was a long season before he could do this. Yet the Lord brought 2 Peter 1—you have a sure word of prophecy whereto you should attend till you be, etc.[2] And he thought (1) they were holy men, (2) they speak more from the holy ghost, and those were undeniable evidences to prove that those were scriptures, and so came out of those temptations.

Now going on in the use of means, he thought that when any duty was performed, he thought something in the duty was amiss and so thought that all he did was to no purpose. And being in conference with a young man, he said means he did use, [yet] he had no comfort because something he saw amiss. Then he said, wherefore serves Christ if we could serve God perfectly? 1 John 2:1–2—if any sin, we have an advocate with the Father. This did melt his heart, and the Lord made him to look not upon him so. And then the Lord helped him to look toward him by that means, Isaiah 50:12—he that heareth and obeyeth, let him trust in the Lord and stay himself upon God.[3] This stayed him. And here he found much hardness, deadness, and seeing many promises made, but conditionally made, his heart stood here. But at last he saw the Lord had promised to work the condition and hence in the sense of the want of the condition to go to the Lord to work it. And here he found the Lord silent long, Exodus 6:4–5. He saw, being Jehovah, that he

2. 2 Pet. 1:19.
3. Correctly, Isa. 50:10.

would do it, and from Habakkuk 2:3—the vision is for a certain time, and it will come and not lie. And so the Lord made him see the promise is for an appointed time, and then it shall speak. There by one minister preaching out of his fullness one received grace for grace.[4] There he answered all his objections against closing with the Lord and so having continued in this place. And then in those times the heart was much taken up in secret meditation and being so. And then when sin or Satan came to draw his heart from God, the Lord helped him to see it before it came as to be delivered from it. And hence he found much sweet communion with the Lord in meditation. And here the heart was not much taken off from the Lord, and this was then presented, that if he took that course, he should not only expose himself to melancholy but to a consumption, and so was beaten down again. And looking upon this frame, it cost him something in sorrow for it.

Then the Lord stirred up men that neither sought God's honor nor his good to put him forth to suffer for the cause of God. And being glued to the place, he considered whether it was not better to suffer than to cast himself upon dangers in flying. Many ministers and others took his case to heart and sought God and could not tell what to say. And it pleased God then to bring Mr. Glover[5] to him, coming out of Lancashire, and I and he should think of it, and the counsel was that he should not stir till he saw the Lord leading him and be contented to be where he will have him. But in this interim the case was clear, and was brought to Northumberland. Some told him of Mr. S[hepard], but he thought things could not be so as reports went. Men might admire, but it was not so. I was desired to go to hear him, going with a prejudicial opinion. The word had not yet efficacy upon him and teaching of the branch, John 15:5 and Revelation 22:17—take water of life freely. After sermons were done, some asked how I liked. I spake very freely, but next day, I having conference with some, I wished them to take heed upon what grounds they believed what I [Shepard] taught. And my heart was against him [Shepard], so diverse people came to him [Sill] to hear the notes. And so he read over the notes, and reading

4. John 1:16.
5. See above, p. 149 n.1.

them over to them the Lord let him see there was more in them than I [Sill] apprehended. And so [at] night in prayer, he was convinced of that sin in being set against him [Shepard]. And from something that he [Shepard] taught next day and before he was put to a plunge and so to question what was formerly done. And sometime he could not what to say concerning his condition and desired others to keep them away. But it pleased God to help him, John 3 and from Romans 5:6, how far he might be enlightened, wounded, terrified that from those things he was much troubled. But he could not conclude all to be naught, but blessed God he did hear those things. And by how much the more his heart was against him [Shepard], by so much the more afterward was his heart knit to him. So for some of the promises that did stay me formerly and then, there was more than I can now remember or call to mind, but sometimes, come to me all that are weary.[6] And at that time, being troubled from Romans 5, then something a child of God went beyond a hypocrite, and so in examining those things he found. And so to clear up himself in that estate of poverty of spirit, so Romans 6—sin shall not gain dominion—and Ezekiel 36—I will take away the stony heart.[7]

Since this time, I came hither. Upon my first coming, I thought that then my heart was in a pretty frame. But being here some little time and some things coming in my way that troubled my mind for my place of settling, my heart began to be troubled and so lost that frame I had. And sometimes the world did trouble me and take up my mind with some opposition and striving against it, yet there was not that against it which I desired. Then upon an occasion at a lecture, Colossians 3—if risen, seek things above[8]—I saw the thing more fully, and by this means I had some power against them. I have found much deadness and security, and then the Lord out of John 13:4–5, that when a Christian is to reflect upon his own glory, he was made to look upon that it should not be so with one that professed. And so the Lord helped him out of that. So from Matthew 25 the Lord let me see the truth and provocations and how it comes. By degrees the Lord hath let him see something.

6. Matt. 11:28.
7. Rom. 6:14; Ezek. 36:26.
8. Col. 3:1.

Question. How came you to see your sin?
Answer. Seeing myself only a bare hearer, I saw my vileness.

Joanna Sill

—if the Lord should damn her, yet to be content

Joanna Sill (d. 1671), John's wife, joined the Cambridge congregation in 1638. A woman of independence, she maintained the family estate after her husband's death and served on one occasion as "attorney" to recover debts for a widowed friend from Newcastle.

It pleased the Lord to help him [*sic*] to attend upon the Lord, and . . . , Dr. Jenison[1] had this text, Matthew 11—woe to these Chorazin and woe to thee, Capernaum[2]—and here was much troubled. And I was much troubled, and then the Lord laid a sad affliction upon me where I saw all my sins in order and apprehended nothing but death and wrath. And diverse ministers came to apply promise, but she could apply none. Yet when almost ready to sink, from 139 Psalm seeing that the Lord knew her[3] and that she could not fly from him, and here stayed. Then she heard Mr. Glover,[4] Psalm 136—the Lord hath done great things for us, and we rejoice—and reproving them that come not affected with great things. And from 15 Jeremiah—thou has forsaken me for I am weary of repenting[5]—and so she thought God would destroy her. And so she desiring to live under his ministry and so she did, and every sermon and word ready to sink. And the Lord stayed her sometime by seeking them that were lost[6] and not to call righteous but sinners.[7] There she stayed, yet in a doubting condition she was, he being gone, and she could not but be quiet but followed him

1. Robert Jenison (1584?–1652), lecturer at All Saints in Newcastle from 1622 to 1639. He was suspended for nonconformity in 1639 but was reinstated in the 1640s.
2. Matt. 11:21–24.
3. Ps. 139:1ff.
4. See Edward Hall's confession, above, n. 1.
5. Jer. 15:6.
6. Matt. 18:11; Luke 19:10.
7. Matt. 9:13; Mark 2:17; Luke 5:32.

and lived under his ministry four years. And though he applied promises, yet she could apply none till at pit's brink, nearly to sink. And from Zachariah 13:1 she saw she was unclean. Then coming to Northumberland, hearing from Matthew 15—Lord, Lord[8]—she saw there one maid['s] need of Christ. Yet she could not apply him and [had] many afflictions. She had never tripped out of way, but inward terrors or miseries without, and then she saw sin she had committed. Oft troubled since she came hither; her heart went after the world and vanities, and the Lord absented himself from her so that she thought God had brought her hither on purpose to discover her. And though she did not neglect duties, yet she found no presence of God there as at other times. Then hearing out of Matthew 25—them that had false principles, she had no oil in her vessel.[9] And she thought she was not so good as a hypocrite for she never came so far. And so God hid himself, and [she] fell into a sinking condition and could not lay hold on a promise nor call God Father. But Hosea 14:4 supported her—in thee fatherless find mercy[10]—and so she saw her nature, how vile it [was]. She knew many see this and that sin and then see not their nature. Then there saw her nature, and so she was discouraged. And being desired to lay under the Lord, she thought it could not stand with God's honor to show mercy to one professor so long. And so seeing more and more of their vileness, but hearing in a day of humiliation that if she sought the Lord with whole heart, find. She found not that heart but resolved to try the Lord whether he would help. And then hearing Isaiah 28—he that believeth makes not haste[11]—she resolved not to hasten the Lord, let him do what he would with her. And that of Lamentations—why should a living man complain for his sin?[12]—she thought she was living but found it hard if the Lord should damn her and never show mercy, yet to be content. But Lord in some measure subdued his [*sic*] cursed will to lie at feet of mercy, let him do what he would. Not long after, having a day of fast, the Lord helped her to seek

8. Matt. 25:11.
9. Matt. 25:8.
10. Correctly, Hos. 14:3.
11. Isa. 28:16.
12. Lam. 3:39.

him. And the day after, when at her calling, she had much joy and consolation from Luke 1—blessed is he that believeth.[13] But she could not believe indeed, and she knew not where she was. Then she questioned whether it was true joy. But going some, she saw not, and hearing that a deluding spirit drew heart nearer to God and *e contra.* But after this, joy was gone, and then there were questions what her grounds were. And she could not believe, but she found a will that would not believe, though she did pray that the Lord would. But hearing, all that Father given shall come, John 6.[14] So she thought, I'll go to the Lord, but could not. Then thought, Lord, if thou hast elected me. But in deep distress, Zachariah 12:10—they shall look and mourn—there she saw she could not believe in that blood which was shed for her. And hence considering God commanded her and condemned her for not believing. And this brought her to long for Christ. Then Revelation 22:17—let whoever will, drink—there she thought she drank of that promise, so Isaiah 55:1 [and] Matthew 5—I blessed hunger[15]—and Canticles 1—because of savor of holiness of Christ, the virgins love thee.[16]

Nathaniel Eaton

—to neglect duties I durst not, and to do out of love I could not

Nathaniel Eaton (c. 1609–1674), first head of Harvard College and a moral problem for Thomas Shepard, studied at Trinity College, Cambridge, as well as with William Ames in Holland. A schoolteacher, he settled in Cambridge in 1638. Eaton made a botch of his short regime at Harvard. Shepard fretted in his autobiography and journal about his failure to check Eaton.

My education was in a religious manner from a cradle that I was trained up to read scripture and frequenting means and in the ap-

13. Luke 1:45.
14. John 6:37.
15. Matt. 5:6.
16. Cant. 1:3.

pearance of some made a progress. But coming down from under the wings of parents to Westminster and Cambridge, the hidden corruption of my own heart came to discover itself in open sins, in sabbath breaking, and company keeping. Yet in all this time I was not left without a testimony within. My conscience was convinced that my ways were of death, which did etc. And the Lord did still hedge in my ways with thorns.[1] But from sin to sin the Lord followed me with frowns from friends, but those could do nothing for me. But coming from university to London, I heard a sermon from Amos 4—prepare to meet thy God.[2] The coherence of it was from 2nd verse—he would catch them by hooks, and God had smit them, yet they returned not.[3] And the issue was as I will do this unto thee. The Lord was come to this last warning: if not, the Lord would do this unto them. And God set on thus in a sad manner to apply the particulars to my condition and that now perhaps the Lord was come to the last warning. The words did not sit upon me much at first, yet alway when I went to my company, this chapter and verse was before my eye, and I carried the Lord's terrors. And at last, when I could stand it out no longer, then I laid down my sin and set some days apart. And pressing the Lord for mercy, yet I did not seek the Lord to answer me, but I spoke words in the air. And so I thought the time of visitation was past and that it was with me as with Esau.[4] It was very sad to me for the present and cast down by it, but the temptation grew upon me, why should I seek the Lord any more? And seeing I should have no portion but in this world, better not to take this than to lose the Lord also. And temptation so far strengthened as that I neglected all. Satan having found the house swept,[5] and I was worse, yet I never went on with peace in my sin. And Lord at last brought this place to my thoughts of Simon Magus, who though in gall of bitterness, yet he was advised if perhaps by praying, Lord might forgive him.[6] The Lord blessed this unto me, yet I became resolved to seek and

1. Hos. 2:6.
2. Amos 4:12.
3. Amos 4:9.
4. Gen. 27:34–41.
5. Luke 11:24–26; Matt. 12:43–45.
6. Acts 8:14–24.

wait on the Lord and to resolve to perish at hands of God. Then the Lord put it in the hearts of my friends to go beyond sea to Mr. Ames.[7] And there I might have used prayer and frequented means, but I received no comfort nor did not meet with the Lord in any duty. But yet I went on in the duty till Dr. Ames expounded divinity that God must be the first and last in every service and that it was an idolatry for a man to exalt a man's self above the Lord. And this made me see why my duties were empty because [not] performed out of love to the Lord. And this I could not because I could not see any evidence of the Lord's love to me. Hence to neglect duties I durst not, and to do out of love I could not, and hence I begged the Lord would manifest something unto me that I might love him, else all duties would not be sweet. And when I considered common mercy that I was alive and that many were in hell, and that there was scripture on this side the pit, and I saw I had not only time but I had a light to know how to use it. And there some work of God upon my spirit. It was not for nothing that God had spent so much pains upon me, and this gave me glimmering hopes that the Lord that had gone so far as that there might be more behind. And sure I was that the Lord had given me cause to see that I should love him, though I saw no more. Hence I went to prayer that the Lord would work my heart to a love to himself. And I did find my heart not so come off so deadly as before. I could not see I did love the Lord as I should, and I saw more unwillingness in me than to stand with love. I did not see my heart closing with the Lord, yet the Lord revealed more unto me the freeness of his love in Christ and that it could not stand with the Lord's nature and glory to depend his decree on anything I did. And hence I did think the Lord might reveal his love to me in time, and that by Christ. And hence the Lord did draw my heart to close with Christ. I saw an emptiness in myself; there was no grace nor peace there nor nothing in the creature. They were empty, and hence I saw there was life revealed and bound up in Christ. And here I went to the Lord that since none could come to

7. William Ames (1576–1633), Puritan master of systematic and polemical theology. Silenced in England, he moved to Leyden, Holland, where he made the case for Calvinism and Congregationalism.

Christ unless the Father did draw him,[8] and here I did seek he would draw my heart. And hereupon I found I did not live without Christ in the word in sabbaths and prayers, especially if any open the door, I will come to him;[9] if any love me, I and my Father will love him and will manifest myself unto him.[10] And hereupon I saw I was come to him and that the promise did belong to me that I should be eased and that the Lord would dwell with me. And so I stayed upon the Lord and rested there. And then I went to England, and the Lord betrusted me with the care of bringing up of children. I labored to keep a good conscience, though with danger, and to seek to keep my scholars in the observation of the sabbath day, and so to leave the issue with him. And from this place I was called to another place, but the place was profane and but one sermon and people haters of the truth. Yet being encouraged by religious friends, thither I went, but I found I lost much of God's presence, and the temptations were too strong for me. They invited me; I must do the like for them. And if I was familiar with any that were godly, they would dissuade. And hence strung to them, and this cost me many prayers, and at last I saw if I would keep a good conscience I must leave it. So I was in many thoughts to leave the place, but I let fall my thoughts again, and so I began to settle. But when things were in this agitation, they intimated to me their resolutions to come hither, and they spent some time in reasoning about a common prayer book and church government. And before they had done, I saw the truth and was persuaded to close with it, and so I resolved to come along with them. And hence before I came I did manifest and witness against that place and their manners and proceedings. And afterward I saw what cause to be humbled for losing my first love,[11] and hence I questioned with me whether the Lord had not a controversy against me for losing my first love and closing with his enemies. And I lost my self-assurance, and at last that of 1 Samuel 12 came to him—the Lord would not cast off his people because he had chosen me to be his people.[12] And since that time the Lord hath cleared his love to

8. John 6:44.
9. Rev. 3:20.
10. John 14:21.
11. Rev. 2:4.
12. 1 Sam. 12:22.

me to give me greater experience of it. Only since I came hither, I have not found my heart to walk so closely with God as I should, and when my heart hath been ready to cast off all, the Lord hath awakened me and hath not suffered me to relapse but to rise again, etc., and persuaded me that the seeds cast upon me shall last unto eternal life.[13]

Robert Daniel

—I want a heart to honor God

Robert Daniel (c. 1592–1655), a farmer, settled in Watertown with his wife in 1631 and five years later moved to Cambridge, where he did well. He had one child by his first wife and acquired five stepchildren by his second marriage, to the widow of William Andrews, whose confession appears below. Daniel's confession dates from 1639.

The best and choicest of my time was spent in a civil course of life, friends and others restrained[?], not questioning my estate. But yet the Lord made me see my case to be miserable and so carried many years under a spirit of bondage and fear of God's wrath.[1] Yet when my soul was at lowest, the Lord held forth some testimony of love, but yet I did depend upon him without assurance. And after this I had some assurance, for whenever I did delight in my pleasures, after I felt I did not. And in former times it was from fear of punishment, but now all my trouble is because I want a heart to honor God. And now the chiefest desire is that I may live to honor him, though I find myself barren and fruitless.

This generally. Particular questions asked; thus he answered.

(1) How did the Lord bring you out of that estate of security into a state of fear and spirit of bondage? Answer. I sinned against God after light. Others did not, and hence I the greatest of sinners. This was by attending to the word, so fearing the wrath of God. And hence I sought to God for mercy and resolution of heart

13. Matt. 13:18–23; Mark 4:3–20; Luke 8:5–15.
1. Rom. 8:15.

against sin. I was convinced of sin against sabbath, yet that sin against resolution overcame it again and I found my will exceeding contrary to the will of God, though I have seen more of my own enmity than before. The wrath of God I apprehended to be the casting of soul from presence of God.

(2) How hath the Lord brought you out of this estate unto the Lord Jesus? Answer. In this estate I saw how just it was for the Lord to destroy me, yet the Lord brought me to rest and rely upon his mercy. 1. Question. Did you find it hard to lie down and yield to mercy? Answer. By seeing the equity of it for my own vileness. 2. Question. How did the Lord draw you to mercy? Answer. Seeing his love to me, 2. seeing the freeness of his mercy. He saw some likelihood in Christ mine, yet I would seek though I did perish.

(3) Question. How came you to assurance? Answer. By feeling a qualification, as mourning not only for wrath but because of my sins, to sin against such a God.

(4) How have you walked with God and what effect have you found of mercy in this land? Answer. Faith hath been wrought more and Christ more revealed more savingly unto me. I fall short in that obedience that should be, which is my burden when I see how the Lord hath led me.

Nathaniel Sparrowhawk

—*The Lord hath let me see*

Nathaniel Sparrowhawk (1598–1647) came to Cambridge in 1636 from Dedham, Essex, with his wife, Mary. There he soon acquired several houses and over a thousand acres. He was a deacon of the church. He was married twice and had at least seven children.

In my childhood his mother took much pains with him. The Lord inclined his heart toward himself when he came to some understanding, and then the Lord let me see my estate was such and not to be trusted unto. And seeing the people of God changed in another condition and the means appointed for that end, hence in ordinary and extraordinary means he sought the Lord. And here he abode in his own strength, striving for a better condition, looking to means and the best means which was precious in many places, yet all could not help. Sometimes he had some warnings of heart and convictions under means as brought him to look to the Lord and his people with a loving heart, not only rich but poor also. And sometime it pleased the Lord to let in himself in a gracious manner in the meditation of those things which Lord made known, that I could walk up and down the room rejoicing in him and hitting those out of the window that were otherwise employed.

Sometimes the Lord, especially in a fast day morning, refreshed my heart at Dedham, and so God inclined my heart to close with the Lord most. But on the fast day morning, desiring to be alone and to bewail my condition and there entreating reconciliation, the Lord revealed himself so as never before, with abundance of the sweetness of himself, which rejoicing made me to break out to weeping, and hardly could I refrain from speaking to others to let them see what Lord had done. But that day he found least of God, and heart locked up most when he thought to find Lord nearest.

And so the Lord after this made me see more and more my follies. Though my life had been ever fair, yet I saw my natural disposition to other ways; and yet Lord stood behind me with his voice saying, this is way, walk in it.[1]

Now coming to deal in the world and seeing others distrusting of God's providence, he was full of carking cares till a servant of his [i.e., of God] spake to me to walk with God and saying that the liberal man shall have plenty[2] and that God was able to provide. And this counsel I took, and the Lord helped me over it. But when the Lord cast in blessings in my calling, I let out my heart too eagerly after them when it should have been drawn nearer to him. Yet the Lord did not let me go but to attend on the means and to carry me in a course and form of worshipping him. And the means I thought had been sufficient to work that which yet I see my soul aworking in. And thus I did lie long in this condition and sometime thought I was cast out of favor of God, and yet the Lord made me plead with him and to remember his covenant. And finding daily the fruit of prayer, here I kept and held.

But the Lord let me see that I looked to men too much and that

1. Isa. 30:21.
2. Prov. 11:25.

the old score was not crossed, and hence I had no rest but desired to come to New England to enjoy them in purity and helped me to be contented, though in a prosperous way. Yet I thought the superstitions clouded God in ordinances and had thought to find power and thought to prize means here, but the Lord hath helped me to see my own heart reaching after things of this world. But the Lord hath let me see the insufficiency of means, and the Lord hath let me see I must look to the Lord Jesus in it and in all means. But the assurance of Lord's love I have not found. In sad times of temptation I have had great support from what I have had in coming.

Since I came hither I have sensed a spirit of enmity and looking after great things, but Lord hath much abated them and lately hath let me see my enmity. When I saw others filled with spiritual good, my soul could not bear it, but the Lord hath let me see it. Is thy eye evil because mine is good, and may I not do with mine own as I list?[3] And the Lord hath lately let me hear his voice in his hand in my family.

I cannot remember many things which I cannot now express myself. And the Lord brought to mind the story of withered hand,[4] that it was his power, and I have entreated the Lord to help my unbelief, and other things whereby I found my heart enlarged.

Mary Angier Sparrowhawk

—Lord is more merciful than I to myself

Mary Angier Sparrowhawk (d. 1644) seems to have joined the church with her husband in 1639. She, too, came from Dedham, Essex. She gave birth to one child there and five more in Cambridge before her early death.

She had parents that kept her from gross sins, yet living under a powerful ministry of Mr. Rogers of Dedham,[1] she was convinced

3. Matt. 20:15.
4. Matt. 12:10–13; Mark 3:1–5; Luke 6:6–10.
1. John Rogers (1572?–1636), vicar of Dedham, Essex, 1605–1636, a formidable Puritan preacher.

that her estate was miserable, yet these convictions did often wear off. And when God changed her estate, she went to a place of more ignorance and so rested more quietly, yet under powerful means had often stirrings. But finding no good, she thought better sit still than go. Yet considering that it was the means appointed to go, she went, and hearing of New England, she thought if any good, here it was. But when her husband was resolved to come, she feared if God should not help, all would rise to greater condemnation. Yet one she spake to of this said, though sure to go to hell yet may go under means. And I thought there I should be kept from many sins and even to betray people of God but thought this temptation would not be if here. Yet unwilling to come from this fear of no blessing, yet thinking that her children might get good, it would be worth my journey. And Mr. Wilson[2] in praying said it—maybe, Lord, thou dost deny to do good to till come thither—and this gave her more cheerfulness of spirit. And so she came to the ship thinking to get good. But there she found her heart more hard and [in]sensible, but hoped to be better here than worse than ever before. Every sermon made her worse, and [she] sat like a block under all means and thought God had left her to a hard heart and that her fears were come upon her.

Hence I thought if we were there where I purposed to abide, then I might find, and hence I could not desire to be here. But hence continuing under means, the Lord made me more and more sensible of my condition, and so my condition very sad. Yet she durst not neglect any public means and thought that the Lord might speak something now, yet saw herself far from humiliation and thought it was a shame to discover her condition. But hearing, better to begin twice than to go to hell once, and so she thought none would think bad enough of her, but she could not speak to anybody and thought also that they would not be plain with her. And sometime keeping her condition close, though sometime sinking, the Lord carried to Roxbury. And hearing of fears, if they carried to Lord they were good, etc. And speaking of them that kept their conditions, that some were in hell lamenting it, hereupon she

2. John Wilson (1588?–1667), preacher at Sudbury, Suffolk, 1618–1630; then longtime minister at Boston in New England.

resolved to make her condition known. But speaking with one which did encourage her which was odious to her, she continued under means and grew worse and worse and so thought it was in vain to use any more means and began to neglect Lord in private. Yet one of our neighbors speaking of her condition, coming to her and wishing her to leave the Lord to his own ways, telling her that it may be the Lord would let her see her blindness and hardness, and God that way to work and that she was God's clay.[3] And asking if she sought God in private, she confessed no, for some weeks. And then she set upon it again but continued worse and worse. But hearing sermon of the woman that had the bloody issue,[4] saw it was her condition and worse and that she [the woman] had a heart to seek after Christ, [but] she had none. And she saw she had no faith at all, and there were many encouragements to such, though all means made them worse. And the Lord did incline her heart hereby to seek help from him and had some encouragement from that sermon and so sought the Lord.

And so had encouragements from other scripture, Hosea, as he that had brought her to a wilderness would speak comfortably[5] and that the Lord would have mercy on them that had no mercy,[6] by which I pleaded with God. And that of Isaiah—I will gather others beside them that be gathered[7]—and hence Lord might help me. But in this furthering the Lord showed her sin more and more, but hearing what an enmity there was in the will against God, she saw it so clearly from Matthew 23—you would not.[8] There she saw that, and this did lie sad upon her and thought, did I think I could take Christ on any terms? And yet had a will to resist him. And being in that sermon exhorted to go to him, to plead with God to subdue her will, which she did, yet saw her rebellion still exceedingly. Sometime after these first thoughts in a morning, could I eat and drink and sleep and no part in Christ? Yet sometime after, what she heard came to mind: Lord is more merciful than I to myself, and the Lord stayed my heart by that.

Sometime after she went on in this condition and in as bad a

3. Isa. 64:8.
4. Matt. 9:20–22; Mark 5:25–34; Luke 8:43–48.
5. Hos. 2:14.
6. Hos. 2:23; Rom. 9:15.
7. Isa. 56:8.
8. Matt. 23:37.

condition as ever, and some scriptures brought me in to submit to the Lord, being hard to submit to the condemning will of God, Isaiah 30—the Egyptians help in vain, but thy strength is to sit still.[9] I saw I had nothing by quarreling but by being contented and that she was the clay and Lord her potter,[10] and so Lord calmed her heart, and so in the same chapter—in returning and rest shall be your rest.[11] By leaving her soul with the Lord, let him do what he will, and thus the Lord gave her a contentedness of spirit and she saw more sin she never saw, yet something that did support her, Isaiah 44—thou hast made me weary with thy sins, yet I will blot out thy sins.[12] And hence I pleaded with Lord of his name's sake, and so look unto me and be saved, all ends of earth.[13] And she thought she was one of them all, and seeing her insufficiency to look, she entreated him that commanded her to look would enable her and that the Lord would lead the blind in a way they went not in,[14] and the stouthearted ones to harken to him.[15] She hence wondered at God that he should speak thus to such a one.

And after this, a question made whether she had closed with person of Christ, yet she saw if she had not, yet she saw the fault was in her. And then that place—fury is not in me, let him take hold of my strength[16]—and she saw that strength was Christ. And she [saw] there was but two ways, either to stand out or take hold, and saw the promise and her own insufficiency so to do. And that other scripture—he had laid salvation on Christ[17]—and she thought now she closed.

And hearing, how know whether united to Christ, and mentioning a scripture, was asked whether she had assurance. She said, no, but some hope. Yet hearing other scriptures—in thee the fatherless find mercy[18] and so many as received him[19]—and hence feared her estate again, hearing nothing for or against her condi-

9. Isa. 30:17.
10. Isa. 64:8.
11. Isa. 30:15.
12. Isa. 43:24–25, 44:23.
13. Isa. 45:22.
14. Isa. 42:16.
15. Isa. 46:12.
16. Isa. 27:4–5.
17. Acts 4:12; 1 Thess. 5:9; Heb. 5:9; 2 Pet. 3:15.
18. Hos. 14:3.
19. John 1:12.

tion, and hence resolved to look out those scriptures where person of Christ was set forth, as first of John—full of grace and truth.[20] And she saw her own emptiness and Christ's fullness, and such a suitableness between Christ and me, and chapter 7—if any thirst, let him come to me and drink.[21] And hearing Lord called to any, she thought she was one of those any, and seeing nothing would satisfy her but the Lord, and nothing in heaven or earth she desired nothing like him, she thought the Lord called her to himself.

John Stedman

—I resolved against ill company and hence [was] hated

John Stedman (1601–1693) settled in Cambridge with his wife, Alice, whose confession appears below. Over the years he filled numerous public offices including those of constable, selectman, militia ensign, and county treasurer. Poor when he arrived, he acquired much land as well as a local monopoly on the fur trade. The Stedmans kept a store in Cambridge.

It pleased God about fifteen years since to move my heart to harken to God, and the first thing that convinced my conscience was a funeral sermon of my uncle's which showed me out of 2 Thessalonians 1—flaming fire[1]—showing the woeful estate of men. It brought me to consider of former courses and sadness of spirit for former courses. Another time, hearing that place, 1 Thessalonians 5—be not drunk with wine[2]—where he showed the greatness of the sin of drunkenness, and being found guilty of that fearful sin, I was much affected with the sermon. And when it was done, it appeared in my countenance to my vain and idle companions, who asking me what ailed me, I said there was cause enough to see them walk so idly after such means. And so I labored to pray and hence got a book, but I entreated the Lord to help me to pray and so was cast off gross sins and was affected with hardness of

20. John 1:14.
21. John 7:37.
1. 2 Thess. 1:8.
2. 1 Thess. 5:7; cf. Eph. 5:18.

heart. And hearing 1 Peter 5—God resists the proud[3]—and here I saw a great worth in humility and saw more of vileness of my hard unsubdued heart, and so seeking to the Lord. And I went to others to help me against a hard heart, and they told me if I was obedient to the Lord, it was enough. And that I found, and so I was admitted to private societies of saints, where I found much sweetness. And so I sought for pardon of sin, and hearing Galatians 2:19 from Mr. Langly[4]—where Christ was, sin was subdued—and so I saw the Lord had pardoned by those signs. After this I came to have many fears and doubts about my estate and condition, and I heard that God did let after faith Satan loose to try men by.[5] And so I followed the Lord and found communion with God and his people so sweet that I resolved against ill company and hence [was] hated. And after this I saw that sad sin of unbelief and hence entreated Lord to humble me for it and persuade my heart of Lord's love. After I was troubled for want of growth, that saints are like willows and palm trees,[6] and hence feared I wanted grace. But I felt my heart longing after grace and want of grace, and that was poverty yet, and this supported [me].

After this I questioned my estate and came to New England, and hearing Mr. C[otton][7] speaking how far a man might go under a covenant of works, and so had great fears that was my condition and not sleeping quietly that I had received Christ nor could find no sense of my need of Christ. And after many weeks I came by providence to this place and heard 2 Corinthians 5:20 treating about justification and calling. God spake to me as if I had told him and so found my hardness of heart subdued in some measure. And since have been carried through many fears and doubts.

Jane Holmes

—I was taken with joy with his delusions

Jane Holmes (d. 1652) married Robert Holmes in Cambridge and

3. 1 Pet. 5:5.
4. Henry Langley (1611–1697), rector at Newington, Surrey.
5. Job 1:6–12.
6. Lev. 23:40; Ps. 92:12; Isa. 44:4.
7. John Cotton: see above, p. 57 n. 32.

bore the first of their nine children in 1638, at about the time she made her confession. Her husband's confession appears below.

It pleased the Lord to take my mother and give a mother-in-law[1] who had many children, which was an affliction to me. And [I] thought it good to make use of it, hence began to read the word and began to think it good to follow the Lord. And I would do what I could to walk in his way because they that did should be happy and others damned.

So I thought I could not live holily in father's house and hence thought to live in a minister's house better, so went to vicar of town, an opposer of the truth, yet I thought he did not live holily enough, an Arminian, one that taught free will and opposing openly puritans. I thought the word taught us to be pure, and he was not. Yet I thought my condition happy, praying morning and evening and not doubting, and though puritans spake against, yet I took their parts and to enquire after that way. And so they told my father. One told me of a new birth, and she spake of her misery and what a life we lived when at school, and she charging others in her letter to hear but one and not the vicar, and she did write of necessity of new birth and that all righteousness out of Christ was nothing. And so I thought I would enquire after that way.

But Lord followed me with sore afflictions, and God denied me comforts I sought for after. And I resolved to go to hear a sermon, and my heart was so endeared to that man to live with him and so desired my father to live there and resolved to come away whatever came of me. But other minister said ministers were turned into an angel of light, and so I thought of them.

And so I came away to my father's, who entertained me, yet content to go to service to anywhere I might live under that ministry. And I wondered at God to carry me to such a house where ministers met, and there, I that found no rebellion, now I found my heart rebel against the Lord and every word and so wounded out of belief, which melted my heart, and [I] thought, though to hell, yet mercy to acquaint with misery. Yet my heart cross to command as I rebelled, and I sought the Lord and could not rest and

1. That is, stepmother.

thought it impossible to have mercy for me that so rebelled against light. And hence Satan set against me that I durst not go to prayer, and I found I was not humbled, yet sought the Lord not to cast me down with false fears nor lift me up with vain hopes.

And hearing in ministry, those that were in love with brethren and trying it if they loved a poor saint as well as a rich saint, some support. And though some support, yet hearing of some much humbled, then I feared, and when I heard a threatening I could embrace that and promise durst not, and so thought I saw the damned in hell and being very sad. God brought in a servant of his that held forth a promise, but [I] could not lay hold on it. And coming to house of God again and hearing, thou thinkest there is no grace because no love to the brethren, etc., but thou art like one in a consumption—if neglect means at first past remedy, then return betimes. And so I resolved to follow the Lord for the same graces again and did find love to saints and had [a] little support. Yet hearing a sermon that feeling follows faith of saints, and I labored to feel it, and Lord making way for New England, I thought I should find feelings. And coming to London, hearing that Paul, when before for himself, now what wilt have me do?[2] I thought I could do so and leave all.

Now coming to the sea coast by providence in that ship where that wretch was, and he expounding in ship, and hearing he did not teach true doctrine, hence I resolved not to hear him and wished others not to hear. But he said he held nothing but what Mr. Cotton[3] held.

Yet he began to insinuate himself into my company and said of all others he could not get our companies, and hence I thought, why should I judge? And then I heard him, but woefully neglected God before, and I was taken with joy with his delusions that I knew not how to renounce it. Yet looking on former evidences and considering if I was driven from sanctification, I knew not what to do. Yet he told me Lord would come with a first. Yet reading Psalms, which comforted me, I thought I would not deny those truths. Yet when I came to hear him, I thought what he said

2. Acts 9:26, 22:10.
3. See above p. 57 n. 32.

true, in private *e contra*. And then when I thought of other Christians, that this was their way, he told me they were no better than Paul before his conversion. But I thought them more holy than he. He said he was as sore against them as I, but he was forced to it, so with me. For he said he was suffered to fall into a foul sin, and he was tempted to lie with another wife and fled to another place to [be] free but at last got his desire. And she thought she was damned but being that place, in me is fruit found,[4] and so quiet. So himself was Lord's, and no sin could separate.

And he heard another's confession that she never came to be driven from her own righteousness but by a gross act, so God would do so to me.

I asked if he was ever taken from her, but he said, no, but could enjoy her three or four times a day.

And I laid open diverse places bad women lewd with lusts,[5] but he said it was his bitterness. But I said he would leave it, yet he said he knew whom he had believed[6] and how it was betwixt God and him, and take heed how he judged him.

So I thought, shall I leave this way for him? So I would seek, yet he by insinuation got within me, and I would not leave him, which I speak it to horror of that which it left me. I had been the vilest wretch.

So some friends coming to me when I came hither, I desired to be at Boston, and I desired to know right way, and I told them. I did find my heart drawing after that way, yet they entreated me to refrain his company. And so, being at Roxbury, Mr. Wells[7] being on that text—return, you backsliding children.[8] No sooner text named but I thought I was a backsliding wretch, and so, my condition being discovered, I went and told him my condition and to cleave spirit, water, blood, whether spirit was first. He said that water was before blood,[9] and so I acquainted him with my ship entanglements, yet by him I was encouraged to go to the Lord and

4. Hos. 14:8.
5. 2 Tim. 3:6.
6. 2 Tim. 1:12.
7. Thomas Weld: see Shepard's autobiography, n. 17.
8. Jer. 3:14–22, 31:22.
9. 1 John 5:7–8.

considered once how precious God and his ordinances once were to me. Yet troubled so I followed God in days of humiliation yet long I could not get my heart in any good frame. But my heart at last was struck with admiration at God's mercy to deliver one from such a wretch and errors. And when I saw others afflicted with pox, I thought I wished I were so, if not left to errors. And so my heart was saddened to the Lord and thought it mercy if I might find least glimpse of favor at last. And seeking the Lord, to submit in anything to his will that if never show mercy, yet I might submit and not blaspheme. And thus following the Lord, the Lord in his ordinances gave me some support. Yet I fearing I was a hypocrite, and that appeared the more because I was ready to take comfort. So going to hear Mr. Wells—thou art Lord our God—and showed a false reliance and true that nothing could content soul that truly relied but the Lord, and that I found. And they had tokens, as Tamar's ring,[10] and will not Lord own those tokens, and are these nothing? So I. And finding a rebellious heart, by many trials I found Lord in me, and I found Lord. I loved him, and I found that my grief was that sin parted between me and God. And on sabbath day morning, 1 Mark—I will be thou clean, Lord, if wilt[11]—and in prayer I found Lord persuaded my heart of his love. And was endeared to Lord and thought, if it might ever be thus, yet since fears, seeing greatness of the sin I am turned from.

Edward Collins

—I was convinced I was the man

Edward Collins (c. 1603–1689) moved from place to place in England until coming to Cambridge in the 1630s with his wife, Martha, and four children. A large landowner, he served as constable, court clerk, and representative to the General Court, the colony's assembly. He was a deacon of the church and one of Shepard's executors. Martha Collins's confession appears below.

10. Gen. 38:18, 25.
11. Mark 1:40.

The Lord gave me that privilege to be brought up of godly parents. Hence I received some restraint from them, who, seeing an evil nature in me, were more careful to restrain me. Next to this he gave me a ministry where I was capable of God, where my father lived and died. And somewhat God did by his catechizing dropped somewhat unto me about fundamentals. But God taking away my father, I was cast into a gentleman's house, a profane house, where I contracted much guilt to my soul as undoing what I had had before. Yet such was God's care to remove me from thence more speedily than was expected. And my mother going to Wethersfield, and they there hearing of the ill family where I was, I was removed from thence under old Mr. Rogers[1] of Wethersfield, where I stayed a year and got some good.

After this, my friends put me prentice to a godly family, where by their care I met with restraint from youthful vanities. And during that time I held forth a profession of religion for sinister ends, and I did increase in some external gifts, and God gave me my ends, repute in the family, whereby I had many advantages.

When I was at liberty at my own disposing, I began to think of my carriage, aims, and ends, and I saw I had done all out of base ends and so had no peace upon good grounds.

Hence I looked after further means and helps and so attended on the means in the city. And some more knowledge and gifts I got, which added to former peace, but I rested not here but searched after more searching means. And so hearing by letters that there was a lecture in Colne, hence I visited my friends, and so hearing doctrine of man's misery, the Lord discovered myself more and more than before, which I desired to see and hear. And he from Luke 12—seek this righteousness[2]—which God set upon my soul and to strike a terror and amazement on myself of my own estate. And by a private meeting of private conference I heard divers questions propounded and answered. And question being made when a man rested in duties, I was convinced I was the man,

1. Richard Rogers (1550?–1618), minister at Wethersfield, Essex, eminent preacher and author in the Puritan cause. Shepard in his autobiography calls his *Practice of Christianity* "the book which did first work upon my heart." See above p. 45 n. 15.

2. Luke 12:31. The minister was Shepard; the lecture sermons were published as *The Sincere Convert.*

and the grace I saw in Christians did ashame me before the Lord, that Christians so young should manifest so much, I having had means so long.

Hence I endeavored to get into private Christian meetings at London, and after, by other notes, I saw I was never all off the old stock. So I prayed to see the evil [of] sin, and saw it, and entreated the Lord to discover the remedy, Christ. And I saw no way but to take Christ upon his own terms, for I saw I had taken Christ but not upon his own terms but had love to some secret lust. And here I found a difficult work how to take him and to live to him. And I thought if Christ was to be had upon no other terms but to part with every lust, then I thought I should never have him, it was so hard.

And so came to my own place, where though an orthodox minister, yet by going to Dedham and Mr. Greenhill[3] and others, and there God carried on his work by himself and wrought peace. And there I took notice of covenant, that it was free, and saw promises made to such dispositions—to lost, to meek and hungry and thirsty,[4] and to such as were confessors and forsakers of sin, and hence I thought Jesus Christ was mine and so stayed my heart. And in searching my heart, seeing sin die and growing in grace, and I thought God would carry on his own work.

And all this time I saw how God would be worshipped, I could not find God's presence in ordinances, being full of mixtures. Hence I sought Lord to bring me to enjoy those liberties because I had some little light as not to join in those ordinances. And so the Lord in his time, though not in mine, to make way for. And since the Lord hath brought me hither, several providences. At the first coming, seeing the great change from this and that place did much transport my heart. Yet after this, this frame was quickly lost by distractions and thoughts and cares, which deadened my spirits, which God seasonably took care to cure by a heavy hand of God. And then I saw and was convinced of unthankfulness and discontent, and so by a servant of his I was brought upon my knees. And

3. William Greenhill (1591–1671), Puritan minister and writer. He brought several of Shepard's publications to press. Shepard's dedicatory epistle in *The Sound Believer* addresses him as "dear friend."
4. Matt. 5:5–6.

I blessed God that he would not let me lie still but to show me my unthankfulness. And so at last I came to see need of all God's ordinances, watchfulness that I might answer the end for which he sent me. And I saw his hand to bring me to the same ministry that first Lord did me good by and to beget me to himself.

John Stansby

—I would have my lusts and haunts

John Stansby, a farmer and clothier in England, joined the church in Cambridge before 1641. Beyond that fact, hardly anything is known of his life there; his confession is almost the only evidence of his existence. Selement and Woolley identify him as the nephew of Robert Stansby, rector of Westthorpe, Suffolk, and quote the uncle's letter of March 17, 1636, to John Winthrop, hoping that "the Lord have wrought in him a great change; outwardly it seemeth so, time (especially in New England) will tell us more."[1]

'Tis a mercy I have long begged and waited for, and then I bless God for this. I know I came in the world a child of hell, and if ever any a child of devil, I. I had a father that brought me up to eleven years. He [being] gone as I grew in years, I sought a match for my lust; and herein I have been like the devil not only to hell myself but enticing and haling others to sin, rejoicing when I could make others drink and sin. And for aught I know, others in hell for them. And the Lord might have given me my portion, but when I lay in my blood,[2] love came to me in Cambridge. And hearing that no adulterers, drinkers should enter into the Kingdom of God,[3] and so I knew my condition naught, yet my heart was so naught that I would have my haunts. Yet I have been greatly affected in or-

1. Selement and Woolley, eds., *Shepard's Confessions,* p. 85.
2. Ezek. 16:6.
3. 1 Cor. 6:9–10.

dinances, and I have had many resolutions then in my base rotten heart. And spirit many a time would have come into my heart and proffering blood and mercy, yet I would have my lusts and haunts that I would have them dearer than God and Christ and mercy and heaven. And just it had been with God to give me up.

But the Lord let me not alone but followed Lord in use of means, and there I saw my hellish, devilish nature opposite to God and goodness, between light and darkness. And I saw how I lay at the brink of hell, and had not the Lord supported me, I had sunk. And here I found mercy of the Lord breaking my heart. And here I saw how the evil of sin, how it separated me and God, greatest God, and that nothing provoked the Lord nor grieved him more than sin. And I saw as soon as ever I committed sin, I was condemned, and that if pardoned, it must cost the heart blood of Christ, and that I did as much as in me lie to drag Christ to the cross.

And hereby, by seeing my vileness, I was drawn to hunger and thirst after Christ and made me feel my need of Christ. And hearing those promises—come to me, ye that be weary[4]—though I knew not whether Christ died for me, yet I saw myself laden and hence begged of the Lord that I might run after him. And in this promise I found the Lord let in a sight of his beauty and glory and excellency,[5] and hereupon I went with boldness to throne of grace[6] and was an earnest suitor for pardon and power from Christ. And I found Christ's death destroying sin and, though to hell, yet I feared to sin because to grieve the Lord. And hence I have an evidence my nature is changed, because when my sin ariseth, I go to the fount opened.[7] And hence, though sin be in me, yet I find the growing nature of it cut off.

And in old England, seeing ordinances polluted, my soul desired to be there where Christ is feeding of his flock in this place, but saw many stumbling blocks, yet prized. Yet since I came hither, my heart hath been straitened for God. I have been under vines

4. Matt. 11:28.
5. Isa. 35:2.
6. Heb. 4:16.
7. Ps. 36:9, 37:9.
8. 1 Kings 4:25; Zech. 3:10.

and fig trees,[8] but Lord has been a stranger to my soul, and I have forsaken the Lord. And of all sins in world, I thought my heart would never run after the world. Yet sin growing in season, I found my heart set upon the pinnacle showing me glory of this and that.[9] And not seeing that I could have them in death's place, but I could not tell how to go away from hence. God shot arrows in my heart,[10] for though I found the word greatly working upon my heart Lord's day and week day, yet other days my heart was carried after the creature. I answered, I am alone, but temptation said, you may.

I could not go from hence, for then I must go with God's arrows in my heart. And temptation said, if stayed from friends, then provided for, but here you must sit down. And hence I found temptation by degrees eat sup and savor of goodness out of my heart that ordinances came to be hell to me. And hence I found in hearing word I thought two hours too long and wished myself not in a meetinghouse. Hence my heart hath been shut up that I could not pray at all. But finding a heart for God and devil, I found the Lord gone and could not tell cause till heard out of Matthew 25—full of self. And hence the Lord let me see I sought myself, and so I have seen hellish frame of my heart. When the Lord has been gone, then I found no life but dead and sluggish and found Lord as a wayfaring man, and chariot's wheels off.[11] And hence faintings, droppings, and unbelief and thought I did well to cast away faith. But if Lord let in some beams of himself, how ready my heart was to rest upon heartbreakings and to be puffed up with them. Though I have nothing to be proud, many devilish ends. I think I have been as devilish a hypocrite as ever lived. Yet Lord hath brought me to judge myself and loathe myself and to wonder at the boundless mercy of the Lord at his feet. And Revelation 3—because poor[12]—hath much supported. And when I could not go to Christ, yet to gaze for him, and hence have gone to Christ for evidence.

9. Matt. 4:8–9.
10. Ps. 64:7.
11. Exod. 14:25.
12. Rev. 3:17.

Barbary Cutter

—*Lord hath let me see more of himself as in doubtings*

Barbary or Barbara Cutter (c. 1622–c. 1707), a teenager at the time of her confession, came to New England from Newcastle, Northumberland, with her father, mother, and two brothers. She married Elijah Corlet, master of the Cambridge Grammar School, raised three children, and lived long. Her mother's confession is printed below.

The Lord let me see my condition by nature out of 16 of Ezekiel and by seeing the holiness of the carriage of others about, her friends, and the more she looked on them, the more she thought ill of herself.

She embraced the motion to New England. Though she went through with many miseries and stumbling blocks at last removed and sad passages at sea. And after I came hither, I saw my condition more miserable than ever. [I] knew not what to do and spoke to none as knowing none like me. Yet hearing 2 Corinthians 5:19—the Lord was in Christ—and there hearing what need there was of coming to Christ and what need it stood of Christ and that need of him to take away iniquity of holy things and to wash robes.[1] Thereby I saw my vileness. Hence being desirous to seek Lord, saw vileness, hence discouraged, but heard again that soul was not farther off when stripped of excellencies and that when soul comes for reconciliation, must see nothing but (1) condemned for best desires, (2) to look on Christ on parole, (3) soul should not find a reason why Lord should pity it for if so, God would unbottom, but hence to hang on good pleasure of will, which God made precious to me, if he would pity me and honor himself in me. And hearing preciousness of Lord's will and seeing my own will, those [were] dear. And hearing the excellency of person of Christ in five particulars, Lord much affected her heart with it, as first was it was full of beauty and glory, 1 John, full of grace,[2] (2) that grace

1. Rev. 7:14.
2. John 1:14.

was poured out on his lips, Psalms.[3] (3) His heart was full of love and pity,[4] (4) mind full of wisdom.[5] God broke her heart at those things. And hearing price was paid, redemption finished, God [the] Father satisfied, 2. more particularly, for ought knew for vilest. Then God and Christ did tender themselves, and hearing what a sin it was to sin against Gospel, against remedy, and that it stirred up a twofold anger in God if [the soul had] not accepted the Lord by that time. Lord inclined my heart to some secret strife and question in secret whether I would go on and anger Lord or no. And hearing Lord would supply wants,[6] cleaved to him. Then questioned whether grace or no. And hearing manner of every saint's washing, John 13,[7] and by certain notes, I found that the saints sometime took Satan's part, if found affection, and at other times not. And hearing because it felt not what it would, denied what it had, yet discouraged.

Yet hearing sin of unbelief, to bring heart to a strait, either to receive or reject him, and so heard as Balaam, then stopped in a strait,[8] so found sweetness. But I lost that which I found in the Lord, sweetness lost. And on a sacrament day, John 21, some affection—Lord bear to Christ to all.[9] And hearing elder brother and what respect he bear his, I sought nothing yet to end giving two notes: (1) when a soul had seen Lord falls and went running to Lord; (2) it looked on promises and begging and saying as many be it to thee as will. Hence had some hopes again. And hearing John 13—now I tell before come[10]—and hearing when Satan did most assault, Christ preferred it, and being then under some temptation which I knew not what to do and speaking not of them but sunk. But when I heard doctrine, it gave me some hopes. And being laid down in some particulars, as (1) in removing stumbling blocks, [(2)] as a cover head in day of battle.[11] And hearing when earth

3. Ps. 45:2.
4. Isa. 63:9.
5. Rev. 17:9?
6. 2 Cor. 9:12.
7. John 13:4–17.
8. Num. 22:24–26.
9. Probably 1 John 2:1–2.
10. John 13:19.
11. Ps. 140:7.

could not go to rain,[12] it opened to receive it and that there was faith when saw nothing but vileness, and could say nothing but Lord, I am vile. And cleaving [to] God's justice and hearing there was faith, I had some support under some trials then on my spirit. And then hearing Matthew 25—Christ would come as a glorious bridegroom to church[13]—and hearing, thought at these: (1) because not their will, because (2) tarried so long, (3) because not love, there was my objection answered.

Question. And there know Lord means me, yet though their name not in the promise, yet in meaning of it and more sure than if named there because Lord by his spirit would boot[14] to soul. And hearing four cautions in laying hold: (1) not to go to Lord in own strength, (2) look not at own wants but look at Lord gave himself to cleanse, not because they are clean. Lord then stayed her heart.

Yet lost that, and Mr. Eaton[15] showing what a sin of unbelief, that mercy and justice was questioned. Hence I had it set on sadly on my soul and so had some resolution to speak of what Lord had done. And hearing at Roxbury that many went on and smother their doubts, hence the Lord broke snare,[16] and so I discovered my estate to some, and so they spake to me as that it was a mercy Lord let me see my unbelief and where never such unbelief. I was recovered first sabbath, Mark ult.—tell my disciples and Peter.[17] Why Peter? Because Peter's faith was more weak than others'. Hence Lord meant him. Hearing hence Lord pitied them and so was stayed. And so wished to beware of sin and so hearing saints apt to cast away faith was want of feelings and providences crossing promises and seeing reminder of corruption and so spiritual agonies and false fears. I saw and was convinced of my sin especially the last out of 35 Isaiah—say to them that be fearful, be strong, your God comes.[18] God set in it and overpowered my heart at that

12. Possibly Deut. 11:17, 1 Kings 8:35–36, 2 Chron. 6:26.
13. Matt. 25:1–13.
14. Advantage or profit.
15. Possibly a reference to Nathaniel Eaton's confession, above.
16. Ps. 124:7.
17. Mark 16:7.
18. Isa. 35:4.

time. And hearing soul should come to Lord in the promise and stay and wait and lie under Lord if he would show mercy; if not, do what he would. And since, Lord hath let me see more of himself as in doubtings. That Lord did leave saints doubting [so] as to remove lightness and frothiness, hence doubtings, and to cause [them to look] for fresh evidence, and by this means kept them from falling. Lord made these suitable to Lord and to draw my heart nearer to himself. And so answered all doubts from Christ. I saw somewhat more, and this day in forenoon.

Alice Stedman

—yet I could not believe

Alice Stedman (c. 1610–1690) accompanied her husband, John, to Cambridge and shared his rising fortunes. They had three children. Alice was not more than thirty years old at the time of her confession.

It pleased God when I was very young to counsel me by a godly minister, which estate, if I had died in it, had been woeful. Many hindrances I had to his ways, but I was encouraged by the word to go on. And afterward I had many sad fears about my estate, whether it was right, because not so humbled as others and because I could not keep my heart alway to the Lord. And in this condition of fear I went on a pretty while. But afterward I went to London and to a minister who wished me to declare my condition, and he found I had rested on my duties and that I was not so deeply humbled. And he labored to convince me not to build my faith on duties but on freeness of God's love in Christ, which I saw I could not. Afterward I was in the country in that condition, finding myself unable to believe and to walk as I should. And so by hearing the word I heard what a sin it was to refuse mercy because it was not so far humbled. And so he set forth great mercy of God, that when the Lord did not do it by a greater, he would do it by a lesser measure. And afterward by 50 Isaiah ult.—who is he that walks in darkness and sees no light?[1]—was stayed by this word to stay upon God; so by Habakkuk 2:3—the vision is for an appointed time. And so I was stayed and carried in means. But after by John 3:16—that whoever believes—the Lord was pleased by that word to overcome my heart and to show me the freeness of his love not only to them that be in greater but in a lesser measure humbled. And the Lord helped me by this, especially if I felt myself lost and undone without Christ. And after this the Lord exercised me with many outward and inward troubles. And at last the Lord by Job—if thou dost evil or good, what canst add to me?[2]—and here I found no rest. And by Romans 7, by considering that what I did, I did not allow and 'tis no more I.[3] And 1 John 2:1—if any sin, we have an advocate with the Father, Jesus Christ the righteous. And afterward the Lord gave some strength and power over those sins. And after this I was exercised with many outward afflictions, wherein the Lord did support my heart. And the Lord stirred up my heart to come to this place, and he made way by unexpected hand in a spiritual manner. When I came to the ship, by straitness and troubles I exceedingly lost my heart, which God set on upon my conscience, that though I had not place, yet I was not so careful as I should and might have been. And many afflictions I met with, yet my heart remained the same. And at land the Lord exercised me with many afflictions, and I found great strangeness from the Lord. And when I came to the means, I felt not what I looked for, which was very sad. Hence some friends put me on to go to the elder, and he asking me what grounds I had of closing with Christ, I felt often as if I never had anything. And Mr. Weld[4] taught, here upon this rock.[5] There he showed how people build upon wrong foundation to close and catch at promise and missed Christ, which I thought was my condition, which was very sad. And [I had] many temptations, especially to hinder me from secret prayer, seeing I never had Christ nor faith, and whatever is not of faith is

1. Correctly, Isa. 50:10.
2. Job 30:26.
3. Rom. 7:15, 17, 19, 20.
4. See Jane Holmes' confession, n. 7, above.
5. Matt. 7:24–27, 16:18; Luke 6:47–49.

sin.[6] And indeed I have not had a word sometime to speak. At last the Lord brought me to a day of humiliation, to which I had much backwardness upon the same grounds. And in the end of the day, desiring my condition might be remembered me, and at latter part of day speaking 56 Isaiah 6—son of a stranger that is a dry tree, yet his prayers shall be accepted.[7] The Lord did much encourage me by it that Lord should hear, and some refreshings by it. But quickly after I was out of it and lost again. And when a neighbor came to me and asking what such a one should do that did think they had grace but since they came here could not see it. He said there is much pride with a professor so many years and thought well of, it's hard to doubt. Yet, said he, 'tis a great mercy he will do it. And by this means I saw my own heart that was my stick, for I was ashamed to open my condition to any. And at that time I considered of Abram, that the Lord did not need to know what was in his heart but that he [Abram] might know it.[8] So I had need to know what was in my own heart. And afterward I went on depending on means when he [God] would speak. Yet I saw much emptiness in ordinances. And thought I saw it was thus and thus with me, yet I could not believe. And when Mr. Buckly[9] taught here out of the 17 of Genesis that great God should enter into a covenant with him [Abram], I was content the Lord should make what covenant he would, especially Abram then falling upon his face.[10] Yet I could not believe. And was a long [time] under the means without faith, and I saw the Lord might justly deprive me and ever withdraw himself. Yet Mr. Shepard speaking what an honor it was to the Lord to believe—we[?] will love them and seek to please them—which encouraged my soul to believe and desired the Lord to help me. And hearing Mr. Cotton out of Revelation—

6. Rom. 14:23.
7. Isa. 56:3.
8. Gen. 22:1–18.
9. Peter Bulkeley (1583–1659), minister at Concord, Massachusetts, from 1636 until his death; author of *The Gospel-Covenant* (London, 1646), New England's principal contribution to covenant theology, with a preface by Shepard. See Michael McGiffert, "The Problem of the Covenant in Puritan Thought: Peter Bulkeley's *Gospel-Covenant*," *New England Historical and Genealogical Register*, CXXX (1976), pp. 107–29.
10. Gen. 17:2–3.

Christ with a rainbow on his head, Revelation 10[11]—I thought there was nothing for me. I thought I was like the poor man at the pool.[12] So I thought if Lord came not with an almighty power to believe. And in midst of that sermon, hearing if ever Lord came in the promise that the Lord was Jehovah and never changed, and then afresh I had John 3:16, that the Lord had begun to humble and subdue and quicken and sanctify. And so by this power of his word I knew he was Jehovah that did never change.[13] And next day coming to one of elders, he asked me what stuck upon my spirit. I said, I was afraid it was not righteousness. And he encouraged me not to give way to those fears. And hearing John 13:20—he that receives him that sent me—the Lord came in much by those words. And so was much confirmed, and many times since the Lord hath spoken to me to help me.

William Andrews

—such a measure of comfort that I could not contain, which did cast me down

William Andrews (born before 1600; d. 1652) settled in Charlestown and moved by 1634 to Cambridge, where he joined Thomas Hooker's congregation. A shipmaster and selectman, he was one of the town's leading men. He married twice and had one child by Mary, his first wife.

I was brought up of godly parents with whom I remained till seventeen years of age, instructed in the principles of religion. After that bound prentice in Ipswich in a religious family and had not much knowledge living out. But I came into godly men's company so that I grew to some knowledge and thought my estate very good and had some comfort in it, performing duties. Yet by sermons of

11. Rev. 10:1. John Cotton preached on Revelation in the late 1630s and early 1640s. Shepard's notes on several of the sermons are in the same book as the confessions. Some of the sermons were published in London in the 1640s and 1650s.
12. John 5:2–9.
13. E.g., Mal. 3:6.

worthy men, as Mr. Carter of Bramford[1]—if righteous scarcely be saved, where shall the ungodly appear?—upon the burial of a very godly man, where he showed the difficulty of being saved and so how that good men came to heaven, one could come at no time to him but [by] reading or praying or hearing or living in his calling. And if such a man hardly to heaven, as if an eel should go through a hole and leave her skin behind her. Now this did mightily strike me, although before I thought my estate good. And old Mr. Rogers preaching on 5 Deuteronomy, how they promised,[2] yet they broke all. So out of 22 of Genesis 1 of Abram gave up Isaac, his only son, of a promise,[3] and hence showed a man ought to slay his dearest sins, though as dear as his only son. Now I knew I was guilty of some sins, and hence it did lay hold on me. So Matthew 5—except your righteousness exceed righteousness of scribes and pharisees[4]—and if such so strict not saved, what would become of others whose hearts were vile and lives too? Hence cast down by this, I was laid up under great torment of conscience, and a long time going to sea. Yet being persuaded that those promises, Matthew 5, did belong to me—blessed be them that mourn and thirst.[5] And indeed I had oft temptation to kill myself, hence durst not carry a knife about me nor go near water. And after some comfort, fell from it again, as out of 57 of Isaiah preached by Mr. Phillips,[6] [verse] 15—I dwell with contrite spirit. This stayed my heart and made me resolve against every known sin. Yet I lay long under trouble and loath to eat much as unworthy of them. And at sea I got books, searching between a true believer and a temporary, as Dyke[7] and Rogers's *Seven Treatises*.[8] And I sought to God to give

1. John Carter (1554–1635), Puritan minister at Bramford and later at Belstead, both in Suffolk.
2. Deut. 5:27. Rogers is probably John Rogers of Dedham; see confession of Mary Angier Sparrowhawk, above, n. 1.
3. Gen. 17:15–21, 22:1–18.
4. Matt. 5:20.
5. Matt. 5:4, 6.
6. George Phillips (1593–1644), minister at Boxted, Essex, 1617–1629, and at Watertown, Massachusetts, 1630 to his death.
7. Assuredly Daniel Dyke's popular tract, *The Mystery of Self-Deceiving* (London, 1615). Dyke (d. 1614) preached at Coggeshall, Essex, until suspended in 1583, and thereafter at St. Albans.
8. *Seven Treatises* (1603) by Richard Rogers (see Edward Collins' confession, n. 1) was among the most read and longest-lived Puritan publications.

peace and search after promises that he would take away stony heart,[9] and lying long thus and bring some promise to light to give me comfort. And at last the Lord sent me thus such a measure of comfort that I could not contain, which did cast me down more than any other things, that the Lord should manifest such mercy to me. And it did much astonish me that the Lord should look upon me at that time. Afterward I doubted whether these comforts were right, because men might taste of heavenly gift, and hence afraid of unpardonable sin. And by another book I saw difference between comfort of hypocrites and others. The one did cast them down, which stayed me. And after this in Spain I fell very sick and sought the Lord but could find no comfort. And some of my men read Psalm 16—my lines are fallen in a pleasant place[10]—which gave me much joy, and so I desired my men to carry me and cast me into sea if I died because I thought papists would dig me up or no. And so I bless God for what I have found here. Temptation—I built a new ship and my mind much upon it even upon the sabbath. And I desired to deliver me from this, whatever he did with me. But that ship was split and all drowned but a few, four of my men [and] myself naked upon the main topsail in very cold weather. And on a morning some on the shore came with a boat. And glad I was that I lost my ship and so lost my sin.

After that I heard of New England. I came hither, God making way, and when I saw the people, my heart was knit to them much and thought I should be happy if I should be joined and united to them. And when I came, God made way both in removing the minister and also in selling off all that I had. And sat down at Charlestown, where I was received. Afterward my wife in my absence came hither, which I bless God for.

Martha Collins

—I persecuted God himself

Martha Collins (c. 1609–1700) settled in Cambridge in the 1630s

9. Ezek. 11:19, 36:26.
10. Ps. 16:6.

with her husband, Edward, and four children, to whom four more were added in the 1640s. She joined the church about 1640.

Father being careful in catechizing me, I looking on myself and comparing myself with others thought my condition very good, being civil. But about nineteen years of age, I began to seek the Lord in private, only from example of others, yet feeling no necessity of it. But in changing my condition I felt no need of change. But being in Essex—thou fool, this night shall they take thy soul from thee[1] and one paper wall between him and hell[2]—which truths somewhat affected my heart. But I thought this was to them that were more vile than I. But going to London, by plenty of means and by my husband's speaking I saw my original corruption and miserable condition and so had a hungering after means which were most searching. Yet I had many objections against mercy and beaten off from offers of mercy by thoughts whether I was elected or no and so refused offer. When husband spake to me of free offer, I thought it was affection to me. And hearing Mr. Shaw,[3] that I should look after the Lord for himself, I looked after that. And coming into the country, I had no good sabbaths nor blessing under that ministry. But hearing of soul's preparation for Christ, I was stirred up to seek. But then blockish and sottish again and so questioned my election.

And so my husband's heart was inclined to come to New England, but when I came to quickening means, then I secretly desired it but yet opposite I was to it by looking upon my miseries here. And yet I saw miseries there toward me and my children and very unwilling and discontent when I was at it to come. Yet I thought if the Lord should bring me here, it would be a great mercy I was alive. And when I came on shore and seeing people living otherwise than I looked for, I was affected. But meeting with sorrows and feeling no life in ordinances, I thought I was sealed up. Then one child was struck, and then I struggled with God

1. Luke 12:20.
2. In all likelihood, Collins remembered the "paper wall" from one of Shepard's sermons at Earles Colne: "God is a consuming fire against thee, and there is but one paper wall of thy body between thy soul and eternal flames" (*The Sincere Convert* (1646), in *Works,* ed. John A. Albro [Boston, 1853], I, 35).
3. John Shaw (1608–1672), Puritan writer and lecturer in Derbyshire, Devonshire, and Yorkshire.

and so then pulled down. And then Lord struck my heart, and I thought it was for my sin and so let the Lord do with me what he will. And afterward I thought they were too strict in examining of members, and at Boston hearing the reasons why they did not receive all that came over, which I forget now. And I blessed Lord that followed me and after hearing when Judas was gone out, then the Lord spake[4] and left sin to strike at some eminent ones. And though I did not persecute, yet I persecuted God himself and struck him and so committed the unpardonable sin and knew not what to do. And hearing on that text—gate is shut[5]—and thinking that surely now gate is shut for me. And so there was my objections answered and taken off, which were never before taken off, and so was persuaded gate was open for me. And reading—I will forgive iniquities for thy name's sake[6]—and here stay. And coming to Mr. S[hepard], (1) I was asked if had not neglected means, (2) if no need of Christ, and so showed nothing but will between you and Christ. Meeting with another, she said, let them be precious to you, and meeting with that, 'tis not in man to direct his ways,[7] it answered my objections against inability.

Brother Crackbone's Wife

—I had a new house yet I thought I had no new heart

Mistress Gilbert Crackbone, given and maiden names unknown, joined the Cambridge church about 1640, soon after the burning of her house that climaxes her confession. The Crackbones had come from London with one or two children. They were moderately prosperous. Gilbert held a number of public posts, including that of selectman.

Her brother sending for her to London in a good house, there I considered my course and ways, especially of one sin. And thought the Lord would never accept me more and was terrified and out of

4. John 13:19–31.
5. Ezek. 44:1–2.
6. 1 John 2:12.
7. Jer. 10:23.

hope. And hearing 1 Isaiah—white as snow[1]—I had some hope. And hearing out of Mr. Smith's book[2] what Lord required, *viz.,* the heart, and if heart given, then eye and foot were given. And so I wished my parents knew me. And so being married and having poor means and having afflictions on my child and took from me, and so troubled what became of my children, and to hell I thought it was because I had not prayed for them. And so came to New England. I forgot the Lord as the Israelites did, and when I had a new house yet I thought I had no new heart. And means did not profit me and so doubted of all Lord had done. Yet hearing when Lord will do good, he takes away all ornaments. And so thought of seeking after the ordinances, but I knew not whether I was fit. Yet heard I was under wings of Christ, one of them, yet not under both. And so saw sloth and sluggishness, so I prayed to the Lord to make me fit for church fellowship and Lord. And the more I prayed, the more temptation I had, so I gave up, and I was afraid to sing because to sing a lie. Lord, teach me, and I'll follow thee,[3] and heard Lord will break the will of his last work. And seeing house burned down, I thought it was just and mercy to save life of the child and that I saw not after again my children there. And as my spirit was fiery to burn all I had, and hence prayed Lord would send fire of word, baptize me with fire.[4] And since the Lord hath set my heart at liberty.

Robert Holmes

—Still I am doubting, but I know I shall know if I follow on

Robert Holmes (c. 1614–1663) and his wife, Jane, were among several confessors who came to Cambridge from Newcastle, Northumberland, where he must have heard Shepard preach. He joined the church in 1641. A farmer of decent means, he served the town as constable and highway surveyor.

1. Isa. 1:18.
2. Selement and Woolley (*Shepard's Confessions,* 40 n. 2), identify four clerical Smiths whose published sermons Mistress Crackbone may have heard read: Henry (1550?–1591), John (1563–1616), Miles (d. 1624), and Samuel (1584–1662).
3. Ps. 86:11.
4. Matt. 3:11; Luke 3:16.

In days of ignorance I contented with common prayer and homilies and sometime went to word but lived above twenty years in disobedience to parents and subject in my will to every lust that since I have wondered the Lord cut me not off then. And so I removed from my father's house in Northumberland, and there I was rude as ever before. And we heard a sermon once a month, and where I heard nothing but sleep, and there I fain would stay. For my spiritual estate, I never looked after it. I was sick to death but took no care for my soul if I died so, and sought to buy cattle when well. And at last I came to Newcastle, where I was much given to work and covetousness, and at last I saw all things here were empty vanities. And I was terrified about my estate, doubting of a sin I lived in doubtfully, and hence at last left off that doubtful sin from a book. But could not find repentance for sin and my life past, and hearing Dr. Jenison,[1] Zechariah 12:10—spirit of mourning—and hence heart melted and I had joy. And thought plague was great, I asked what promise I had to live on, and Isaiah 26—stayed on thee.[2] In my heart I purposed at last came to New England and found heart and all ordinances dead but saw sin of common prayer. And so affected and established by Mr. Cotton's white horse,[3] hearing—I am oppressed; undertake for me[4]—I prayed to help me and reveal himself to me. And my heart was melted all sermon time, and being sacrament time I went home and cried to him. Still I am doubting, but I know I shall know if I follow on,[5] and if he damn me, he shall do it in his own way.

Elizabeth Cutter

—he that comes to me I'll not cast away

Elizabeth Cutter (c. 1576–1663) appears in Shepard's record as Old Goodwife Cutter, being then in her mid-sixties. After the death of her husband, William, she lived with her daughter Barbara, whose confession appears above.

1. See Joanna Sill's confession, above n. 1.
2. Isa. 26:3.
3. Rev. 6:2, 19:11. See Alice Stedman's confession above, n. 11.
4. Isa. 38:14.
5. Hos. 6:3.

I was born in a sinful place where no sermon preached. My parents, I knew not father; mother sent me to Newcastle, where placed in a godly family as I think. And hearing—fear God, keep his commandments[1]—two of which, third and fourth, I saw I broke. And six and seven years I was convinced thus. And I went to another family, where the people were carnal, and there fell to a consumption and after followed with Satan and afraid he would have me away. Mr. Rodwell[2] came to me, and he was an instrument of much good to me. And afterward Lord's hand was sad on me, husband taken away and friends also to this place. And I desired to come this way in sickness time, and Lord brought us through many sad troubles by sea, and when I was here, the Lord rejoiced my heart.

But when come, I had lost all and no comfort, and hearing from foolish virgins, those that sprinkled with Christ's blood were unloved, so I saw I was a Christless creature and hence in all ordinances was persuaded nothing did belong to me. Durst not seek nor call God Father nor think Christ shed his blood for me.

And afterward I went to T[homas] S[hepard] and found more liberty and so had less fear, but hearing of foolish virgins were cast off,[3] so should I, being a poor ignorant creature. Going to servants of the Lord, I told them I could not be persuaded one lived so long. Hearing Mr. S[hepard], if I were as Abram and had such gifts,[4] then Lord would accept, but if poor creature, so I sought the Lord the more. And hearing in day of humiliation Lord by sundry places Lord rejoiced my heart—Christ came to save sinners,[5] Christ came not to save righteous but sinners,[6] and to find lost and broken hearted.[7] Come to me, weary.[8] But I thought I had no repentance, yet I was encouraged to seek the Lord and to be content with his condemning will to lie at Lord's feet. Seeing such

1. Eccles. 12:13.
2. Unidentified.
3. Matt. 25:1–13. Shepard's sermon series on *The Parable of the Ten Virgins* (London, 1660) fills the second volume of his *Works*.
4. Gen. 25:5–6?
5. 1 Tim. 1:15.
6. Matt. 9:13; Mark 2:17; Luke 5:32.
7. Luke 4:18.
8. Matt. 11:28.

need of Christ, was not knowing whether else to go and that he that comes to me I'll not cast away,[9] and so desired Lord to teach me and desired to submit.

Jane Wilkinson Winship

—hearing . . . hearing . . . hearing

Jane Wilkinson Winship (d. before 1651) came with her husband from Newcastle, Northumberland, in the 1630s. They seem to have been members of Thomas Hooker's Cambridge congregation. Edward Winship became one of the town's prominent and affluent citizens. The couple had four children.

Hearing 2 Jeremiah 14—two evils broken cisterns[1]—I was oft convinced by Mr. Hooker[2] my condition was miserable and took all threatenings to myself. I heard by T[homas] S[hepard] the evil of sin that separated from Christ though so much pity, and hence I was convinced of evil of sin. And was afraid to die and should forever lie under wrath of God, and I heard, he that had smitten, he could heal, Hosea 6.[3] And hearing T[homas] S[hepard]—terror to all that were out of Christ—wondered how they could eat, sleep that had no assurance of Christ. Hence troubled yet prayed Lord takes outcast of Israel.[4] Hearing one say one thinks I have no Christ, I heard of David, if any pleasure, he'll bring me back again. And hearing Mr. Eaton[5] out of 80 Psalm—sickness in every family yet no peace made—and so went under many sad fears.

Hearing Mr. Rogers[6] speak every sermon account and Mr. Rogers[7] of Rowley—woman, great is thy faith.[8] And hearing Mr.

9. John 6:37.
1. Correctly, Jer. 2:13.
2. Thomas Hooker: see Shepard's autobiography above, p. 48 n. 18.
3. Hos. 6:1.
4. Ps. 147:2; Isa. 11:12.
5. Perhaps Nathaniel Eaton.
6. Nathaniel Rogers (1598–1655), minister at Becking, Essex, and Assington, Suffolk, until settling in Massachusetts in 1636. The next year he became one of the ministers at Salem.
7. Ezekiel Rogers: see Shepard's autobiography above, p. 53 n. 27.
8. Matt. 15:28.

Wells[9] caused by want of confession I went, I opened my heart about sin against holy ghost.

I thought it impossible to have my heart changed; 2 Jeremiah—is there anything too hard for me?[10]—I was comforted.

Hearing of doubts of saints, one was waverings of the minds, other of wills and minds. The one drew them from God, the other near to God. I saw it was not so with me.

Hearing, say to them that be fearful in heart, behold he comes[11]—Mr. Wells—pull off thy soles [i.e., shoes] off thy feet for ground is holy.[12] And hearing Exodus 34, forgiving iniquity,[13] I thought Lord could will, was he willing. But I saw how rich to forgive, and hearing John 13, hearing in use, offer of Christ to offer will love lose glory by me that have been so vile? Yes, there is hope, for God hath recovered his glory[14] and that nothing is required but to accept. But I cannot. Lord will draw[15] but how know that I take Lord to free from misery and wrath and as king? And hearing of lecture sermon use, if content with Christ alone, Lord will visit. Hearing whether ready for Christ as his appearing, had fears,[16] city of refuge.[17] Hearing had not Lord done that as if I could say there is no God like this, I found that by hearing, in him fatherless find mercy.[18] Hearing oppressed undertake for me,[19] eased. Hearing whether Christ was accepted (1) whether content with him alone, (2) when absent, mourns under it. Hearing many apprehended Christ, and Christ had not apprehended them, and one was if overcoming love of Christ had been upon their hearts. Doubting by reason of passion whether any grace, I desired in a day of humiliation Lord would meet. Hearing humble yourself under God's hand,[20] comforted. Hearing of Thomas's unbelief,[21]

9. See Jane Holmes's confession, above, n. 7.
10. Jer. 32:27.
11. Isa. 35:4.
12. Exod. 3:5.
13. Exod. 34:7.
14. John 13:31–32.
15. John 6:44.
16. Matt. 24:44; Luke 12:40.
17. Num. 35:11ff.; Josh. 20:2, 21:13ff.
18. Hos. 14:3.
19. Isa. 38:14.
20. 1 Pet. 5:6.
21. John 20:25–29.

he showed trust in Lord forever, for there is everlasting strength, and stayed.

Jane Palfrey Willows

—though I had let my hold go, yet he would not let his hold go of me

Jane Palfrey (dates unknown) moved from Northumberland to New England as a young widow with two children in the 1630s. In Cambridge she married George Willows, by whom she had two sons. She joined the church in 1640.

It pleased the Lord to let me see sin of ignorance; I used a form of prayer and came to Newcastle, where I used a form. And there being a great sickness and all to go from their families, I was cast in a place where Mr. Glover[1] lived, at Heddon, and there was cast down and brought low inwardly. Neither can I speak any particulars, but I was convinced of such sins as I durst not commit afterward.

And I came again to Newcastle, but I could not live there but rather desired to go to a more private family where I had more liberty. And went under many doubts and fears and was sometime encouraged and sometime cast down. And when husband gone, I thought all I had was but a form, and I went to Mr. Morton[2] and desired he would tell me how it was with me. He told me if I hated that form, it was a sign I had more than a form. But I could not be quiet but to him and asked, when so far humbled as to be accepted in Christ Jesus? He said they would not think they had enough but that they would hunger after him the more. And Dr. Jenison[3] and Mr. Morton encouraged me.

And then I had a mind for New England, and I thought I should know more of my own heart. So I came and thought I saw more than ever I could have believed that I wondered earth swal-

1. See Edward Hall's confession, above, n. 1.
2. Unidentified.
3. See Robert Holmes' confession, above, n. 1.

lowed me not up. And 25 Matthew 5—foolish virgins saw themselves void of all grace—I thought I was so and was gone no farther and questioned all that ever the Lord had wrought—I'll never leave thee.[4] I could now apprehend that yet desired the Lord not to leave me nor forsake me, and afterward I thought I was now discovered. Yet hearing, he would not hide his face forever,[5] was encouraged to seek. But I felt my heart rebellious and loath to submit unto him and was long under it. And that, Romans 9—hath not potter power over the clay to make me a vessel of honor, etc.?[6]—was quieted but could not resolve to speak to any. At last I was left to a discontented frame, and I considered what a woeful frame I had, distrusting God's providence, and so was in a confusion in my spirit and could not speak to my husband. So I went sadly loathing myself [that] I should rise against any providence of his and durst not lift up my eyes to the Lord, being so great. Yet 25 Psalm—be merciful because my sin is great[7]—and this encouraged me to go, but then I thought I should dishonor Lord the more in going to him. But seeing Lord's command in obedience to it, I was encouraged to go to the Lord, Matthew 8—when centurion said, speak word, I shall live[8]—that enough. And when heard, I will have mercy on whom I will,[9] but I was made by that word to lie down and entrusted Lord to keep down my spirit. And hearing Christ had received gifts for the rebellious, I was made willing and wondered I was out of hell.

Afterward I felt no hungerings and so far from loving as that I hated the Lord, yet I entrusted Lord though I had let my hold go, yet he would not let his hold go of me, and this stayed. And I went to the elder and then to a friend and asked if any had such a heart and such temptations. And they said, yes. When I came home again, Lord came to me and showed me need of Lord's strength and support every moment and was afraid to fall to the same condition again. Yet I lost it again. Yet heard Lord would give strength

4. Heb. 13:5.
5. Ezek. 39:29.
6. Rom. 9:21.
7. Ps. 25:11.
8. Matt. 8:8.
9. Exod. 33:19; Rom. 9:15.

to them that have no strength[10] and went to Elder Frost,[11] and he asked me a question which I could not answer, whether I saw a willingness and readiness in Lord to show mercy to me. And hearing Psalm 42—still hope in God[12]—was encouraged, and hearing what a sin it was to resist the Lord, I entrusted the Lord to help me against it. And hearing greatest mercy to be under sin, and I had a fellow feeling of Christ's sufferings and so had many objections and doubts answered, which I forget.

Nicholas Wyeth

—are you not one unfruitful tree to be hewn down?

Nicholas Wyeth (c. 1595–1680), mason and farmer, came to New England from Suffolk about 1638 with his wife and two children (one died on the way). His confession is dated January 7, 1645. After his wife died a year or more later, he married a widow with three children; together the couple had two more children.

It pleased the Lord acting first out of his free mercy he let me see the evil of not keeping the sabbath. About sixteen years of age, being a prentice, wherein I went to that company that drew to idleness, and Lord helped me out of 16 of Ezekiel—when I was in my blood and when no eye pitied.[1] I saw he was the refuge for pity, for I had profaned the sabbath much. But I saw through Lord's help I was not in my way, and I was much troubled that I had so spent the sabbath. And hence I went out to hear the word, and having none at home, I desired to hear them that were most suitable to my condition to stir up my heart. And going to hear one Mr. Salby,[2] I did much affect his ministry, and I did somewhat profit by it, and so I had much love to the word, for I saw that I was lost and that it was the means of help. And preaching out of Canticles showing—

10. Isa. 40:29.
11. Edmund Frost (d. 1672), long-time ruling elder of the Cambridge church.
12. Ps. 42:5, 11.
1. Ezek. 16:5–6.
2. Robert Selby (dates unknown), rector at Bedfield, Suffolk, c. 1584–c. 1610.

my beloved is mine and I his[3]—and he showed they that loved Christ, he loved them as his own. And the Lord kept me and encouraged me hereby much still to go and hear other good men. And every sabbath day I went four miles to hear him about a year, but I went on very poorly as I have done ever since. And I took every opportunity I could and could get liberty of my master to go out to hear but yet, though I went on poorly, yet had much love to the word and loved society of them and God's people. And so I lived twelve years, and Lord brought Mr. Burrows[4] some sixteen miles off, and I was then able-bodied then and went often to hear him. And by Brother Danforth[5] went out and having means in the town. But I heard Mr. Burrows out of Galatians. He said, as a man sows, so shall he reap;[6] he showed a natural man did [not] sow anything that was good, everything was evil. And I saw I was in my natural condition, yet I went out to hear and went twenty miles off to Mr. Rogers, out of Colossians—if risen, seek things which are above[7]—but though I did hear much, yet I could not see my heart was brought so near as I did desire, for I had been very careless in remembering what I heard and for sixteen years went on so in old England. Hence I came to New England, being persecuted and courted for going from the place where we lived, and hence I used means to come hither where we might enjoy more freedom. And I had much joy in going about this work; though I had lived very foul, yet my heart much convinced me and that I should live under means most powerful. And so I was much opposed by my friends, and enemies of God discouraging of me, and the Lord helped me to withstand them that did oppose me, for I could not be content to live where I did, and I went through many difficulties before and when I came to sea, yet I went on. And God took away my son,

3. Cant. 2:16.
4. Jeremiah Burroughs (1599–1646), then preacher at Bury St. Edmunds, Suffolk, a leading advocate of Congregational Independency. It was at Burroughs' home in Norfolk that Shepard's pregnant wife, Margaret, tumbled down a flight of stairs. See autobiography above, p. 36.
5. Nicholas Danforth (d. 1638), a prominent resident of Cambridge.
6. Gal. 6:7.
7. Col. 3:1. Wyeth lived near Ipswich, and there were several preachers named Rogers in the general vicinity: Daniel at Wethersfield, Essex; John at Dedham, Essex; Nathaniel at Assington, Suffolk; and Timothy at Pontesbright or Chapel, Essex.

some telling me the Lord was displeased for going on, but discouragements of natural friends I regarded not, and I did not care though the Lord took away all I had. Yet I had many things to call me back, my wife all the time going through many afflictions. And then I thought of what others said—the Lord would meet with me—but I did not look as coming to New England was the cause but did believe if the Lord should bring my child and self hither, the Lord would recompense me by means. When we came here, the Lord raised up my wife, and I did much rejoice to see the place and see the people and hear God's servants. Only troubled me to see death of Mr. Danforth, yet I thought God's people were a loving people. So the Lord stirred up some friends here and having friends at Long Island, yet I would not go thither. And yet God's hand hath been much against me since I came hither, and I know not but it hath been for my carelessness in not watching over my child in regard of the sin of the family, which God sit on. Though I have been much drawn away unto new plantations, though I could never see a clear way to go away, for I saw so much of love of God's people here that I thought I should bring much evil on me if I did remove. But for that sin which brake out, it had been good for me if I had never come hither to this place. The Lord's hand hath been much out against me and is so still. He gave me a child after my own heart, and God hath taken it from me, and 'tis so just for I have gone on so formally and coldly since I came here. Though I have enjoyed much in public, yet I have been very unfruitful and unchristianlike.

E:[8] Question. Do you remember nothing about your misery and way of mercy? Answer. Yet I have since been much affected out of 25 Matthew and 14 John, but I am shallow. Question. Do you remember nothing how God hath tendered Christ to you? Answer. In Ephesians 2 I heard when far off, then made near,[9] and Lord let me see no way to be saved but by his own free grace. Question. What effects did it work? Answer. I saw it was his free grace to encourage me to go on. The Lord let me see I had nothing in myself. Question. Did the Lord ever give you any assurance of his love in

8. E. is unidentified. Selement and Woolley suppose Richard Eccles, a member of the congregation (*Shepard's Confessions,* 195 n. 11).
9. Eph. 2:13.

Christ? Answer. The Lord let me see if not born again, I could not enter into Kingdom of God.[10] Question. What supports your heart with hope? Answer. Nothing but free grace in Christ. I did fear I should not be able to speak the truth, but I have been very unprofitable, and so it appears. Yet I desired to enjoy society of God's people.

S:[11] Question. What ground of assurance? Answer. Because love began. Question. How know that? Answer. Because of that good I see in them and would get from them, and I think myself unfit to come into their society. Question. Have you no fears? Answer. Yes, of death in regard of unprofitableness, unsensibleness of my condition, and want of assurance.

C:C:[12] You complain of unsensibleness; what is cause you said drowsiness? Question. Is there no other evil but that? Answer. Yes, I have a wandering eye, not attending upon the word, but helped since I saw it; again I have not made use of God's people to get into their societies. Question. Are you not one unfruitful tree to be hewn down?[13] Answer. I am convinced by this that my unfitness, unfit to partake sacraments. Question. You rejoiced much when sabbath came? Answer. Though this be and yet sleepy. Answer. I have had when sabbath comes great hopes to see what I have not seen for I and hence joyed, yet it hath been with a great deal of deadness. And I labor against it and have striven against it and have hoped the Lord would then meet with me.

E. F.[14] Question. What did you mean when you said you comfort yourself with vain hopes? Answer. Because I have heard as unprofitably after hearing as before, though I went with much expectation.

Question. What have you read or heard that might make you hope the Lord might meet with you? Answer. I did believe that was the means, viz., hearing word and prayer, and so I knew I was in way because draw near to me and I'll to you.[15] Question. Would

10. John 3:3.
11. S. could be Thomas Shepard or any one of a number of laymen.
12. Selement and Woolley suppose layman Christopher Cane (*Shepard's Confessions,* 196, n. 15).
13. Matt. 3:10.
14. Undoubtedly elder Edmund Frost.
15. Jas. 4:8.

Lord deny? Answer. No want in him but in myself, yet I have comforted myself in waiting upon the Lord. Question. Are you privy to any guile in your way? Answer.

Question. Whether if your course be too tall or no or sense of that makes you lie down? Answer. I have had continual strivings against it according to light, but I have been of a very forward, hasty nature.

Question. Have you had some profit in God's ways? Answer. Yes. Instance? Answer. I have seen more of the love of the Lord Jesus by such truths I heard not in old, as how to observe sabbath and prepare for it and others which I cannot speak. I have here much of Christ's love but cannot remember and been much supported and heard of love hath brought me into awe of his will. Question. Have you not seen more into your heart and life? Answer. Yes, out of commandments. E. F. Then there is something of fruitfulness.

Question. What use make you of Christ in regard of sin? Answer. I knew out of John—without me you can do nothing[16]—I have seen by many of.

Question. What is your chiefest desire in secret when no other? Answer. That the Lord would manifest himself more to my soul in Christ and power of ordinances. Question. Why do you forget things, brother? Answer. I see cause enough in my own heart why Lord should deny me. I know many things in my practice. I have not so meditated on the word.

Elizabeth Oakes

—what would become of me if I was taken away?

Elizabeth Oakes, a single woman, may have been a daughter of Thomas and Elizabeth Fanning of Earles Colne, Essex. The parish register shows a child of that name and family baptized there in 1625, when Shepard was the Puritan lecturer. After her parents' deaths, she was adopted into the Oakes family of Dedham, Essex.

16. John 15:5.

Stepbrothers Edward and Thomas were prominent in Cambridge at the time Elizabeth made her confession, dated May 10, 1648.

After the Lord brought me to this country, my father being taken away, Mr. S[hepard] told me that he had laid up many prayers, and after that, thinking of those words, I thought I had no father to take care for me nor pray for me. But I read, God would be a father to fatherless,[1] after which, the Lord laying affliction and sickness on me, and thinking it was for my sin, I was little affected, yet sought God in private duties, yet thought God would not hear because all wicked prayers are abomination to God.[2] After which the Lord left me to neglect seeking him, and then I thought God would never give me a heart to seek again. Yet the Lord visiting me with his hand, yet I not sensible. And hearing out of catechise[3] (1) the Lord make me see, (2) to be sensible, I thought I fell short. Yet reading catechise, (3) the Lord set upon me upon question, what [were the] beginnings of second death[?][4] (1) terror of conscience; (2) Satan's power; (3) curse on all blessings.[5] And I thought I was troubled in conscience yet under power of Satan, and I a curse. After this I saw my sin but thought I was not humbled. I was troubled but spake to none and could [not] desire to speak. And Mr. S[hepard], coming to my father, said now was acceptable day, if now God gave me a heart to seek him. And he told me God would make the self sensible of it as the greatest evil, and hence I thought whether the Lord ever intended any mercy to me—Hosea 6, They that follow on to know me shall know me[6]—and the Lord gave me a heart to seek him in some measure. And after this, being afflicted and examining myself what would become of me if I was taken away, yet hearing that place, They that come to him, he would not cast away,[7] I having little hope, yet seeing promise not only to faithful but to their seed, I had some hope. After that, hear-

1. Ps. 68:5.
2. Prov. 28:9.
3. Mary Rhinelander McCarl identifies the source as Thomas Shepard's *A Short Catechism . . .*, which circulated in manuscript in his congregation until posthumously printed in Cambridge in 1654.
4. Rev. 2:11.
5. Shepard, *Short Catechism,* pp. 35–36.
6. Hos. 6:3.
7. John 6:37.

ing out of John 13 that when Peter denied Christ he went out and wept,[8] and I thought on those words, and I thought I had denied the Lord often, convincing me by his word yet unhumbled, and out of those words, Out of me ye can do nothing,[9] he [Shepard] showed that the soul could do nothing without Christ, and I saw it then, that of myself I could do nothing good. Mr. S[hepard] preaching out of John 14 of humiliation after soul saw his sin,[10] I thought the Lord now let me see my sin as greatest evil on [illegible] of consolation, if God let soul saw [*sic*] sin though not humbled in that measure, but I thought I was not as others were. Hearing Mr. Symmes,[11] he preach[ed] upon Oft as they denied Christ's offer, they had trod under foot Christ's blood,[12] and I thought I had done so. And Mr. S[hepard] preaching in John, All that were called not elected,[13] and how shall I know whether I was elected, and I heard if the Lord gave the soul a heart to choose Christ, Christ had chose[n] Christ [*sic*] before. And I thought the Lord gave me a heart to choose him above all things here in this world. After the Lord giving me a heart to seek him to enjoy him in all his ordinances,[14] I thought I was so unfit and unworthy that I was unfit, and I heard that some might not find God because they did not seek him in all his ordinances, and that the sacrament was a means wherein the Lord would coming [*sic*] more.

Upon question what she saw in Christ to make her prize Christ. Answer: peace, life, light, all things; for I saw I was dead and darkness, and Christ was peace and life and light.[15]

Jane Stevenson

—I knew not but I might be next at grave

Jane Stevenson came to Massachusetts Bay with her shoemaker husband, Andrew, and a small daughter before 1643. They subse-

8. Correctly, John 18:15–27. Matt. 26:75; Mark 14:72; Luke 22:62.
9. John 15:5.
10. John 14:21–24, but see Acts 8:32–33.
11. Zechariah Symmes (1599–1670), pastor at Charlestown, Massachusetts, 1636–1670.
12. Heb. 10:29.
13. Correctly, Rom. 11:5–7.
14. 1 Cor. 11:2; Heb. 9:1. See Shepard, *Short Catechism,* pp. 22–23, on ordinances.
15. Phil. 4:7.

quently had seven more children. Mistress Stevenson made her confession in 1648.

When the Lord was pleased to convince me of sin, it was by affliction, the plague being in the place; I [was] in the midst of wrath of God,[1] and some whom I have been in company with, within 24 hours laid in grave, and yet the Lord spared me, and I knew not but I might be next at grave by reason of my sins. And I had sinned against God and disobeyed parents, and hence I thought God would visit me, and I was unfit to live and [would] die by my sins, and hence prayed God would spare me. The Lord afflicted me among the rest, yet the Lord gave me my life and spared me. And hence I had a greater desire to hear the word. And hence sin no more lest a worse befall thee[2]—that came to me. And a godly man asked me how I walked now, and I told him I desired to know more of God, and he asked me what I thought of my prayers: would they carry me to heaven, and Lord accept of them[?] I said so. And he told me that then every prayer was abomination,[3] and he might damn me for them, so long as I rested upon anything I did. And I asked him what I should do; if ever he did me good, it must be for his name sake and out of his grace, and hence I saw my own unworthiness more. And hence having way made to New England, I desired God would glorify himself by my coming. And here I met with difficulties and trials and fell to great discontent. And when I heard [on] the Sabbath what God would bring on discontented creatures and how the Israelites did so, and then, though they had their desire, it was with a curse, and this made me fear. And the Lord departed from me, and my sins were so great against such deliverance as I did enjoy. And the Lord brought that scripture, All you that are weary, I will give you rest,[4] and Though sins as crimson yet Lord would make them as wool.[5] And I heard Mr. S[hepard] that Christ would come in flaming fire, etc.[6] and hence desired the Lord that I might know him. And

1. Rom. 1:18.
2. John 5:14.
3. Prov. 28:9.
4. Matt. 11:28.
5. Isa. 1:18.
6. 2 Thess. 1:7–8.

hearing Mr. S[hepard] that the Lord would search for secret sins, vain thoughts,[7] and I desired the Lord to set his fear in my heart. And that place in Scripture, I have chosen you, that they who will not lay down father and life is not worthy,[8] I have oft thought whether I should ever do so unless Lord gave me strength. And Mr. S[hepard] showing how ready we were to content ourselves with things of this life.

Asked where Christ was a spirit. At right hand was all righteous.[9]

John Shepard

—plowing was sin; eating and drink and sleep, all was sinful

John Shepard (1623–1707)—no relation to the minister—was the son of mariner Edward Shepard, a member of the Cambridge church. At the time of his confession he was operating the ferry across the Charles River to Brighton. He later became a cooper. He had three wives and eleven children by the first of them, Rebecca Greenhill.

It pleased God at time to awaken my conscience by Mr. Shepard speaking at baptizing of a child to parents to encourage child to seek God, though [I was] but young, 8 or 9, in private d[evotions?]. And here I saw myself guilty of neglect, and put on to th[e] duty by mother, I sought after God. And keeping the ferr[y] being a fit temptation to forsake God, called away at fit seasons, yet should [have] sought God sooner or later. Yet I took some time, yet conscience would not let me alone. And coming up from waterside, I answered conscience that I sought God as oft as I could or had opportunity, yet conscience not quiet. And carrying Mr. Waters[1] over ferry, he took occasion to bid me seek because others had more labor to take up their time and thoughts. But after this God would

7. Ps. 90:8.
8. Matt. 10:37–39.
9. Acts 2:32–33.
1. Unidentified.

not let me alone. Ye ask and have not because ye ask amiss out of fears.[2] And here I was put to seek God more seriously because I did only to quiet conscience.[3] And so I thought I had to quiet men, and this might be well enough, and so continued a season. But hearing out of catechize about original sin,[4] and I never knew the filth of that sin as then the Lord let me see. Answer to question is the contrariety of whole nature of man to law of God, and actual sins of the actions. And here had showed whatever a man did unregenerate was sinful, and plowing was sin, and all what they did perform, and eating and drink and sleep, all was sinful. Now after this, being convinced of original sin and that nothing I could do did displease [*sic*] God, though in itself lawful, yet as from me sinful, and having some thoughts of wrath to come, I was amazed to think of wrath, what a long time eternity was, and that there was but two ways, and one I might go to.[5] Yet Lord having awakened my heart, I made this request [that] God would smite his root that the branches might wither.[6] And the Lord never broke my heart till now, for the Lord made me mourn for this sin of my nature, and hence I set myself against this sin, whereas before it was against actual [sin]. And when Mr. S[hepard] came to open 3 Commandment about preparation,[7] though I sought God, yet I was guilty of neglect of preparation to seek God [illegible] in either for Sabbath or privy duty. And I saw my inability to prepare for any and unfitness to come to God in it. Now after this, Mr. S[hepard] came to show John 15:16, You have not chosen you [*sic*].[8] Doctrine: Greatness of Christ's love is seen in the freeness of it. At which time, being in great trouble for want of love and fear of God's love, not knowing what would become of me, and I promised him if he would clear up his love, I would cleave to him, and walk in his way,[9] and after my resolution was to continue seeking for mercy.

2. Jas. 4:3.
3. Shepard, *Short Catechism,* p. 31.
4. Ibid., p. 35.
5. Ezek. 21:19–21.
6. Mal. 4:1; Ezek. 31:3–14.
7. Exod. 20:7; see Shepard, *Short Catechism,* p. 23.
8. John 15:16.
9. Ps. 86:11, 143:8; Isa. 30:21; Jer. 42:3.

And [I] heard out of 5 Commandment[10] how inferiors should go to superiors, and I went to J. Sill,[11] and he was glad and did encourage me, and I told him my condition, and telling him of this sermon, how Christ did choose the soul: (1) Christ chose it [before] 1,000s, (2) freely, (3) everlastingly, (4) for this end, to enjoy all fruits of election. And so soul choose[s] Christ. Now the Lord gave me some hopes he had chosen me. But telling him what my fears were, he asked me whether my fears were only for wrath of God, or did I mourn for sin as it grieved God. I told him I could not answer him, and I was under fears God would separate me from him. Then upon a time I went to him again, and after some time of meditation I thought I did mourn for sin as it did grieve God, as well as making separation. And [I asked him] how was my heart when I was not enlarged to seek after God, and he said it was a mercy if my trouble was that I had not a better heart to seek God. And after this I had some hope of love, that he had chosen him. Yet I purpose to continue praying, hearing no man had the least desire yet should go to God to make it come, and was much encouraged that if the Lord has begun to blow up the spark, he would not quench it,[12] and sin shall no dominion over you,[13] this encouraged [me]. And by that: Come to me and ye shall find rest.[14] Mr. Norton[15] [preached on] My iniquities are too heavy for me.[16] Was sin so to me, and intolerable, and I saw it such a burden unless Lord give rest, and that nothing could satisfy conscience but what pacified wrath of God, which was Jesus Christ. And hearing Psalm 119, I shall not be ashamed when [I] have respect to all thy commandments,[17] and this was to be willing to see every commandment and what was contrary to them, and [to be] humbled when [I] did cross any. And upon examination of my heart I found God had given me great hopes that the Lord had given me such a heart.

10. Exod. 20:12.
11. John Sill—see his confession above.
12. Isa. 1:31.
13. Rom. 6:14.
14. Matt. 11:28.
15. John Norton (1606–1663), minister at Ipswich, 1636–1653, and First Church, Boston, 1653–1663.
16. Ps. 38:4.
17. Ps. 119:6.

But the Lord awakening my conscience, I thought there might be some secret sins between me and mercy, and I went to God to take away my secret sins. And that there was no sin hid from God, though from me many. Hearing Mr. Allin of Charlestown[18] concerning the rest of the soul, that nothing in world but had its rest, and [he] showed that Father was rest and way to it was by Christ, and [there are] divers false rests, and men go far and fall short of rest: some rest in duties and [so] show no rest. Now upon examination I found God had let me see I did not rest in anything I did but to come to him through Christ, I hope of love because God hath heard my prayers for the subduing of my sin and mortification of sin I have lived in.

Isabell Jackson

—he would not break the bruised reed

Isabell Jackson, first wife of Richard Jackson, died in Cambridge in 1661. The first paragraph of her confession was recorded by Shepard. The rest is in another hand, probably that of one of the elders, Edmund Frost or Richard Champney; it repeats the initial reference to Isaiah. The confession, like that of Nicholas Wyeth, is distinguished by a long interrogation showing the church's concern about the applicant's spiritual capacity.

In ministry out of Isaiah, Hear, Oh child, I have brought up rebellious child,[1] and I thought I was a rebellious wretch against God, and so I continued long. I was in a sad condition long together, and I heard, They that seek the Lord shall find him,[2] and hearing, Fatherless find mercy in me.[3]

Isaiah the 1:2: Hear, oh heavens, and give ear, oh earth, for the Lord hath spoken, I have nourished and brought [up] my children, and they have rebelled against me. A minister preaching out of

18. Thomas Allin (1608–1673), minister at Charlestown, 1638–1651.
1. Isa. 1:2.
2. Matt. 7:7; Luke 11:9.
3. Hos. 14:3; Ps. 68:5.

those words and showing the rebellion of the heart against the Lord, she thought the Lord did convince her that she had a heart as all others had which did rebel against the Lord, which did much affect her.

So out of the 2 of Corinthians 4:3–4, For if our gospel be hid, it is hid to them that are lost, in whom the God of this world hath blinded the minds of them that believe not, which was made known unto me to be hid from me, and that I was lost, which did affect my heart a long time, till one did preach out of 42 Isaiah and 3, A bruised reed will [he] not break and the smoking flax will not be quench[ed], from which scripture the Lord did let her have some hope that though she was weak, yet he would not break the bruised reed, and by some godly minister's instruction she was somewhat help[ed]. And a godly minister preaching out of the whole prophecy of Malachi, I thought I did receive much good, although I cannot remember and was but a poor silly creature as I am still, which she saith is a great trouble to her that she is so bad that hath had so much means to make her better but she is not.

Again the minister preaching out of the 23 of Jeremiah 29, Is not my word like a fire, saith the Lord, and like a hammer that breaketh the rock in pieces[?] Where, saith he, If thy heart be as hard as a stone, this hammer, if it come at it, it will break it. And I, finding my heart hard as a stone, did pray to the Lord that he would break it, and the Lord did affect her heart.

So out of 17 Jeremiah 9, The heart is deceitful above all things, where the deceit of the heart being opened, I did not think there had been so much deceit in my heart till then that the minister did discover the same. And though she said, My memory is weak, and [she] cannot remember what was said, yet this she did desire, that the Lord would humble her heart for that deceit, and that she had spent her time and got no more good.

And after this Mr. Shepard [preached] out of the 38 Isaiah wherein it said, I am oppressed, for I thought I was oppressed: but, said the minister, though thou can but sigh and breathe or chatter after the Lord.[4] That did refresh that there should be any hope for such a poor creature as I am. And when I was come to New En-

4. Isa. 38:14.

gland, I did look on myself as cast in the open field,[5] and so saw myself in a sad condition, and though[t] others thought ill and meanly of me, and I thought worst of myself, and I was in a sad condition, and my sleep did depart away from [me], so that I did not know what to do. Then that in 14 Hosea was brought to me: In thee the fatherless find mercy.[6] That place did much refresh me, that the Lord should look on so poor miserable sinner as I was. I might have been better, but I thought the Lord saw I would be lifted up; therefore the Lord did leave me so much. More comfort and refreshment I might have had if I had made use of what I did enjoy.

1 Question: What need have you observed of Christ and coming to him[?]

Answer: A great deal of need of him, for there is nothing to be had without coming to him.

2 Question: By what means did you see need of Christ, and by what scripture were you helped[?]

From that place out of 42 Isaiah 3 of the bruised reed, where it was showed that what the Lord did for a poor creature, it was out of free mercy, and though it were but a little that the Lord had wrought in the soul, the Lord would not quench it.

But had you not prayed to the Lord Jesus that he for free grace and mercy sake would pity you[?]

Answer: Yes, for I thought there was no free grace without him, nor no free mercy without him, and I thought it great mercy that the Lord should stoop down so low, to such a distressed one that was nothing but sin and corruption, and that he would look on such a poor creature.

Question: What did oppress [her] and what kind of undertaking did she desire[?]

Answer: My sins was great and many, and I did desire that the Lord would pity and pardon her of all.

Question: Whether it was the guilt or power of sin that did oppress her.

Answer: Was both.

5. Ezek. 16:5.
6. Hos. 14:3.

Upon an occasion of some words that did fall out between her and one other, I saying to that party, Why did you not speak to myself? the party answered that I was without. The word "without" did much trouble me, not knowing what the party meant, whether I was without Christ or out of the church. But I put me upon examining of my estate, and being thereupon in a very sad condition, not knowing what to make of myself, then that place again in [scripture], The fatherless find mercy. The beginning of this trouble was before that party [spoke to me], only that did further evil to my trouble. But my trouble was chiefly for my sin, and misery by reason of my sin.

Having been asked, because she did much complain of ignorance and rebellion, if she did find any help or healing of them.

Answer: She had in some measure, though much did still remain which she did apprehend did so unfit her that it did keep her back, and complained of the proneness that was in her heart to evil, which was so much as no man did know how much was in her heart.

Question: When the Lord do let you see the sin and misery that is in your heart daily, what then is your refuge[?]

Answer: By going to the Lord by prayer to humble her soul. She went to the Lord, she said, for her prayer was sinful.

Question: But do you find the Lord a refuge to support her soul[?]

Answer: Sometime I do, and if the Lord will not support me, still I think with Job to stick to him and mourn and wait till he help me.

At what gate or promise do you stay for help[?]

Answer: 61 Isaiah 1: To bind up the brokenhearted, to proclaim liberty to the captives, and the opening of the prison to them that are bound. For I have sometime looked on myself as a prisoner shut up in sin and corruption. Yet that place being once opened, I was much helped by it, and though I do not feel help from it daily, yet sometime I do. Once being in discourse with a godly minister, he bade me take that as my own and not let it go, but she told him she could not. Then, said he, You will lose the benefit of it by your unbelief. And inward[ly] I had not the benefit of it till she was come here, being in very great trouble. Yet that word came in, that he doth open the prison to them that are bound, and God did give me great comfort. I thought myself unworthy of any such mercy and did much fear my falling away.

And the question being what other scriptures was there that did afford her any comfort[?]

Answer: Galatians 5:6, For in Jesus Christ neither circumcision now availeth anything nor uncircumcision but faith that worketh by love. The chief thing she noted there was her love to the saints.

So out of the 18 of Matthew where it is said, Except you become as little children, you cannot inherit the kingdom of God,[7] which did holp her when she had troubles upon her, both inward and outward, and her heart did not so quietly lie under them as she thought it should. Then that scripture coming in made her heart glory when she thought she might become as a little child.

So Isaiah 11, The wolf shall dwell with the lamb and the leopard shall lie down with the kid, and the calf and the young lion and the fatling together, and a young child shall lead them.[8] All which did show her of what a meek spirit she should be of, that was naturally like to leopard and lion.

She did also express much how she was afraid of her falling away, having known and been well acquainted with some that had been eminent in profession yet falling away to the great dishonor of the Lord and scandal to religion, and they being strong and tall cedars and she but weak and a low shrub. This did much affect her heart.

Question: But do you not fear deceit in your own heart[?]

Yes. And she did pray to the Lord to direct her heart in the right way, and so to cast low weight that hung so fast on, and the sin that be [i.e., do] so easily beset, and to run with patience the race that was set before her.[9] And [she] also did desire to set the Lord always before her and to seek him in the first place.

Question: What is the evil in sin that you have seen[?]

Answer: [It] is because it is a dishonor to the Lord, how as Adam did dishonor the Lord by breaking of the Commandments.

7. Matt. 18:3.
8. Isa. 11:6.
9. Heb. 12:1.

Abraham Arrington

—little mind or heart to seek God

Abraham Arrington (b. 1622), the town blacksmith, was the only one of the sixteen confessors recorded for 1648–1649 who failed to gain admission. His wife, Rebecca, had already joined, but he was not accepted until 1663. McCarl speculates that time was needed to live down the wildness of his youth as reflected in his remark (in 1677) that "it was a pit[i]full thing that a young man and mayd could not be together but such reports must come of it, and he did beleuiv ere long the young men must pass by the mayds like quakers and take no notice of them."[1]

The first time Lord did me any good was what a friend, a godly man, brother Isaac,[2] being at work together, he spake to me how it stood with me about my estate and asked me whether God gave me a heart to seek him. So I told him I had little mind or heart that way. And he then said it was high time to look to it, for now was a fair season. And his words affected me, and he took much pains in his family. Ecclesiastes 12: Remember Creator.[3] He pressed it upon me as my duty now in my youth to seek after God. And coming to hearing word [of the] Lord out of John 14, penultimate, The Prince of the world comes,[4] [which] showed that Satan did assault Christ at time of his departure, when [he] found no sin [in Christ], and hence terror to all wicked men, the Lord will find something in them. And I was affected with this sermon, and he let me see that there was that sin in my heart for which the Lord might justly condemn and cast me out of sight. But going on in use of [m]eans, another man, Mr. Newman,[5] [preached on] If gos-

1. McCarl, "Thomas Shepard's Record of Relations of Religious Experience, 1648–1649," *William and Mary Quarterly,* 3rd Ser., XLVIII (1991), p. 437, quoting Roger Thompson, *Sex in Middlesex: Popular Mores in a Massachusetts County, 1649–1699* (Amherst: University of Massachusetts Press, 1986), p. 88.
2. Joseph Isaac, who had settled in Cambridge in 1636, was a selectman and deputy to the General Court.
3. Eccles. 12:1.
4. John 14:30.
5. Samuel Newman (1602–1663), minister at Weymouth, 1639–1643, and Rehoboth, 1644–1663.

pel be hid, 'tis to them that be lost,[6] and I saw I was lost and under wrath. And going on, Look to things which are eternal,[7] and I saw I minded nothing but sin and my own pleasure and lusts. And hearing another [preach on] God be merciful to me a sinner,[8] he saw nothing but sin and misery and hence cried out to God for mercy but yet thought mercy did not belong to me, had not made it such a misery,[9] yet 6 Hosea, If [ye] follow on to know the Lord, ye shall know him.[10] And thus the Lord spake by Mr. Shepard concerning sight and sense of sin, that it must be an intolerable burden to make it restless to seek after Christ.[11] And hence I thought I wanting this, I was not fit for mercy. But that scripture, Lord came to seek that which is lost,[12] which did somewhat encourage me to seek after God still. And so by Mr. Mather[13] [preaching on] John 6:37, All given shall come to him, use of exhortation to come to Christ unless prove yourselves reprobates, Lord's desire was. And hence I was encouraged to seek after himself. Lord let me see my desires were after him and to seek him.

Robert Browne

—here God hath endeared my heart more to himself

Robert Browne (1611–1690) arrived in New England in 1635 a bachelor and possibly an indentured servant. He married in 1649. The record is otherwise bare.

The Lord in England showed me the evil of sin by a godly man who showed miserable estate of wicked men, that they were without God in world and without hope. And I thought I must be one of those which were so. And so I saw evil of sabbath breaking and of not praying, for people of God do not [*sic*] pray. And then Psalm

6. 2 Cor. 4:3.
7. 2 Cor. 4:18.
8. Luke 18:13.
9. In margin: "1 desr., 2d, called."
10. Hos. 6:3.
11. See Shepard, *Short Catechism,* p. 36.
12. Matt. 18:11.
13. Richard Mather (1596–1669), minister at Dorchester, 1636–1669.

8 [of] David, [God] makes man master of all,[1] and hence I thought God requires something of me to live as I list that [received] so much mercy from God. And I saw evil of company keeping, and if I went on, there was no hope of mercy for me. And so I thought I would reform myself and endeavored to pray and to keep sabbath, and so I thought it would be better with me than others who had no regard. Yet seeing others sport, I was tempted to break off all but was struck with such a fear and trembling that I must go back again. And I lived under a bad master, and I thought I would go hear one 3 miles off [preaching on] As newborn babes,[2] and how precious he was to believers. And hence he showed the miserable condition of them out of Christ, and I saw myself such a one, for I was ignorant if Christ knew me, what Christ was, and without knowledge heart cannot be good. And then the Lord brought innumerable sins I could not tell them, and I thought there was no hope of mercy for me. Yet I thought I would use means. I could read a little, and that place, Matthew 11, came to me, Come to me,[3] and I was glad of that scripture as of anything in my life. And I desired Lord to rid me of sin and that burden. And [I remembered] Isaiah 1, Though sins of crimson [they shall be] whiter than snow.[4] And so in seeking God I found some refreshing and ease and strength against it, and love to God's people. And then I could go by my companions and loathe them. And I found delight in sabbath word [and] ordinances, and then the word was not tedious, but [I was] sorry [it was] done so soon, and I loved to keep their company that would speak of it. And so the times being bad, and good people departing, I thought to come to New England. And here God hath endeared my heart more to himself, hath showed me more of my vileness and wretchedness, and needing all his love to look upon such a wretch to show me evil of sin and love me. John 6, I'll not forsake you: draw near to me, and I'll draw nigh to you;[5] Seek and find.[6] Consideration of Christ's excellency made me love him.

1. Ps. 8:4–6.
2. 1 Pet. 2:2.
3. Matt. 11:28.
4. Isa. 1:18.
5. John 6:44.
6. Matt. 7:7.

Jonathan Mitchell

—nothing to pray for but God to break my heart all to pieces

Jonathan Mitchell (1624–1668) came with his parents to Connecticut from Yorkshire in 1635 and graduated from Harvard twelve years later. He succeeded Shepard in the Cambridge pulpit and married Shepard's widow.

My parents being both godly saints, my lot [was] to hear many means of good, so my childhood and my carriage was fair, and I had some childish religiousness, but as I grew in years gracelessness manifested itself in me. And though I had stirrings against [it], yet I returned quickly to my un[illegible] actions. I lived without God in the world. Mr. Hooker's[1] sermons about sight of sin and sense of it did stir up prayer, but I returned to the vanity and carelessness of my life. But by my parents' words again I began to consider of sin against all light I had, and so I continued for some time. Christ coming to save sinners of whom I was chief, I began to give up myself to Christ, and I had some raised apprehensions of God to me. But I knew not my heart but was taken with conscience of my sin. And at Southampton[2] where way was more spiritual, I was more affected. I saw I was at enmity with God and God with me, and my convictions increased, and I waited on God when I was in general blindness. Isaiah 42: He will lead blind in way they knew not.[3] This was sweet to me, as also, To them that have no might he increases strength.[4] So also the Lord let into my heart some sweet apprehension of God's love to me, and so I was suddenly and strangely filled with my atheistical thoughts about truth of God and being of the Scripture, and I looked on them as my bane, and so my conscience forbore to seek him, and I had a heart that received [not] God, and then my will was full of evil and a positive enmity against Christ, and I found light though goes against Christ. I could not find it [in] my heart to relish Christ, and

1. Thomas Hooker, then at Hartford, Connecticut.
2. Mitchell studied under Abraham Pierson, minister at Southampton, Long Island, 1640–1644.
3. Isa. 42:16.
4. Isa. 40:29.

I found my heart unwilling to stick to Christ, and hence I begged for this more than life, the Lord overcoming my heart, yet I followed Lord to draw me to Christ and prized him above all things. After I came here [I heard a] sermon about conviction of sin. I was, I saw, to seek to be humbled for sin and to feel it as untolerable burden, and the hardness of my heart was exceeding great and was often ghastly to look upon, and I had nothing to pray for but God to break my heart all to pieces and to feel what I saw, and the Lord did bring in some visions of sin and wrath of God. And what was spoke last did suit me, that a man might feel sin as an untolerable burden, when never at rest till Lord look down from heaven and when spirit was putting soul forward and, though quiet, yet made soul mourn for it the more. And I saw also that the Lord led me in a way which no man passed through,[5] and here the Lord's counsel was to follow God, and the more I followed him, the more the Lord showed me it was not in vain to seek him, and not long after, [hearing a sermon on] Philippians 3, Them that are in a constant progression, some that rested in some beginnings, as them that had great sins but little humility,[6] every word in this sermon took hold on my heart and wounded me and convinced me, for I ought before to make work of it, and I thought God made it to my hand. And the counsel given at that time and place was against me. My heart was hardened, and so continuing in that estate, when my heart was desolate, I thought that [there] was no way but God to Christ. And he said, They that come I will not cast off.[7] And I heard directions how [to come] to Christ: (1) Come empty and poor and answerable with sense of want of everything; that took my heart greatly to think the Lord would have me come to him with need of everything.[8] (2) Come to him and let him do with thee what he will.[9] Peace, leaves it with them.[10] And my spirit was greatly charged and with sweetness raised up to look for mercy in that promise, They that come to me I'll not cast off. But sense of

5. Exod. 13:17–18.
6. Phil. 3:14–19.
7. John 6:37.
8. Heb. 4:16.
9. 1 Sam. 3:18.
10. John 14:27.

this was overwhelmed again, yet Lord left in something of his love and Christ and, especially of late, some more feeling of aching and sweetness in that [illegible], Christ power is liberty,[11] and that, Go to Christ for eternal life, Christ having all power in heaven.[12] Though my iniquities keep good things from me, yet I walked [hi]therto in darkness and death daily,[13] and that is able to foresee to offer me all that come to God by Christ.

Elizabeth Cooke

—God would spew me out of his mouth

Elizabeth Cooke married Joseph Cooke, a prominent citizen of Cambridge and a personal friend of Shepard. Little else is known of her.

We lived in a very ignorant place, with little means, and hence I desired to come to New England, though before now. And then I was in fear that the Lord would not bring me hither because I would not when I might, but when I came here I found my heart altogether dead and unprofitable under means. And I saw myself indeed in a miserable condition because ignorant of Jesus Christ. And I was sensible of the unfruitfulness of my heart under means, though many times hearing offer of grace in Christ, yet I thought it was to them that were humbled for sin, and I thought though the Lord left me not to sin as others, yet I thought myself so much the worse because lukewarm, and I thought God would spew me out of his mouth.[1] Though many times hearing of power of grace, yet I thought it was presumption in me to do it. But out of catechize, that it was not measure but so much as brought the soul to Christ that was supposed,[2] and I thought my heart was overcome, and I thought it was free grace. And many times I was in a sad condition and in many fears, but could not get over them to make known my condition to any. The Lord humble me for it.

11. Gal. 5:1.
12. Rom. 6:23; 1 Cor. 1:24.
13. Isa. 50:10.
1. Rev. 3:16.
2. John 3:34; Shepard, *Short Catechism,* p. 16.

Could not answer (1) what answer from humility, (2) what of Christ she saw in him or tasted from him to make her prize him.

Elizabeth Dunster

—I saw an unbelieving heart

Elizabeth Dunster, sister of Henry Dunster, first president of Harvard College, married Simon Willard about 1651 and died soon after. The family had come to New England from Lancashire.

About half a score years since, being brought up in my father's family, I saw myself by nature a child of wrath, and I knew not what would become of me. And though I might have company of godly [people], yet I did not care for them lest reproved. And so I went on, with many convictions, and brother Imlet,[1] If hid, 'tis to them that be lost.[2] I found myself ignorant, and I was lost, and I had several temptations, and I had no rest [from the conviction] that I was in a lost condition. And reading of rich glutton, Oh look, whose is now thy part![3] and considering how soon I might be taken away, and [this] made me see I stood in need of a savior, and I went mournfully, and I thought time was past and [I had] chosen sin because I gave not to God's people in misery. And I desired the Lord to pardon me and humble [me] and of mercy to show me it, and so I begged it. And one was speaking out of James 1, Sin when finished brought death,[4] and showed was it not [for] God's restraining grace we should fall into all sin, and hereby I saw need of a savior. I had knowledge of a savior but not that he belonged to me.[5] And Luke 15: Prodigal, when he went [home], his father ran and met him.[6] And I gathered some encouragement, and I saw that the Lord might come to me, and this I prayed for. And another time, Come to me, all ye weary and heavy laden, I'll ease

1. Perhaps William Hamlet, a lay preacher who settled in Cambridge.
2. 2 Cor. 4:3.
3. Perhaps Luke 16:20.
4. Jas. 1:15.
5. Rom. 3:31–32; Shepard, *Short Catechism,* p. 51.
6. Luke 15:11–32.

you.[7] And this broke my heart and made me willing to come, and some encouragement to me, and that the Lord would take off this burden. But I felt an inability to come, and I entreated the Lord to draw me, and that I might close with him. And when I was reading John, This is will of him, that whoever come, I'll not cast them off.[8] This sunk deep into my soul, and this encouraged me to come boldly. Genesis 39, Shall I do this wickedness and sin[?][9] One showed the people of God, though they could sin greatly and sin against God. And I was troubled for speaking against another, and it turned to me as a testimony that Lord had done me good. And meditating on John, We know we are passed from death to life because [we] love brethren,[10] and I looked: they were precious who were sacred burden. And so by this, Ye shall know that ye are children of God, and his commands are not grievous.[11] And then I was visited with sickness, and I was then much refreshed with Lord's presence, Fear not, I am with thee,[12] and so from Lamentations, The Lord is my portion, saith my soul, and it's good to wait upon the Lord.[13] And I saw much mercy to me when days were let out. Then trial in our family forced [us] to fly, and we fled in the night. The enemy came and took away much of our substance, and because I had been means to forward then in the cause, and I was much satisfied that they that forsake not lands and houses were not worthy of him, and count it all joy when persecuted for righteousness.[14] And since I have seen God going before me, but sometime I have found deadness and departing from him, but [he] hath chastised me and let me see some sin and some mercy. And when I came over seas, I had God's presence. I was assured I was where God would have me, and so I submitted. Since I came, I thought I was not profitable, considering what mercy Lord had shown. And that place, That sins against mercy provoke God,[15] and one sin was

7. Matt. 11:28.
8. John 6:37.
9. Gen. 39:9.
10. John 5:24.
11. 1 John 5:2–3.
12. Deut. 31:6.
13. Lam. 3:24, 26.
14. Matt. 5:10.
15. See Luke 20:9–16.

when this came home, none received mercy, and I found my heart dead and sluggy. I thought I was greatly provoked, and I mourned for this sin, and [this] helped me to profit, and having some measure caused me to recall my former condition of death. And so I desired Lord would help when Christ was held forth all that a believer desired, and I thought if I could believe, nothing [would be] wanting, and I saw an unbelieving heart. And God has helped me against some sins and temptations since I came hither.

SELECTED BIBLIOGRAPHY

The Cambridge Texts

The first edition of *God's Plot* (Amherst, Mass., 1972) has the full text of Thomas Shepard's journal. For the whole body of lay confessions see George Selement and Bruce C. Woolley, eds., *Thomas Shepard's Confessions,* Colonial Society of Massachusetts *Collections,* XVIII (Boston, 1981), and Mary Rhinelander McCarl, "Thomas Shepard's Relations of Religious Experience, 1648–1649," *William and Mary Quarterly,* 3d Ser., XLVIII (1991), 432–66.

On the Uses of the Cambridge Texts

Caldwell, Patricia. *The Puritan Conversion Narrative: The Beginnings of American Expression.* New York: Cambridge University Press, 1983.
Reads the confessions as an imaginative literary form—"the first faint murmurings of a truly American voice."

Cappello, Mary. "The Authority of Self-Definition in Thomas Shepard's *Autobiography* and *Journal.*" *Early American Literature,* XXIV (1989), 35–51.
This exploration of "the problem of self-construction in these most self-conscious of texts" finds signs of the emergence of a modern concept of self.

Cohen, Charles Lloyd. *God's Caress: The Psychology of Puritan Religious Experience.* New York: Oxford University Press, 1986.
This study recognizes the Puritans' fears but amplifies their hopes and places their experience of divine beneficence at the core of piety: "an analysis of conversion must be a tractate on love." Has a valuable annotated bibliography.

Delbanco, Andrew. *The Puritan Ordeal.* Cambridge: Harvard University Press, 1989.
Shepard epitomizes the immigrant generation as a man in physical and psychic flight who sought an ambiguous security in the disciplines of self-criticism and self-control.

———. "Thomas Shepard's America: The Biography of an Idea." In *Studies in Biography,* edited by Daniel Aaron, 159–82. Harvard English Studies 8. Cambridge: Harvard University Press, 1978.
Traces the outline of Shepard's intellectual life with reference to the "moral crisis of migration."

Hall, David D. "On Common Ground: The Coherence of American Puritan Studies." *William and Mary Quarterly,* 3d Ser., XLIV (1987), 193–221.

The most up-to-date review essay; calls attention to a "sea change in our understanding of Puritan piety" involving recognition of a "structured movement from anxiety to assurance" through an "ethic of self-discipline."

———. "Toward a History of Popular Religion in Early New England." *William and Mary Quarterly,* 3d Ser., XLI (1984), 49–55. See Selement.

———. *Worlds of Wonder, Days of Judgment: Popular Religious Belief in Early New England.* New York: Alfred A. Knopf, 1989.
Accepts the confessions as definitive for Puritan piety in early New England while emphasizing the structured ritual as a support for spiritual assurance.

Hambrick-Stowe, Charles E. *The Practice of Piety: Puritan Devotional Disciplines in Seventeenth-Century New England.* Chapel Hill: University of North Carolina Press, 1982.
Shows how piety was geared to the enhancement of assurance through a well-constructed regimen of private and public devotional exercises.

Hoopes, James. *Consciousness in New England: From Puritanism and Ideas to Psychoanalysis and Semiotic.* Baltimore: Johns Hopkins University Press, 1989.
Psychoanalytic concepts are brought to bear on the Puritan conversion "understood as an interpretation rather than a religious 'experience.'"

Knight, Janice. *Orthodoxies in Massachusetts: Rereading American Puritanism.* Cambridge: Harvard University Press, 1994.
Defines within the Puritan movement a distinctive persuasion of divine grace, to which Shepard's relation is ambiguous.

Porterfield, Amanda. *Female Piety in Puritan New England: The Emergence of Religious Humanism.* New York: Oxford University Press, 1992.
This gender-sensitive essay finds in ministers such as Shepard a feminine posture of devotion, deference, and emotional dependence marked by fear of abandonment, longing for love, and association of humility with erotic desire.

Rutman, Darrett B. "New England as Idea and Society Revisited." *William and Mary Quarterly,* 3d Ser., XLI (1984), 56–61. See Selement.

Selement, George. "The Meeting of Elite and Popular Minds at Cambridge, New England, 1638–1645." *William and Mary Quarterly,* 3d Ser., XLI (1984), 32–47.
This article and those of Hall and Rutman in the same issue discuss the question of "collective mentality" in early New England.

Swaim, Kathleen M. "'Come and Hear': Women's Puritan Evidences." In *American Women's Autobiography: Fea(s)ts of Memory*, edited by Margo Culley, 32–56. Madison: University of Wisconsin Press, 1992.
Explores gendered differences between women's and men's inscriptions of self in the Shepard confessions.

Tipson, Baird. "The Routinized Piety of Thomas Shepard's Diary." *Early American Literature,* XIII (1978), 64–80.

Underlines the importance of the diary form for Puritans and sets Shepard's journal in the perspective of English Puritan piety.

Werge, Thomas. *Thomas Shepard.* Boston: Twayne Publishers, 1987.
On Shepard's imagination and rhetoric, underlining "the persistent Puritan awareness of the polarities inherent in every form of ordinary and sacred experience." Useful bibliography.

Sources for the Study of Puritan Spirituality

Bercovitch, Sacvan. *The American Jeremiad.* Madison: University of Wisconsin Press, 1978.

———. *The Puritan Origins of the American Self.* New Haven, Yale University Press, 1975.

Bozeman, Theodore Dwight. *To Live Ancient Lives: The Primitivist Dimension in Puritanism.* Chapel Hill: University of North Carolina Press, 1988.

Daly, Robert. *God's Altar: The World and the Flesh in Puritan Poetry.* Berkeley: University of California Press, 1978.

Elliott, Emory. *Power and the Pulpit in Puritan New England.* Princeton: Princeton University Press, 1975.

Foster, Stephen. *Their Solitary Way: The Puritan Social Ethic in the First Century of Settlement in New England.* New Haven: Yale University Press, 1970.

Gilpin, W. Clark. *The Millenarian Piety of Roger Williams.* Chicago: University of Chicago Press, 1979.

Godbeer, Richard. *The Devil's Dominion: Magic and Religion in Early New England.* New York: Cambridge University Press, 1992.

Gura, Philip. *A Glimpse of Sion's Glory: Puritan Radicalism in New England, 1620–1660.* Middletown, Conn.: Wesleyan University Press, 1984.

Hall, David D. *The Faithful Shepherd: A History of the New England Ministry in the Seventeenth Century.* Chapel Hill: University of North Carolina Press, 1972.

Haller, William. *The Rise of Puritanism.* New York: Harper and Brothers, 1938.

Hambrick-Stowe, Charles E., ed. *Early New England Meditative Poetry: Anne Bradstreet and Edward Taylor.* Sources of American Spirituality. New York: Paulist Press, 1988.

Hammond, Jeffrey A. *Sinful Self, Saintly Self: The Puritan Experience of Poetry.* Athens: University of Georgia Press, 1993.

Holifield, E. Brooks. *The Covenant Sealed: The Development of Puritan Sacramental Theology in Old and New England, 1570–1720.* New Haven: Yale University Press, 1974.

Kibbey, Ann. *The Interpretation of Material Shapes in Puritanism: A Study of Rhetoric, Prejudice, and Violence.* New York: Cambridge University Press, 1986.

Lang, Amy Schrager. *Prophetic Woman: Anne Hutchinson and the Problem of Dissent in the Literature of New England.* Berkeley: University of California Press, 1987.

Leverenz, David. *The Language of Puritan Feeling: An Exploration in Literature, Psychology, and Social History.* New Brunswick, N.J.: Rutgers University Press, 1980.

Lowance, Mason I., Jr. *The Language of Canaan: Metaphor and Symbol in New England from the Puritans to the Transcendentalists.* Cambridge: Harvard University Press, 1980.

Maclear, James Fulton. "'The Heart of New England Rent': The Mystical Element in Early Puritan History." *Mississippi Valley Historical Review,* XLII (1956), 621–52.

Miller, Perry. *The New England Mind: The Seventeenth Century.* New York: Macmillan, 1939.

Morgan, Edmund S. *Visible Saints: The History of a Puritan Idea.* New York: New York University Press, 1963.

Murphey, Murray. "The Psychodynamics of Puritan Conversion." *American Quarterly,* XXXI (1979), 135–47.

Pettit, Norman. *The Heart Prepared: Grace and Conversion in Puritan Spiritual Life.* New Haven: Yale University Press, 1966.

Rutman, Darrett B. *American Puritanism: Faith and Practice.* Philadelphia: J. P. Lippincott, 1970.

Schuldiner, Michael. *Gifts and Works: The Post-Conversion Paradigm and Spiritual Controversy in Seventeenth-Century Massachusetts.* Macon, Ga.: Mercer University Press, 1991.

Selement, George. *Keepers of the Vineyard: The Puritan Ministry and Collective Culture in Colonial New England.* Lanham, Md.: University Press of America, 1984.

Stannard, David E. *The Puritan Way of Death: A Study in Religion, Culture, and Social Change.* New York: Oxford University Press, 1977.

Stoever, William K. B. *'A Faire and Easie Way to Heaven': Covenant Theology and Antinomianism in Early Massachusetts.* Middletown, Conn.: Wesleyan University Press, 1978.

Stout, Harry S. *The New England Soul: Preaching and Religious Culture in Colonial New England.* New York: Oxford University Press, 1986.

Tipson, Baird. "Invisible Saints: The 'Judgment of Charity' in the Early New England Churches." *Church History,* XLIV (1975), 460–71.

Wakefield, Gordon Stevens. *Puritan Devotion: Its Place in the Development of Christian Piety.* London: Epworth Press, 1957.

INDEX